THE THEATER IS IN THE STREET

The Theater Is in the Street

Politics and Performance in Sixties America

BRADFORD D. MARTIN

University of Massachusetts Press
Amherst and Boston

Copyright © 2004 by University of Massachusetts Press
All rights reserved
Printed in the United States of America

LC 2004001715
ISBN 1-55849-449-9 (library cloth ed.); 458-8 (paper)

Designed by Jack Harrison
Set in Adobe Garamond by Binghamton Valley Composition
Printed and bound by The Maple-Vail Book Manufacturing Group

Library of Congress Cataloging-in-Publication Data
Martin, Bradford D., 1966–
   The theater is in the street : politics and performance in
sixties America / Bradford D. Martin.
      p. cm.
Includes bibliographical references and index.
ISBN 1-55849-449-9 (library cloth : alk. paper) — ISBN 1-55849-458-8 (pbk. : alk. paper)
1. Street theater—United States—History—20th century.
2. Street theater—Political aspects—United States—History—20th century.
I. Title.
   PN3209.M37 2004
   792.02.'2—dc22
                        2004001715

British Library Cataloguing in Publication data are available.

For Heather

CONTENTS

ILLUSTRATIONS

ACKNOWLEDGMENTS

I thank Hollis Watkins, Charles Neblett, Bernard LaFayette, Bernice Reagon, Leslie Jones, and Reebee Garofalo for their information on the Freedom Singers. Tom Walker contributed unstintingly to the Living Theatre chapter and has provided consistently generous friendship over the years. Judith Malina, Hanon Resnikov, and Mark Hall Amitin have given their insights and guidance as well. Nicole Wills, Arthur Lisch, and Shelly Muzzy shared their remembrances for the Diggers chapter. Jon Hendricks, Irving Petlin, Leon Golub, and Lucy Lippard all were gracious with their time and thoughtful with their responses regarding the Art Workers Coalition and the Guerrilla Art Action Group.

This project benefited from the advice of a group of colleagues in the academic world on whose mentorship I have come to rely. First and foremost, Bruce Schulman helped me conceive of this project, provided sustaining enthusiasm, and patiently responded to every request for help—requests that came early and often. Lois Rudnick encouragingly spurred me to embrace the nuanced implications of my topic. Alexander Bloom, Patricia Hills, Jill Lepore, Joe Urgo, Judy Smith, Cheryl Boots, Sarah Junkin, Barbara Tischler, and David Farber all read various portions of the text and contributed salient insights. The Boston University Americanists also helped me think through the project in its early stages. The staffs of Boston University's Mugar Memorial Library, Bryant College's Douglas and Judith Krupp Library, especially

Colleen Anderson and Paul Roske, and the California Historical Society patiently indulged my research queries. Ivan Bernier and Samantha Khosla assisted this project with expert clerical and administrative help. Janet Mesick's research assistance turned up key documents for the Diggers chapter.

I am grateful to the Boston University Humanities Foundation, whose Clarimond Mansfield Award helped subsidize early phases of this project, as well as Boston University's American and New England Studies Program for its support over the years.

My editor at University of Massachusetts Press, Paul Wright, patiently fielded my numerous questions and provided invaluable help in bringing this project to fruition. Managing editor Carol Betsch was equally helpful and generous in the final stages of the project, and the manuscript benefited greatly from Joel Ray's rigorous copyediting. I wish also to thank Thomas LeBien, an editor with whom I didn't end up collaborating but who nevertheless read the manuscript, offered valuable advice, and introduced me to important publishing world realities. It was great to revive an old friendship, especially with someone of such obvious wit and talent.

There are several family members without whom this project would not have been possible. My parents, Gary and Elizabeth Unger, and my mother-in-law, Joan Abrames, have been supportive in as many senses of the word as one can imagine. My children, Jackson, Hazel, and Harry, are inspiring in innumerable ways on a daily basis. Finally, my wife, Heather, enabled this project at the most fundamental level; without her patience, tolerance, and encouragement its completion would have remained only a distant prospect.

THE THEATER IS IN THE STREET

INTRODUCTION

The Convergence of Art, Politics, and Everyday Life

> I am for an art that is political-erotical mystical, that does something other than sit on its ass in a museum. I am for an art that embroils itself with the everyday crap and comes out on top. I am for an art that tells you the time of day, or where such and such a street is. I am for an art that helps old ladies across the street. CLAES OLDENBURG

> The march was stopped about a block and a half from the campus by 40 city, county, and state policemen with tear gas grenades, billy sticks and a fire truck. When ordered to return to the campus or be beaten back, the students, confronted individually by the police, chose not to move and quietly began singing "We Shall Not Be Moved." BOB ZELLNER

During the 1960s, artists and activists transformed notions of how public spaces might be used, expanding the range of cultural and political expressions beyond the substantial restrictions they had faced in the early postwar era. Echoing a widespread sentiment among 1960s artists, the sculptor Claes Oldenburg asserted that for art to be vital it must do more than "sit on its ass in a museum," embracing subject matter and venues familiar to people's everyday lives.[1] "Public space" or, more colloquially, "the street" provided the locus for this sea change in the arts. Describing a civil rights movement confrontation in Talladega, Alabama, the activist Bob Zellner highlighted the centrality of singing to the struggle for desegregation, which by its nature involved public spaces and accommodations, from lunch counters to public parks and beaches to educational facilities.[2] By mobilizing singing as an organizing tool, communications medium, and tactic of social contestation in the struggle for desegregation, movement activists reintroduced to the public space a vibrant cultural form that had largely vanished during the McCarthy years. Just as focus on everyday life catalyzed a new movement in the arts, singing assumed a key role in the culture of the civil rights movement, infusing American public life with a strong performance element that received considerable publicity from both television and print media. These two trends intertwined throughout the sixties as cultural forms increasingly moved into public venues, frequently conveying pointed political content.

During the sixties, art, theater, and politics permeated everyday life; public performance in the streets served as the principal forum for this development. But what constitutes a public performance? Were civil rights activists who sang freedom songs as part of the civil rights movement performers in the same way as, say, the avant-garde theater company the Living Theatre, who led its audiences into the streets as the climactic act of its 1968 production *Paradise Now*? In modern parlance "performance" has been used to refer to a broad range of sometimes quite dissimilar activities. Marvin Carlson has argued for recognizing "performance" as a "contested concept" and for acknowledging "the futility of seeking some overarching semantic field" to encompass all the term's uses.[3] Nevertheless, the tendency of various sixties collectives to bring their art and politics into public spaces suggests that some narrowing of the performance concept is possible. Erving Goffman's definition of performance as "all the activity of a given participant on a given occasion which serves to influence in any way any of the other participants" resounds with relevance for the public performers of the sixties in both its allowance for a wide range of performative activity and its suggestion of a quest to "influence" and involve audiences.[4] The performance studies scholar Richard Schechner cites eight "sometimes separate, sometimes overlapping situations" in which performances occur, including everyday life, the arts, popular entertainments, business, technology, sex, sacred and secular ritual, and play.[5] At various times, sixties public performers drew from all these areas, including aspects of the business, technology, and sex varieties not usually part of performance-theory discourse. Public performers of the sixties tended most often, however, to mesh some combination of the everyday life, arts, popular entertainment, ritual, and play aspects of performance.

"Public performance" can be defined as a self-conscious, stylized tactic of staging songs, plays, parades, protests, and other spectacles in public places where no admission is charged and spectators are often invited to participate, and it conveys symbolic messages about social and political issues to audiences who might not have encountered them in more traditional venues. In the sixties, arts and cultural groups reconceived the relationship between politics and culture, using public performance to express their politics. While their specific political objectives varied, these groups shared the impulse to stage their performances and actions in public spaces, eschewing museums, theaters, and other halls of culture. This crucial choice allowed the freedom singers of the civil rights movement, the Living Theatre, the Diggers, the Art Workers Coalition (AWC) and the Guerrilla Art Action Group (GAAG) to narrow the gulf between everyday life and politics, broadening the definition of politics in a way characteristic of both the New Left and the counterculture of the sixties, and redefining the uses of the public space.

This process recalls the historian Mary Ryan's analysis of nineteenth-century public ceremonies, festivities, and performances. Ryan contends that such events "brought city residents together in a short-term commitment to some larger civic identity." During the sixties, singing freedom songs, creating street theater vignettes that invited audience participation, and protesting museum policies all embodied performances of the kind of shared identity Ryan describes, though often such performances arrayed themselves in opposition to mainstream values. Yet the "short-term commitment" Ryan mentions, in the sixties as well as in the nineteenth century, could also carry potential long-term effects. Ryan argues that the earlier public ceremonies promoted "cultural cohesion" and facilitated the development of a common language that citizens could mobilize to address other civic or political concerns.[6] Public performers of the sixties nurtured the development of such a common language and hoped to wed this vocabulary to a range of activist concerns and idealistic goals from civil rights to personal liberation to democratization of art-world institutions.

Assessing the influence and impact of these performances is notoriously problematic. On the one hand, it is impossible to quantify the impact of a multifaceted participatory spectacle such as the Diggers' Invisible Circus, since different participants each experienced the same events through the lens of their own experiences and prejudices. There is rarely a "smoking gun" of audience testimonials to attest, conveniently, that the AWC's poster of the My Lai massacre, for example, displayed in front of Picasso's *Guernica* at the Museum of Modern Art, moved a critical mass of spectators to a new awareness of the museum's myriad links to the military-industrial complex and its use of art to "sanctify killing." Thus it would be reckless to claim that these groups' public performances definitively shaped public consciousness about the evils of segregation or the war in Vietnam. Yet palpable trends in anecdotal evidence, as well as the ubiquity of public performance by the late sixties as a cultural aesthetic and protest strategy, suggest the resonance of this idiom. During the Living Theatre's 1968–69 U.S. tour, audiences did accept its invitation into the streets to begin the work of nonviolent anarchist revolution on a nightly basis. Whether or not spectators were in close agreement with the company's politics, various accounts suggest that they regularly got caught up in the participatory spirit of the moment. Similarly, anecdotal evidence demonstrates that even southern white segregationist prison guards could be moved by the freedom songs of incarcerated activists, and the fact that the antiwar movement and women's liberation movement both adopted singing (sometimes using the very same songs as the civil rights movement) to promote unity, build morale, and show resolve indicates that this form wielded considerable power.

The relationship between public performance and activism tended to broaden definitions of politics, since the goals, philosophies, and tactics of these groups reflected the New Left's and the counterculture's expansive rethinking of politics and lifestyle. For instance, freedom singers in the civil rights movement drew from earlier musical traditions within the black church and the labor movement, and through their own struggles influenced the movement culture of the predominantly white New Left. The Living Theatre's landmark production *Paradise Now* reflected the counterculture's communitarian and aesthetic sensibilities. The criticism the AWC and GAAG hurled at prestigious art world underwriters such as the Rockefellers resounded with New Left analysis that linked America's corporate elite to the Vietnam War. Taken together, the careers of these groups refute the notion of the sixties political left and cultural left as separate entities. The heightened social tensions and political crises of the sixties catalyzed public performance as a newer, more symbolic, but also more immediate way of "doing politics" than conventional political protest. Reflecting the New Left's egalitarian ideals, performing in the streets allowed arts and cultural groups to lessen the distance between performers and audience, which in turn allowed political ideas to be discussed more freely. One of the main accomplishments of this phenomenon was to reintroduce political discourse to art, theater, and cultural life in the sixties after its virtual eclipse in the early postwar era. As cultural and political expressions intertwined and influenced each other, these groups manifested considerable overlap between the New Left and the counterculture in terms of personnel, ideology, and culture. Finally, the careers of individuals in these groups after the groups changed or disbanded gives the lie to the motion of sixties radicals as abandoning politics after the decade ended. Their activism and concern for social change persisted into the 1970s and beyond.

Public performance links these groups and provides a window on larger political and cultural transformations, such as the civil rights movement, the antiwar movement, and the counterculture. The SNCC Freedom Singers and other civil rights activists sang songs such as "We Shall Overcome," "This Little Light of Mine," and "We Shall Not Be Moved" on the front lines of sit-ins, marches, and other protests. After performances of *Paradise Now* (1968–70), the Living Theatre accompanied its audience into the streets to begin what it called the "beautiful nonviolent anarchist revolution." The Diggers performed puppet shows on the streets of San Francisco's Haight-Ashbury neighborhood and distributed free food in Golden Gate Park. Sculptors, painters, and other artists in the AWC staged imaginative public protests against the Vietnam War in New York City's streets and museums. GAAG's guerrilla actions subverted museums' institutional prestige by disturbing business-as-usual, provoking authorities and challenging the art world by exposing its relationship to the American military-industrial complex.

These groups reflected a broad set of political influences, which resulted in diverse connections to larger cultural and protest movements. The Freedom Singers' music embodied their commitment to the nonviolent direct action politics of the civil rights movement in the early sixties. Living Theatre founders Julian Beck and Judith Malina enjoyed relationships with the writer and philosopher Paul Goodman and Dorothy Day of the *Catholic Worker*, producing some of Goodman's plays and getting arrested with Day in the General Strikes for Peace of the 1950s; Goodman's anarchism and Day's pacifism inspired the Living Theatre's work. The Diggers, a community-oriented group with theatrical roots, drew from a variety of political influences, including the seventeenth-century English utopian sect which was their namesake. Anarchism pervaded Digger politics. They advocated circumventing the money system, which they saw as "blocking the free flow of energy."[7] Influenced by the broader New Left, the AWC and GAAG spearheaded the antiwar movement within the art world, also focusing on issues concerning artistic freedom.

The diverse realms of cultural life these groups represent demonstrate the pervasiveness of politically oriented public performance in the sixties; that the Freedom Singers, the Living Theatre, the Diggers, the AWC, and GAAG all gravitated toward a shared sensibility of expression suggests the vitality of this broad-based phenomenon. Several theater groups along with the Living Theatre combined politics and public performance during the sixties, but the activity of cultural groups from a variety of media confirms that this trend transcended the theater world. The AWC and GAAG, for instance, followed the art world lead of Happenings in staging events outside museums and galleries. The Diggers' theatrical background and position at the counterculture's Haight-Ashbury epicenter allowed them to create festivals, performances, and events on their neighborhood's streets. The Freedom Singers provide an especially useful measure of this use of public spaces, since they were a predominantly black group, originating in the rural South, with stronger ties to the civil rights movement than to the artistic and cultural worlds per se. Freedom singing's emergence in the early sixties provided a precedent for the use of public spaces for performance, and the practice flourished as the decade progressed.

The move of cultural performances into the streets marked a sharp contrast to the early postwar era.[8] The 1947 House Un-American Activities Committee "Hollywood" hearings, designed to uncover Communist subversion in the motion picture industry, served harsh notice about the limits of cultural expression in cold war America. The episode heralded a period of retreat from overtly political subject matter in the arts during the fifties, reinforcing the prevailing view that art and culture ought to be separate from politics. "During the McCarthy era," the Living Theatre's cofounder, Julian Beck, recalled, "the repression was so great that even the critics would say 'You cannot mix art and politics.'"[9] The trend toward "apolitical" art also marked the visual arts, where abstract expressionism became the dominant form. The art historian Serge Guilbaut has shown how abstract expressionism, though a rebellion in artistic form, was so "neutral" and devoid of ideology that American politicians deployed it as cold war propaganda symbolizing the "freedom" of the individual artist under American capitalism.[10] Abstract expressionism's hegemony persisted until the sixties, when new forms emerged that were inspired by the materials and routines of everyday life.

Prior to the cold war era, there were several important antecedents to groups such as the Living Theatre and the Diggers. In the 1910s, the Provincetown Players produced innovative theater that stressed both personal liberation and community goals based on the premise that cultural expressions could transform society. The Provincetown Players even practiced a form of what the Living Theatre (and Students for a Democratic Society) later called "collective creation." Many of the Players participated in the 1913 Paterson Strike Pageant, a theatrical spectacle written by John Reed, in which fifteen hundred silk workers reenacted their strike before an estimated audience of fifteen thousand at the old Madison Square Garden. The Paterson Strike Pageant blurred the lines between art and everyday life, creating a spectacle in a venue not usually used for theater, staging the performance to maximize audience participation, and anticipating sixties participatory events such as Happenings, the Diggers' Invisible Circus, and the Living Theatre's *Paradise Now*.[11]

Likewise, in the 1930s, groups such as Harold Clurman's Group Theatre and Orson Welles's Mercury Theatre led the "People's Theatre" movement that has been called "the left-wing theatrical renaissance of the depression."[12] Even the government-funded Federal Theatre Project, part of the New Deal's Works Progress Administration, often addressed contemporary social issues and did not shirk controversy. In particular, the Federal Theatre's Living

Newspaper unit, led by Joseph Losey and Nicholas Ray, staged innovative dramas that explored specific social problems and their solutions and anticipated the Living Theatre's interest in the anti-naturalist theater of the Soviet director Vsevolod Meyerhold and served as an antecedent to the Diggers' creation of spectacles that collapsed the boundaries between art and everyday life. In the visual arts as well, from the influential Mexican muralists Diego Rivera and Jose Clemente Orozco, to the public art of the Treasury Section of Fine Arts under the Public Buildings Administration, to the radicalized striking cartoonists at Walt Disney Studios, artists' work reflected the dignity of work and collectivism central to the Popular Front's cultural agenda.[13] Although the seeds of later repression were sometimes evident, as in the scrapping of Rivera's now infamous Rockefeller Center mural with its image of Lenin and in Congress's cutting of the Federal Theatre's funding from fear of Soviet influence, on the whole the cultural milieu of the Depression encouraged artists, writers, and playwrights to grapple with the pressing issues of the day. This encouragement contrasts sharply with the repressive period following World War II.

While the McCarthy-era injunction against combining art and politics weighed heavily on theater groups in the fifties, the Living Theatre drew on another innovative cultural influence to expand its range of expression: the Beat literary movement. The Living Theatre's production of Jack Gelber's *The Connection* (1959), inspired by Beat experiments and improvisations, shattered the taboos of fifties artistic expression in form and content.[14] These elements of the Beat literary aesthetic were themselves influenced by improvisational jazz, and many of the characters in *The Connection* were jazz musicians, whose performances featured extended live jazz interludes. *The Connection* combined scripted dialogue and improvisational sections to depict the daily lives of junkies. At times, the staging was such that audiences were convinced that the junkies the actors portrayed were real, an effect enhanced by the Living Theatre's use of actual junkies to play some of the minor roles.[15]

The Connection marked a watershed in the Living Theatre's culture, introducing an unprecedented level of improvisation, topical subject matter, and an interracial cast, all of which proved hallmarks of the company's subsequent work. Jazz musicians involved with *The Connection* introduced Julian Beck and Judith Malina to smoking marijuana, which was part of a complex of communal activities that shaped the Living Theatre's identity in the sixties. The Diggers, too, often used drugs recreationally or to augment their creativity. Popular memory associates the Diggers and the Living Theatre with the counterculture, and (as opposed to the SNCC Freedom Singers, the Art

Workers Coalition, and the Guerrilla Art Action Group), marijuana, LSD, and amphetamines played a significant role in the culture of these groups.

The sense of group identity—the self-conscious understanding by individual members of belonging to a collective—varied among these groups, but it typically played an important role in their cultural sensibilities. The SNCC Freedom Singers represented a more formal manifestation of the larger body of freedom singers in the civil rights movement. For this larger group, singing was just one element, though probably one of the most important elements, of their identity as activists in the civil rights struggle. The Living Theatre embraced communal living well into its career—while in residence in Europe during the mid-sixties—but this new collective ethic soon came to inform the company's process and politics in fundamental ways. The Diggers functioned as a collective from the start, almost from the minute that key Digger personnel split with the San Francisco Mime Troupe in 1966. Though the struggle for individual freedom, construed as pursuing the authentic self, figured prominently in the Diggers' message, it did so in a communal context that increasingly required personal preferences to be subordinated to group needs. The collectivist ethic was weakest among the visual artists in the AWC. At the outset, the AWC adopted the word "coalition" as part of its name, as the word implied a more tentative alliance than "union." Individual participants could thus coalesce over discrete issues rather than embracing an entire ideological platform. Indeed, the AWC first convened as an umbrella organization to lobby for the artistic rights of visual artists. Only later did the AWC, and its related but more radical offshoot, GAAG, begin to protest the war in Vietnam. At no point did communal living play a vital role in the careers of the AWC or GAAG.[16]

Why did these diverse collectives thrust themselves outside traditional arenas of cultural expression and into the streets in the sixties? The answer involves a pervasive effort to move beyond bourgeois cultural venues such as theaters, concert halls, and museums, and to democratize culture by trying to communicate with broader audiences where the performer-activists encountered them, most often, in the streets. In the SNCC Freedom Singers' case, artistic considerations always remained subservient to their commitment to the larger civil rights movement. As movement activists, the Freedom Singers had already participated in direct-action protests in public spaces. Moreover, singing represented a widespread movement practice that publicly symbolized its ideals of unity, equality, and freedom. When the Freedom Singers were organized as a formal group for fundraising and to publicize the movement outside the

South, they simply expanded the work that the larger body of freedom singers had already begun. Integration and voting rights constituted the movement's key goals in the early sixties, reflecting the activists' desire for inclusion in mainstream American life as opposed to its radical overhaul.

These goals of full citizenship might suggest that the Freedom Singers embraced the mainstream to a greater degree than the Living Theatre, the Diggers, the AWC, and GAAG. Certainly they differed from these groups by remaining political activists first and foremost. Yet they also established a precedent of using the streets to dramatize their political beliefs, creating cultural space for public performance from which the other groups benefited. Though the other groups shared an antipathy to American capitalism that seemingly set them apart from the Freedom Singers and propelled them into the streets, it is important to remember the more radical turn the civil rights movement took after 1965 toward issues of economic justice and cultural identity. The music changed to reflect this turn. For instance, the Chicago movement adapted "This Little Light of Mine" to reflect the movement's new urban, economic focus in the song "I Don't Want to Be Lost in the Slums." Other Chicago movement songs derided hazardous lead paint and threatened rent strikes if landlords failed to address substandard housing conditions.[17] Thus the post-1965 songs of urban discontent and economic rights constitute important context for understanding the complete trajectory of freedom singing.

Both the Living Theatre's and the Diggers' work featured criticism of the money system as a central theme. The Living Theatre's *Paradise Now* opened with the "Rite of Guerrilla Theatre," in which the actors intoned five key phrases to provoke audience response. The *Paradise Now* production notes explained one of these phrases, "You can't live if you don't have money," by arguing that "there is no way to sustain yourself on this planet without involvement in the monetary system."[18] "The Rite of Guerrilla Theatre" criticizes this state of affairs; taken further, however, the critique implied by "You can't live if you don't have money" was that it was morally and ethically inconsistent to make theater calling for social transformation in traditional theater venues with their high ticket prices. The Living Theatre's eventual shift to street theater in the seventies was a logical outgrowth of this critique.

The Diggers adopted a more direct approach to fusing politics and action during the sixties, distributing free food in the Panhandle of Golden Gate Park and clothing in their free store. The group's numerous broadsides and manifestos labeled the food and clothes "free because it's yours." That slogan emblematized the Diggers' more communal understanding of property than existed in mainstream American society. While the Living Theatre lamented about the impossibility of living without money, the Diggers staged a "Death of Money Parade." This street theater action featured a bizarre funeral procession with Diggers and members of the San Francisco Mime Troupe (SFMT) clad in eclectic beggar costumes carrying a black-draped coffin around Haight-Ashbury.[19] Though members of the SFMT started the Diggers, and some Diggers possessed traditional theater backgrounds, the group's presence in the streets and public spaces was driven by the hippie scene in Haight-Ashbury during the mid-sixties. The emergence of hippie street culture in the Haight coincided with the apex of the Diggers' influence in the community.

Opposition to the Vietnam War became the principal focus of the AWC, but its earliest demands in a protest directed at the Museum of Modern Art included two free evenings a week for working people to visit the museum. The AWC sought to make the New York art world more accessible to a broader economic cross-section of the public. Resistance to such demands contributed to the AWC's decision to stage their guerrilla action protests in the public spaces in and around New York's museums, making the actions accessible to the general public. GAAG, though not embracing any specific anticapitalist program, engaged in a critique of capitalism that exposed the art world's links to the corporate underwriters of the Vietnam War and railed against the commodification of art. GAAG's public actions dramatized this critique, which owed much to the New Left's efforts to redefine legitimate corporate behavior during the sixties.[20]

These groups are not the only ones that combined politics and public performance during the sixties. Certainly the mix can be seen in several highly theatrical, symbolic, public protests in the late sixties, from the Yippie-led initiative to "levitate" the Pentagon as part of the 1967 Stop the Draft Week activities to women's liberationists crowning a live sheep to protest the 1968 Miss America Pageant for its objectification of women. This element defined the aesthetic sensibility of a critical mass of the era's socially conscious artists. In the theater alone, collectives such as the SFMT, El Teatro Campesino, and Bread and Puppet Theater also brought their work to the streets. The groups featured here, however, comprise a cross-section of the cultural world, whose primary backgrounds represent not only theater, but music and the visual arts as well. My focus on groups representing different media suggests the pervasiveness of public performance as a strategy for addressing politics during this period. Analysis of the diverse obstacles, challenges, and pitfalls that confronted groups in various media allows for a richer, more nuanced discussion of politicized cultural expressions than would restricting the study to a single medium.

These groups enjoyed considerable notoriety and influence during the sixties. The SNCC Freedom Singers published books of the songs used in direct action protests, performed in Carnegie Hall, and eventually spawned the popular African American a cappella singing group Sweet Honey in the Rock. The Living Theatre's 1968–69 tour resulted in mass arrests in several cities, usually for public nudity, and garnered national media attention. The rock singer Jim Morrison's highly publicized 1968 arrest in Miami on obscenity charges occurred shortly after he attended *Paradise Now*, which encouraged spectators to take off their clothes.[21] The Diggers figure centrally in contemporary media coverage of the development of Haight-Ashbury's hippie scene and the emergence of the counterculture. The AWC and GAAG were the subject of extensive, often hostile, debate in the mainstream art press, including the writings of the *New York Times* art critics Hilton Kramer and Grace Glueck, and art journals such as *Artforum, Arts Magazine,* and *Studio International.*

The work of these groups conveys a strong sense of the sixties as a time of expansive possibilities. The title of the Living Theatre's *Paradise Now* proclaimed that personal and communal liberation loomed as a tangible, immediately gratifiable possibility. These groups shared a fundamental optimism, fueled in part by the spectacular economic growth of the early and mid-sixties. "We thought we were going to change everything," the Living Theatre's Malina recalled, underscoring the period's buoyant mood.[22] Despite rising inflation, the still-expanding economy generated a sanguine outlook on politicized cultural expressions as a legitimate vehicle for change. Economic abundance empowered these groups to assume that positive political and social change was attainable, and that art, theater, and culture had a role to play in this transformation. It seemed possible that sympathetic affluent liberals would generously fund such work; after all, liberals dominated the American political mainstream for most of the decade. Though sixties arts and cultural groups may have putatively opposed liberals, they shared some of the same core values, such as a sympathy with the civil rights movement, a desire to ameliorate poverty, and a commitment to free expression. At the very least, these groups existed in a climate that did not overtly attempt to repress culture that criticized American capitalist society.

Simultaneous with an expanding economy, an emerging set of values associated with young people in the sixties, which the historian David Farber has called the "values of consumption," informed the sizable expectations with which these groups approached their work. Personal creative freedom, liberated self-expression, and immediate gratification, the mainstays of the consumption ethos, became institutionalized in youth culture.[23] Not only did the values of consumption influence artistic and cultural work, they provided a rationale for "authentic" public self-expression as consistent with the egalitarian politics of the era.[24] The groups featured here believed in the imperative for authenticity epitomized by the Diggers' credo, "Do your thing," and felt compelled to express their beliefs publicly. Thus the movement to the streets with politically charged theatrics represented an attempt to "re-enchant" and re-animate politics by self-consciously eroding the boundaries "between politics and art, politics and culture, politics and everyday life."[25] This book examines groups enmeshed in this process of re-enchantment through authentic public expression.

Chapter 1 investigates the SNCC Freedom Singers and others who used music to support the political activism of the civil rights movement. In the process, these activists were key players in resurrecting a tradition of protest song largely dormant since the thirties, despite the efforts of the less-publicized folk movements of the fifties, such as the one associated with the Highlander Folk School in Tennessee. Singing in SNCC was often led by local songleaders who had been trained by SNCC field-workers to use freedom songs as organizing tools in meetings. This process reflected SNCC's philosophy of trying to develop local leadership at the grass roots and thus embody the equality of their social and political agenda within the organization. The Freedom Singers and other civil rights activists worked from an eclectic body of songs drawn from a variety of sources, such as African American spirituals, the labor movement, and contemporary rhythm and blues. With only a few exceptions, they tended to avoid original compositions, choosing rather to adapt and rework their existing repertoire to fit new situations of social contestation in the civil rights movement.[26] The chapter concludes by considering why singing declined in importance just as the civil rights movement shifted toward separatism and black nationalism in the mid-sixties, suggesting both that the freedom songs reflected an integrationist ethos that no longer held relevance to the movement's vanguard after 1965, and that on some level, the music remained, but was transformed to reflect the movement's focus on economic justice.

Chapter 2 examines the Living Theatre's transition from poetic drama and formal experiments in the fifties to overtly political theater in the sixties. The collaborative process the Living Theatre developed, "collective creation," strove to embody the politics of equality in a manner similar to that of SNCC. The Living Theatre developed collective creation while in European "exile" from 1964 to 1968, as the company self-consciously adopted a communal identity.[27] The company's European experience marked its U.S. tour of 1968–69, when its pacifism proved discordant with the cultural moment following the assassinations of Martin Luther King Jr. and Robert Kennedy. *Paradise Now* and the other works in the repertoire on the 1968–69 tour sought to minimize the distance between performers and audiences, ultimately propelling the Living Theatre into the streets, as street theater became a mainstay of the company's work after the late 1960s.

Chapter 3 considers why the Diggers focused on questioning and subverting the money system. The Diggers asserted themselves as a political conscience for the Haight-Ashbury counterculture, holding this new community accountable for living up to its ideals of love and personal freedom. The group's prolific broadsides, which they posted on neighborhood streets, furnish evidence of this sensibility. Digger writings criticized countercultural festival concessionaires for marketing "pseudo psychedelia," rock bands for aspiring to conventional music industry success, and hippie merchants for collaborating with the police to protect their private property.[28] In October 1967 the Diggers staged a "Death of Hippie" parade through Haight-Ashbury, attempting to rescue countercultural ideals from their perversion by "media poisoners."[29] This public performance and others like it dramatized the Diggers' utopian vision of a "post-scarcity" society. Finally, the chapter examines how key Digger personnel, frustrated by the deterioration of conditions in the Haight despite the Diggers' efforts, attempted to pursue their utopian inclinations in the hinterlands as part of the rural communard exodus of the late sixties and early seventies.

Chapter 4 considers the Art Workers Coalition and a related but separate group, the Guerrilla Arts Action Group, examining the political agenda behind their protests and actions. For example, the AWC's list of demands in 1969 to the Museum of Modern Art (MoMA) included greater representation for black and Latino artists, issues of artistic freedom, and making the museum more accessible to working people. Ultimately, the most noteworthy AWC/GAAG protests centered on the Vietnam War. In April 1969 the AWC initiated a "Mass Antiwar Mail-In," in which members paraded with mailable antiwar art works, addressed to "The Joints Chiefs of War," to the Canal Street Post Office and mailed them to Washington, D.C. GAAG staged its "Blood Bath" action in MoMA, littering the museum floor with lists of their demands, ripping off each other's clothes, and spurting fake blood to dramatize the "mess" of Vietnam.[30] As the AWC and GAAG increasingly engaged in antiwar protest, the content of some members' artwork became more politicized. Yet many artists kept politics out of their art; rather, they chose to politicize themselves by adopting a set of conditions under which they gave and withheld their art. The various strategies for politicizing art, and the reaction to such strategies by the larger art world, constitute a central concern of this chapter.

These groups and their efforts to take artistic expression into the streets have received little sustained scholarly attention that examines the relationship between their artistic and historical contexts. For instance, the Living Theatre has figured prominently in dramatic criticism, but such accounts dwell on the company's theatrical innovations rather than on how its notoriety coincided with a particular cultural and historical moment. Most of the material published on the Living Theatre focuses on its history through the 1968–69 tour, scarcely mentioning the company's seventies work, which most successfully blended its artistic and political sensibilities.[31] Histories of the civil rights movement often treat singing as an anecdotal sidebar to the larger movement, albeit a positive one, never foregrounding the significance of the singers' presence in public spaces, or the songs' role in maintaining courage and resolve and in sending messages to segregationist forces.[32] Early historians of the sixties typically either dismissed the Diggers' antics as outrageous, alluded to them anecdotally as emblematic of countercultural zaniness, or cast them as foils to the "straight" New Left, but recent scholarship has focused more sustained, serious attention on the ideas and politics undergirding Digger actions; it is my intention to contribute to this trend by examining the Diggers' public performances and participatory events.[33]

The AWC and GAAG have attracted the least scholarly attention of these groups. Though the art historian Lucy Lippard has assessed their contributions, she focuses primarily on the groups' relationship to developments and institutions in the larger art world.[34] The meaning of the AWC's and GAAG's innovative public performances in a larger trans-media cultural context is only a secondary focus in Lippard's insightful work. The present study identifies the political and ideological commonalties of these two groups, focusing on their public performances and arguing that they deserve a place among the dominant cultural and political trends of the sixties and early seventies.

My work rejects many of the earliest interpretations of the sixties which tended to treat culture and politics as separate categories and acknowledged only those individuals and groups who tried to achieve legislative and structural political changes as legitimately political while portraying the counterculture as a sideshow separate from politics.[35] I contend that cultural groups' own understandings of their political purposes furnish the most appropriate starting point for a discussion of their political content. The groups I discuss were linked to the New Left and to the counterculture. Thus they resist the conventional definition of an apolitical counterculture bent on "tuning in, turning on, and dropping out" without confronting mainstream American institutions directly. By the same token, that the groups' ideologies reflected influences rooted in the political Left demonstrates the applicability of New Left ideas to the cultural sphere. Their experiences argue for a closer relationship between the ideas and lifestyles of the counterculture and the New Left than occurs in works that conceptualize the two as separate phenomena, contend that the counterculture folded when faced with the "pressures of politicization," or maintain that New Leftists viewed "the crush of countercultural hedonism" as destructive to their movement.[36]

Recent scholarship articulates a more nuanced view of the relationship between the counterculture and the New Left. Rejecting the theory of a split between the New Left and the counterculture as the sixties wore on, one line of recent scholarship argues that the two increasingly intertwined as the decade progressed. Though initially "the hippies maintained an arm's length relationship with the politicos," beginning with the October 1967 Pentagon demonstration, the distinction between the antiwar movement and the counterculture "blurred" as Vietnam policy and mainstream values became targets of the youth challenge.[37] In another variation, Todd Gitlin, a veteran of Students for a Democratic Society, portrays the political Left and the cultural radicals in a halting, tenuous alliance that was alternatively nurtured and ruptured in the second half of the decade. For instance, according to Gitlin, while the 1967 Human Be-In self-consciously sought to fuse the sensibilities of Haight-Ashbury hippies and Berkeley politicos, it also underscored tensions between these groups. By contrast, the cathartic street rioting of the 1968 Chicago Democratic Convention and the Columbia University confrontations unified radicals and counterculturalists against the authoritarian brutality both faced.[38] Several scholars have noted the role that "consciousness-expanding" drugs played in promoting and discouraging, fusion between the two groups.[39] By contrast, the People's Park movement in Berkeley, which again self-consciously attempted to facilitate collaboration between cultural and political radicals, actually proved divisive when these groups were challenged by the armed repression of the National Guard called out by Governor Ronald Reagan. Political radicals interpreted the violence as a call to heighten both their rhetoric and resistance, sometimes invoking the need for paramilitary training, while the People's Park's countercultural contingent shifted to an ecological sensibility or abandoned politics altogether.[40] The cultural historian George Lipsitz characterizes the counterculture as alternative rather than oppositional, arguing that its imperative that personal transformation and enlightenment precede changing the world "did too little to interrogate the axes of power in society." Lipsitz cites institutionalized racism and sexism, the imperialistic brutality of the Vietnam War, and the ease with which capitalist society co-opted hippie social and economic innovations as forces too powerful for the counterculture's alternative lifestyles to combat.[41]

Though Lipsitz's distinction is compelling, it represents the counterculture's political content as a zero-sum game: either the counterculture was political or it wasn't. The communal identities and collective approaches that the groups featured in this study embraced, together with a sense of politics that owed much to the New Left, suggest a picture of convergence between the counterculture and the New Left as a complexly textured phenomenon. Overlapping ideas and influences between the two were fluid rather than static, were analyzed, selected, rejected, and transformed freely and for reasons that were sometimes opportunistic, capricious, and even whimsical. Interlocking personal and social relationships and overlapping personnel tied these arts and cultural groups to the counterculture and the New Left. For instance, in June 1967 four Diggers (a group usually associated with the counterculture) deliberately disrupted a Students for a Democratic Society alumni conference, leaving a large faction of New Left veterans "turned on by their theater of cruelty" and "shaken, intrigued, and tempted by the Diggers."[42] Emmett Grogan, a Digger and countercultural icon, discussed guerrilla theater with key organizers of a forerunner of AWC, "Angry Arts against the War in Vietnam," a week-long festival held in New York in the winter of 1967; performers in "Angry Arts" included musicians associated with the folk revival with whom the Freedom Singers often performed. Another AWC precursor, Artists and Writers Protest, published its condemnation of the Vietnam War in the SDS magazine, *Caw*. Not surprisingly, upon its 1969 founding the AWC bore a marked resemblance to the New Left in its goals, ideologies, and tactics. Julian Beck and Judith Malina, whose Living Theatre later became identified with the counterculture, participated with folk revival figures and the civil rights activist Bayard Rustin in the General Strikes for Peace of the early 1960s. During its 1968–69 American tour, the Living Theatre's audiences consisted of not just the student Left but young people identifying with countercultural rebellion. *Paradise Now*, the tour's centerpiece, linked immediate political issues such as Vietnam to a larger array of social and personal freedoms which the counterculture embraced.

These relationships demonstrate a convergence between countercultural figures and the "political Left" that involves a broader definition of politics than the traditional view that cultural expressions are separate from politics since they occur outside the parameters of elections, party politics, and organized social movements. This book fits into a growing body of scholarship that reconceptualizes what constitutes "authentic" political activity as broader than solely that which takes place within established institutions.[43] One emerging line of argument is that far from serving simply as a weak substitute for politics, culture can become a sort of pre-political form, or a "rehearsal for politics." Within this framework, culture is seen as possessing a viable "oppositional potential."[44] Some observers have ventured further, suggesting that radical artistic expressions and cultural forms serve not merely as rehearsals for politics but rather amount to a form of "counterculture" or "oppositional stance," contesting mainstream values and society.[45] The groups featured in this study not only "rehearsed" deeply felt political beliefs, they performed their visions of politics publicly. Central to their politics was the moral conviction that personal choices, lifestyles, and acts of artistic creation are infused with important political dimensions. These groups shared this vision of personal politics with a larger movement that included the New Left, the counterculture, and the emerging feminist movement during the sixties. Most important, they addressed the relationship between politics and lifestyle, boldly imploding these categories in dramatic and provocative public spectacles.

CHAPTER ONE

Freedom Singers of the Civil Rights Movement: Delivering a Message on the Front Lines

The civil rights movement achieved its greatest triumphs by bringing to the fore issues of human and constitutional rights, morality, power relations, race, and culture, and giving these abstract concepts concrete shape in the hearts and minds of the American public. Movement activists accomplished this through a series of direct action nonviolent protests designed to call attention to the injustices of southern segregationist society. Many of the most celebrated direct action campaigns in the movement, from the Montgomery bus boycott to the lunch counter sit-ins and the Freedom Rides, involved activists' efforts to desegregate public accommodations. Thus the transformation of public space represented one of the movement's most visible and central concerns, and these campaigns spawned a body of freedom songs that became integral to movement strategy. The activists who sang these songs mobilized music as part of the daily struggle waged in the public spaces of the South. The term "freedom singer" applied to anyone who sang songs as part of the civil rights movement. Local campaigns also generated several freedom-singing ensembles that formed to lend their vocal capacities to the struggle. These included the Montgomery Gospel Trio, the Nashville Quartet, the CORE Freedom Singers, the Alabama Christian Movement Choir, and the SNCC Freedom Singers.[1] In this chapter I focus primarily on the activities of the larger, more general body of freedom singers, highlighting at the end the SNCC Freedom Singers, who, apart

20

from television, did the most to spread the movement's music outside the South.

The evolution of the freedom singers' use of music—first overcoming a reluctance to singing in public spaces, then using singing to demonstrate courage and resolve to white authorities, and reworking lyrics to fit different situations of social contestation—demonstrates that they possessed a self-conscious awareness of the performative aspects of public singing and a concern for its effects on various audiences that links them to more overtly theatrical groups such as the Living Theatre, the Diggers, the Art Workers Coalition, and the Guerrilla Art Action Group. Later, after freedom singing was well established as an essential tactic within the movement and as a central part of movement culture, the Student Nonviolent Coordinating Committee sponsored a formal group, the SNCC Freedom Singers, to travel outside the South and perform in concert halls to publicize the cause. With the development of this handpicked group of excellent singing voices who comprised the SNCC Freedom Singers, the performances of the larger, anonymous legions of freedom singers in the South appeared in more conventional ways and in more traditional venues.

Freedom singers sought primarily to advance the integrationist and egalitarian goals of the early civil rights movement. Despite the considerable recognition they received for their music, artistic concerns remained secondary to their roles as activists in a mass democratic movement. Singing, therefore, was important as a tactic, an aspect of movement culture rather than an expression of art for art's sake. Though this difference separated freedom singers from, for instance, the Living Theatre, for whom artistic concerns were always salient, it is less obvious in relation to the Diggers, the Art Workers Coalition, and the Guerrilla Art Action Group, whose expressions were inseparable from the social, political, and cultural upheavals of the sixties.

Though it was not inevitable that freedom singing would play as prominent a role in the civil rights movement as it did, an African American tradition of using music for social protest dated back to the days of slavery. Before the Civil War, slaves used music to resist oppression, singing spirituals about the "freedom train" that served as coded language to help relay practical information for escaping slavery via the Underground Railroad. Runaway slaves also sang to bolster their hope and resolve in the face of danger; Frederick Douglass recounts that the spiritual "Run to Jesus" signified not just the solace of the "world of spirits" but "a speedy pilgrimage toward a free state" in the here and now. This use of music as a tool of resistance continued during the Jim Crow era as African American spirituals were sung to provide comfort in everyday life under racial oppression and in situations of social contestation. For instance, during the Atlanta riots of 1906, the black community sang a version of "Oh Freedom," with its statement of defiance, "And before I'll be a slave / I'll be buried in my grave," which later became a staple of the sixties movement. In the 1930s the Southern Tenant Farmers Union, which included numerous black locals, sang another future freedom song, "We Shall Not Be Moved," in its efforts to confront the poverty and oppression rural sharecroppers endured.[2] Thus singing in the civil rights movement traced a lineage back through African American history; yet in the early sixties, activists came to employ singing on an unprecedented scale, mobilizing freedom songs as a ubiquitous part of the movement's activities from mass meetings to direct action confrontations.

Despite the breadth of singing in the movement, adopting black spirituals did not necessarily come naturally to the middle-class black students in SNCC, the group most responsible for making singing a central element of movement strategy. These students were upwardly mobile, and some of them linked spirituals with slavery and social backwardness. Bernice Reagon has argued that the southern black colleges "as a general rule, attempted to free students from cultural traditions and ties that were distinctly rural, Black and old-fashioned." Rather than the music of the traditional church, black college choirs substituted meticulously arranged "Negro spirituals," which used typically European harmonies and musical structures. This formal training wrought a cumulative effect on black college students. Guy Carawan, music director at Highlander Folk School, referred to the students' singing prior to the sit-ins as "stilted and formal and showing a basic lack of pride in their traditional music."[3]

Yet the traditional spirituals supplied a body of songs with which middle-class students and rural sharecroppers were both familiar, and which could be easily altered or "updated" to address the most timely and pressing issues.[4] Movement activists made a conscious decision to use traditional black music, in conjunction with other forms such as rhythm and blues and gospel, because they believed it could provide a valuable historical link to a tradition of black social contestation. Mobilized in a variety of different situations, singing emerged as the most visible element in the movement culture of SNCC and the larger civil rights movement.[5]

By 1964, SNCC's movement culture included coed and interracial housing in Mississippi's "freedom houses," and even occasional marijuana smoking. The liberalized sexual mores and experimental use of substances that this culture facilitated are phenomena that many historians of the sixties assume that the counterculture invented. Yet SNCC's "communal clustering" anticipated the wider countercultural movement of the mid- and late sixties. SNCC's communal ethos, in which singing functioned as an "organizational glue," links them to groups more closely associated with the counterculture, such as the Living Theatre and the Diggers, both of which pursued communal lifestyles more self-consciously.[6] The continuity of this communal impulse suggests an area of overlap between the political Left and the counterculture.

More than a part of movement culture, singing served as a deliberate and conscious movement tactic. It provided a means of reorienting black cultural identity and affirming a positive link with African American cultural heritage and with traditions of black protest. Prior to the civil rights movement, many African Americans suffered a negative self-image and feelings of inferiority to whites that stemmed from the lingering effects of slavery-era oppressions as well as the legal inequalities of the Jim Crow South.[7] Initially the movement focused on this publicly codified inequality, arguing that blacks should have access to the same rights and privileges of citizenship that whites enjoyed. As early as 1962, however, students in SNCC began to question assimilation, integration, and legal equality as the movement's ultimate goals. They argued that an enhanced sense of black cultural identity and of economic justice were necessary to create a racially egalitarian nation. Ultimately these sentiments evolved into the ideas of "Black Power" and black nationalism that dominated African American discourse by the late sixties, which transformed the civil rights movement from a struggle for integration to a struggle for identity in a society that activists wanted to remake in order to accommodate pluralism. By making the cultural link to traditional African American music, the freedom singers played a vital role in this transition from the early movement's concerns with social relations and voting rights to the focus of Black Power on economic self-determination and cultural expression.

Singing bridged a social gap between the middle-class black college students in SNCC and rural southern blacks, which served SNCC's goal of fostering indigenous leadership in rural black communities. Singing created a sense of unity within the movement and conveyed this unity to the public outside the movement. Moreover, activists regarded singing as crucial to overcoming fear and sustaining courage in the face of violence and hardship. As the forum for freedom songs was increasingly a public one, singing became an outward demonstration of resolve, both to hostile authorities and to Americans outside the South. Finally, singing helped create public sympathy for the civil rights movement. This was accomplished not only through the efforts of the formal group of SNCC Freedom Singers, but through the masses of grassroots civil rights activists for whom such songs, as "We Shall Overcome," "Keep Your Eyes on the Prize," and "This Little Light of Mine" came to accompany almost every movement activity from meetings to mass demonstrations. The freedom singers forged new parameters of public performance, and were thus part of a constellation of cultural shifts that cleared space for groups such as the Living Theatre, the Diggers, the Art Workers Coalition, and the Guerrilla Art Action Group.

Letting the Light Shine: Singing and Black Cultural Identity

The February 1, 1960, sit-in by four black college students at a Woolworth's lunch counter in Greensboro, North Carolina, marked a turning point in the civil rights movement. This demonstration initiated a more confrontational phase of the movement in which students figured prominently, using tactics of nonviolent direct action civil disobedience to protest segregation. The Greensboro sit-in inspired the formation of SNCC in April 1960 and spurred several other sit-in demonstrations, most notably in Nashville, Tennessee. When students from Baptist Theological Seminary, Tennessee State University, and Fisk University started the Nashville sit-ins eight days after Greensboro, singing began to assume an even greater centrality to the civil rights struggle.

With "I'm Gonna Sit at the Welcome Table," SNCC used a traditional tune, kept some verses intact to retain its religious meaning, and added new topical verses typifying the movement's concern with transforming the public space:

> I'm gonna sit at the welcome table,
> I'm gonna sit at the welcome table one of these days, hallelujah,
> I'm gonna sit at the welcome table,
> I'm gonna sit at the welcome table one of these days.
>
> I'm gonna walk these streets of glory,
> I'm gonna walk these streets of glory one of these days, hallelujah,
> I'm gonna walk these streets of glory,
> I'm gonna walk these streets of glory one of these days.
>
> I'm gonna get my civil rights,
> I'm gonna get my civil rights one of these days, hallelujah,
> I'm gonna get my civil rights,
> I'm gonna get my civil rights one of these days.
>
> I'm gonna sit at Woolworth's lunch counter,
> I'm gonna sit at Woolworth's lunch counter one of these days, hallelujah,

I'm gonna sit at Woolworth's lunch counter,
I'm gonna sit at Woolworth's lunch counter one of these days.[8]

Highlighting activists' call for inclusion at the pedestrian "lunch counter" and the exalted "streets of glory," "I'm Gonna Sit at the Welcome Table" infused their worldly goals with a spiritual dimension. Yet the importance to the members of SNCC of access to public accommodations in and of itself should not be understated. The same social ferment that produced the formation of SNCC, a student-led organization in the vanguard of the civil rights movement, propelled many young activists to examine and confront the segregated public spaces of the South in the early sixties. Diane Nash, a student leader in the Nashville sit-ins of 1960 remembered, "When I first came to Nashville, I learned that there was only one movie theatre . . . to which Negroes could go without having to enter through a back door or an alley entrance and climbing up the ceiling or the balcony. . . . I noticed that the lives of the Negro students in Nashville were, for the most part spent on campus . . . simply because there was no place to go." The ensuing Nashville desegregation campaign demonstrated the students' ardor for equal access to the city's public spaces, as lunch counter demonstrators endured cigarette burns and ketchup showers from whites resisting challenges to the prevailing social order.[9]

Further north, in Cairo, Illinois, a campaign to desegregate a municipal swimming pool produced "If You Miss Me at the Back of the Bus," which explicitly emphasized the movement's focus on public life with lyrics such as "If you miss me at the back of the bus, and you can't find me nowhere / Come on up to the front of the bus, I'll be ridin' up there"; "If you miss me at Jackson State, and you can't find me nowhere / Come on over to Ole Miss, I'll be studyin' over there"; and "If you miss me in the Mississippi River, and you can't find me nowhere / Come on down to the city pool, I'll be swimming in there."[10] Like the earlier "I'm Gonna Sit at the Welcome Table," "If You Miss Me at the Back of the Bus" envisioned southern society remade, without discriminatory regulations concerning seating on public transit, educational opportunities, and access to recreational facilities.

In Nashville, young civil rights activists started to use music to overcome ingrained feelings of inferiority to whites. For instance, James Bevel and Bernard LaFayette, two members of a formal group of freedom singers known as the Nashville Quartet, wrote a song called "Dog, Dog" which questioned, from a child's point of view, the southern practice of preventing the social mixing of the races. "I lived next door to a man and he had a lot of children, and so did my dad, but we weren't allowed to play together because they were white," Bevel explained. "But we had two dogs. He had a dog and we had a dog. Our dogs would always play together . . . so we wrote this song for our group." The lyrics to "Dog, Dog" ask the question, "My dog a-love-a your dog / and your dog a-love-a my dog / and then why can't we sit under the apple tree?"[11] By posing the question of why social custom forbids children of different races from playing together as their dogs do, Bevel and LaFayette undermined segregation's paramount ideological presumption, the notion of black inferiority.

"Dog, Dog" represented an atypical freedom song as it was an original composition, yet freedom songs adapted from existing songs also attempted to dispel notions of black inferiority. For instance, "You'd Better Leave Segregation Alone" reworked a rock 'n' roll song originally entitled "You Better Leave My Little Kitten Alone" and included the lyrics "You'd better leave segregation alone / Because they love segregation like a hound dog loves a bone." In this song, the freedom singers aimed the facetious admonition to "leave segregation alone" at prospective activists, wryly weaving cautionary tales of the depth of white zeal for the Jim Crow system with verses such as: "Well I went down to the dime store to get myself some eats / They put me in jail when I sat at them folks seat," and "Well I went down to the dime store to get myself a coke / the waitress looked at me and she thought it was a joke."[12] The phrase "like a hound dog loves a bone" also cast southern whites as canines, portraying white segregationists as less civilized than blacks. The lyrics of "You'd Better Leave Segregation Alone" employed an important strategy of the larger civil rights movement by contrasting polite, civilized young black college students with unruly, brutal white segregationists.

The largest body of freedom songs drew from black spirituals. "(Everybody Says) Freedom" illustrates this most significant group of freedom songs. This song was modeled on "Amen," a spiritual that employed a one-word lyric, "amen," chanted over and over again. "(Everybody Says) Freedom," like "Amen," made use of multi-part harmony and call-and-response vocal techniques from traditional African American music. During the Nashville sit-ins student activists changed the word "amen" to "freedom." In the context of confrontations with Nashville's white segregationist establishment, this song became a powerful statement of the movement's preeminent goal. It also signified racial pride by using the "Amen" melody, affirming the historical link with previous generations of African Americans who struggled under slavery and Jim Crow. SNCC's John Lewis identified "(Everybody Says) Freedom" as "the heart of the Nashville movement," and commented that he felt "uplifted" by the song.[13] Lewis's choice of words suggests that black college students, through freedom songs, increasingly viewed traditional African American culture as a means to promote positive self-identity rather than as an unsophisticated remnant of black life in a rural South they hoped to abandon.

Activists' embrace of traditional black music developed during the sit-ins, but singing had figured in the Montgomery bus boycott, as well, with familiar Christian hymns such as "Onward Christian Soldiers," "What a Fellowship, What a Joy Divine," "Lord I Want to Be a Christian in My Heart," and even "Battle Hymn of the Republic." Julius Lester, then a Fisk University student, commented that during the 1960 mass meetings in Nashville, activists "sang 'Battle Hymn of the Republic' to death, as well as a number of hymns."[14] Lester's comment implies that staid Christian hymns seemed insufficient to student activists engaged in the dynamic and confrontational new phase of the movement that the sit-ins represented. During the Nashville sit-ins, freedom singers replaced the hymns with traditional black spirituals, changing their lyrics as necessary to reflect the daily confrontations and the ideological principles of the movement.

The strategic choice of spirituals manifested black students' growing sense of positive cultural identity. "This Little Light of Mine" overtly reflected the concern with promoting feelings of self-worth. "This little light of mine / I'm gonna let it shine," began the song, affirming a resolution to express oneself as an individual. In the context of the civil rights movement, this amounted to a statement of personal commitment to the struggle for equality. Yet later in the song the subject changes from the first-person-singular "I" to the first-person-plural "we": "We've got the light of freedom / We're gonna let it shine." This shift reflects three significant developments. First, it emphasizes the collective nature of the civil rights struggle in which an affirmation of personal self-worth and commitment became a resolution of action on the part of a larger group of singers. Second, it also suggested the inverse, namely, that the heightened sense of personal identity generated a sense of group empowerment. Finally, deploying the central image of the song, "light," in the same phrase as a key movement goal, "freedom," established light as a metaphor for freedom for the remainder of the song.[15] In the Jim Crow South, where white supremacy was so powerful and resistance so risky that it needed to be carried out surreptitiously, declaring an intention to let the light of freedom "shine" demonstrated an impulse toward self-expression regardless of the costs and a willingness to confront the segregationists.

Movement activists understood that singing helped transform black identity to prepare for the civil rights struggle. "When I opened my mouth and began to sing, there was a force and power within myself I had never heard before," the freedom singer and historian Bernice Reagon remarked of her personal transformation through music, "Somehow this music . . . released a kind of power and required a level of concentrated energy I did not know I had. I liked the feeling."[16] SNCC's Cordell Reagon, who later became Bernice's husband, related the sense of personal empowerment singing provided to the struggle for social and political change: "The music doesn't change governments. Some bureaucrat or some politician isn't going to be changed by some music he hears. But we can change people- individual people. The people can change governments."[17] His comment suggesting that the greatest value of politicized cultural expressions may be in transforming individuals and mobilizing them politically may be applied with at least equal veracity to the careers of the Living Theatre, the Diggers, the Art Workers Coalition, and the Guerrilla Art Action Group.

Within the civil rights movement, recognition of music's ability to empower individuals as activists was not limited to individuals in the vanguard, such as Cordell Reagon; moderate movement leadership agreed on the value of singing as well. For instance, the Reverend Wyatt Tee Walker, executive assistant to the Reverend Dr. Martin Luther King Jr. of the Southern Christian Leadership Conference, noted the diversity of black Southerners he heard singing "We Shall Overcome." Walker concluded that "it generates power that is indescribable" and "serves to keep body and soul together for a better day which is not far off."[18] Dr. King himself observed of the same song, "We shall overcome. That song really sticks with you, doesn't it?"[19]

Bridging the Gap: Freedom Songs, SNCC, and the Creation of Unity

Participants in the civil rights movement came from diverse backgrounds, and singing helped foster a sense of common identity. Bernice Reagon identified the repertoire of freedom songs as one of only a few resources with which SNCC fieldworkers entered local communities. Organizing needs placed a premium on fieldworkers doubling as good songleaders, since singing provided a means by which educated, often middle-class black student activists could effectively communicate with poor rural black Southerners. When the SMCC field secretary and veteran activist Charles Sherrod outlined effective community organizing techniques at a 1963 conference, teaching freedom songs appeared as the first item on his list.[20] Freedom songs allowed diverse groups of black people to bond more closely. "After the song," Bernice Reagon recalled, "the differences among us would not be so great. Somehow, making a song required an expression of that which was common to us all."[21] The songleader Julius Lester claimed that the freedom songs served to "crumble the class barriers within the Negro community." "The professor and the plumber, the society matron and the cleaning woman, the young college student and the unlettered old man," Lester declared, "stand beside each other, united by a song and a dream. They march together and are jailed together."[22] In uniting socioeconomically divergent groups of black Southerners, freedom songs became essential to creating successful mass meetings.

Pointing out the songs' simplicity, the freedom singer and native Mississippian Hollis Watkins explained that anyone could "pick them up" and learn to sing them quickly. According to Watkins, anyone could invent a verse and then "they'd hear their verses coming back to them." Watkins's comments suggest that the process of inventing verses created an equality of musical opportunity, which facilitated greater feelings of equality between the often urban middle-class students in SNCC and the poor rural blacks in the communities where SNCC did fieldwork. Singing was "something that people in the South did," explained Watkins, "if you sang with people, then you could talk about voter registration."[23] Elaborating on how this process worked, Watkins elucidated the rootedness of singing in southern black culture: "Black people, in the South in particular, the vast majority of black people were religious and spiritual beings. And . . . singing was an integral part of their culture because of them being spiritual and religious. They were used to doing a lot of singing, used to being part of that. . . . So, it's deeply embedded into the culture." SNCC field-workers capitalized on music's cultural centrality, adopting singing as a "natural entrée into the hearts, souls, and minds of black people in presenting and offering something that was not foreign to them," and making singing an indispensible part of SNCC's movement culture and organizing strategies. Watkins remarked on the crucial role of singing as a social lubricant at mass meetings: "Mass meetings would generally start . . . with people singing songs—spiritual songs, singing freedom songs—and it was really kind of a warm-up thing to get people involved, to get people to relax."[24] Watkins's remarks highlight how SNCC activists saw singing as a means of establishing rapport with the people of the rural South as a prelude to engaging them politically.

Yet singing exerted influence beyond unifying diverse groups of black Southerners. It also helped to develop indigenous leadership in the southern black communities where SNCC organized. Ella Baker of the Southern Christian Leadership Conference, who convened SNCC's founding conference in April 1960, believed SNCC ought to be a vehicle for "the development of people who are interested not in being leaders as much as in developing leadership among other people."[25] What Baker meant more specifically was that SNCC should try to foster local leadership rather than simply assuming leadership by virtue of the superior educational and class backgrounds of its members. SNCC activists used singing to nurture the kind of indigenous leadership Baker sought by transferring songleading responsibilities from field-workers to local songleaders. To do this, fieldworkers attempted to identify local individuals with the potential to be songleaders. Usually those designated as local songleaders possessed previous singing experience, often in church or school choirs.

Fannie Lou Hamer represents the preeminent example of an uneducated black woman from the rural South who became a civil rights leader thanks in part to her work as a songleader. Hamer worked as a sharecropper for eighteen years before becoming involved with SNCC in 1962 as part of voter registration efforts in Mississippi. She served as a delegate in the Mississippi Freedom Democratic Party (MFDP), which SNCC helped organize through the umbrella organization, the Council of Federated Organizations (COFO.) Hamer received national attention at the 1964 Democratic Convention during the MFDP's bid to unseat the all-white Mississippi regular Democratic delegation, delivering a compelling testimony before the Democratic Party's Credentials Committee, remarking, "If the Freedom Democratic Party is not seated now, I question America." Hamer's nationally televised testimony caused Lyndon Johnson to preempt coverage of her concluding remarks to save the Democratic Party further embarrassment by staging his own impromptu press conference.

Television coverage of the 1964 Democratic Convention showed Hamer leading a powerful rendition of "This Little Light of Mine," which showcased the songleading skills that facilitated her ascent into a leadership position in the movement. Bob Cohen, director of the Mississippi Caravan of Music, a group of folksingers who toured Mississippi as part of the 1964 Freedom Summer, observed, "When Mrs. Hamer finishes singing a few freedom songs one is aware that he has truly heard a fine political speech, stripped of the usual rhetoric and filled with the anger and determination of the civil rights movement. . . . [O]n the other hand in her speeches there is the constant thunder and drive of the music."[26] Cohen's comments highlight the close interplay of music and political activism in the civil rights movement, each one fueling and feeding the other. This mutually reinforcing dynamic between politics and cultural expression characterizes the experiences of myriad groups who used public performance to address political issues in the sixties.

Hamer was forty-four years old when she first became aware of SNCC, but SNCC also helped develop much younger songleaders. In McComb, Mississippi, one of the most hostile locales in the South, Watkins, emerged as a songleader while a high school student. During the Montgomery bus boycott, among the most prominent local songleaders at mass meetings were a group of three elementary school girls. These girls became further involved in the movement as the Montgomery Gospel Trio during the late fifties and early sixties, attending the Highlander Folk School, singing at a Carnegie Hall benefit, and recording with the Folkways Record Company.[27] And of course the college students in SNCC constituted another group of young people in whom songleading experience instilled confidence as activists. Bernice Reagon wrote of her songleading while in the Albany jail: "I found that although I was younger than many of the women in my section of the jail, I was asked to take on leadership roles. First as a song leader and then in most other matters concerning the group, especially in discussions, or when speaking with prison officials."[28] Reagon's account suggests that in the context of SNCC's attempt to function as a "leaderless" organization—and thereby embody within the organization the egalitarian principles they hoped to establish in the South—songleading fostered a kind of organic and tacit leadership necessary to conduct the day-to-day affairs of the movement. Songleading functioned as a de facto authority from which other responsibilities tended to flow. It is not coincidental that some of the most prominent individuals in the history of the civil rights movement, including Fannie Lou Hamer, James Farmer, Cordell Reagon, and Bernice Reagon were prominent songleaders.

Skillful songleaders used the repertoire of freedom songs to generate unity that reached beyond movement activists. Candie Anderson Carawan, a white participant in the Nashville movement, recalled that at the trials resulting from the Nashville sit-ins a group of 2,500 people gathered around the city courthouse to support the arrested students, singing "Everybody Sing Freedom." One of the verses to the freedom singers' adaptation used the words "Civil Rights" as the main lyrical motif. "I looked out at the curb, where the police were patrolling," Carawan remembered, "and caught one burley [*sic*] cop leaning back against his car, singing away—'Civil Rights.' He saw me watching him, stopped abruptly, turned, and walked to the other side of the car."[29] Similarly, one Freedom Rider remembered an initially antagonistic female prison guard in Parchman, Mississippi, who ultimately was "often heard humming our freedom songs."[30] It was a measure of freedom songs' power to achieve unity that during the Albany movement "students were told when they were taken to some of the jails in the surrounding areas, 'I don't want no damn singing and no damn praying.'"[31] This comment indicates that southern authorities themselves recognized the value of singing to movement unity and maintaining high morale.

Activists used singing symbolically to convey unity to people outside the movement who might be sympathetic to its goals. At the 1963 March on Washington singing helped a diverse civil rights leadership demonstrate unity to the general public despite internal conflict between the movement's radical and moderate elements. Most emblematic of the way freedom singers used music to attain unity is the ritual that came to attend the singing of "We Shall Overcome," the movement's most recognizable song.

"We Shall Overcome" originated in black churches in the early 1900s as a song entitled "I'll Overcome Someday," and earlier as "I'll Be All Right." The song also possessed a history of use in social contestation that predated the civil rights movement, as the predominantly black Local 15A of the CIO Food, Tobacco, Agricultural, and Allied Workers Union adapted the song for use on picket lines during a 1945 strike in Charleston, South Carolina. The link to the labor movement is more than coincidental. American workers, from the IWW's preeminent songster Joe Hill to Woody Guthrie, with his ballads of Depression-era labor solidarity, commonly transformed familiar tunes into vehicles of protest by substituting topical lyrics. In Charleston, the strikers added nonvocal modes of participation to the traditional church version of "I'll Overcome Someday," such as hand-clapping and stomping. They also changed the song from first person singular to first person plural: "*We* will win our rights," "*We* will win this fight," and "*We* will overcome."[32] This crucial change in the lyric allowed the song to function as a statement of unity and perseverance, which anticipated its use during the sixties.

The 1945 strike ended successfully, and some of the strikers brought the song to the Highlander Folk School, a progressive adult education school in Monteagle, Tennessee. At Highlander, two women from Local 15A taught the song to Zilphia Horton, the wife of Highlander's founder Myles Horton. She added several verses to the song and taught the song to Pete Seeger, who changed "We will overcome" to "We *shall* overcome," explaining that " 'We shall' opens the mouth wider; the 'i' in 'will' is not an easy vowel to sing well" and added two more verses. In April 1960, Guy Carawan, a white songleader and music director at Highlander, attended the founding conference of SNCC in Raleigh, North Carolina. At the conference, Carawan taught students "We Shall Overcome," and several other songs. SNCC students quickly adopted "We Shall Overcome" into the repertoire of freedom songs, making melodic and rhythmic changes that moved the song closer to its gospel origins.[33]

From the moment of its introduction to SNCC members at the founding conference—sponsored by the Southern Christian Leadership Conference to harness the momentum generated by the student sit-in movement—"We Shall Overcome" demonstrated the ability to create unity. Though SCLC, an established organization composed of black religious and community leaders, tended to be more moderate than SNCC, both groups sang "We Shall Overcome" together at the conference, in effect pledging their commitment and unity.[34] "We Shall Overcome" quickly emerged as the theme song of the civil rights movement, complete with a set of rituals that accompanied its singing. By the summer of 1963 the song typically closed meetings and demonstrations not just of SNCC but of several other organizations as well. Also, activists developed a unique way of physicalizing the sentiment of unity expressed in the lyrics of "We Shall Overcome." Robert Shelton of the *New York Times* observed, "As its stately cadences are sung, the participants cross arms in front of themselves, link hands with the persons on each side and sway in rhythm to the music."[35] This ritual constituted a fervent statement of unity, which television helped disseminate as part of the popular iconography of the sixties (fig. 1).

The following anecdote suggests that activists self-consciously viewed this ritual as a type of public performance, which should follow specific guidelines. SNCC's Cordell Reagon possessed experience as a songleader and field secretary in the Nashville sit-in movement. When Reagon arrived in Albany, Georgia, in the fall of 1961 to help organize that town's black community in a campaign to desegregate public accommodations and fight discrimination in municipal jobs, he found that black students there were already singing a version of "We Shall Overcome." These students had seen and heard the song during television coverage of the sit-ins. In translating the song from what they had heard on television, the Albany students adopted the version with which they were more familiar from their singing experiences in church, which included the use of the first person singular "I'll overcome someday." Reagon quickly showed the Albany students the "proper way" to sing "We Shall Overcome," using the first-person-plural "we," singing it at the end of meetings, and linking hands.[36] That Reagon so carefully taught the Albany students a specific version of the song with its accompanying physical rituals, signifying the collective nature of civil rights activism, emphasized the function of "We Shall Overcome" as a powerful tool with which to express movement unity both to local audiences and to the potentially larger audiences on television. This dimension of the song reached its apotheosis as public performance when 240,000 diverse supporters of civil rights linked arms and joined the gospel

FIG. 1. As the civil rights movement gained confidence, singing played an increasingly prominent role in public demonstrations such as this one. The crossed arms, linked hands, and swaying in time with the rhythm, a ritual linked specifically to "We Shall Overcome," became enshrined in the popular iconography of the sixties. Courtesy Wisconsin Historical Society (WHi-5295).

singer Mahalia Jackson in a rendition of "We Shall Overcome" at the March on Washington for Jobs and Freedom on August 28, 1963.[37]

"We Are Not Afraid Today": Singing to Overcome Fear

Initially freedom songs were used solely in meetings and not at demonstrations. Yet the variety of settings in which activists sang them expanded to a wider array of venues as the movement progressed. The image of civil rights demonstrators clapping and singing movement favorites such as "Everybody Sing Freedom" or "This Little Light of Mine" as they marched through southern streets is now fixed in the popular history of the civil rights movement. Yet it was by no means inevitable that singing in public would become a part of the movement. The earliest sit-ins and demonstrations occurred in silence.

The historian Kenneth Cmiel has pointed out that these early silent, polite, direct action protests were designed to expose the hypocrisy of the southern social order by contrasting black civility with unruly white mobs. To Cmiel this tactic illustrated "the brutality lurking behind established southern etiquette," thereby inverting the presumed white superiority that constituted segregation's ideological basis in what Cmiel refers to as a "bourgeois festival of misrule."[38]

Other factors may have influenced decisions to keep early protests silent. For instance, the leaders of the earliest wave of sit-ins in February 1960 were "very conscious of being charged with rowdiness or uncouth behavior."[39] Certainly singing was beginning to reappear as a form of public protest, slowly reemerging from a period of disuse in the McCarthyite fifties, to regain some of the relevance it had enjoyed as a vibrant part of labor activism from the days of the IWW and the International Labor Defense. In May 1960, University of California–Berkeley students sang and were arrested as part of their public protest of the House Un-American Activities Committee's appearance in San Francisco. Civil rights movement leaders knew, however, that public singing might result in a pretext for local authorities to interfere with demonstrations and make arrests on charges of disorderly conduct. Thus, at the outset of the sixties, when southern segregationist authorities looked for opportunities to reinforce black deference, and when repressive institutional bodies such as HUAC still existed, black activists refrained from singing freedom songs publicly because of their unique vulnerability to hostile reprisals.

In December 1961 the Albany movement decisively changed this, when activists made the crucial transition from singing freedom songs in meetings to singing them in jails and then on the front lines of demonstrations. Police Chief Laurie Prichett deployed the tactic of instituting mass arrests—local authorities arrested 760 demonstrators in December 1961 alone—while mobilizing facilities in adjoining locales to ensure sufficient jail space to remove as many protesters as possible from the streets. Once jailed, the demonstrators sang to overcome fear, maintain unity and morale, and simply to pass the time. The Albany protests yielded mixed results. They did not generate the publicity and media attention needed to pressure local authorities to desegregate the city fully or expeditiously, but Albany represented a clear-cut victory in terms of movement culture and spirit, legitimizing singing in public protests. Since students realized their actions would result in arrest, they believed they might as well sing. "There was more singing than there was talking," recalled Bernice Johnson Reagon. "Songs was the bed of everything." She explained that Albany represented the "mother lode," or the "concentrated essence" of black people's spirit, "our most powerful point in terms of community and peoplehood." The Albany movement received national publicity for its musical creations and innovations, and this attention sparked plans to form a group of traveling freedom singers, which further expanded the public context of freedom songs.[40] By the end of the Albany movement in 1962, freedom songs resonated in marches, during demonstrations, and in jails. As the venues for singing broadened, the freedom singers began to take on a vital public role, which involved quelling activists' fears in potentially dangerous situations.

Direct action protest during the civil rights movement deliberately placed activists in situations designed to provoke southern whites who virulently opposed desegregation. Activists believed that if they could focus national media attention on the violent actions with which some southern whites resisted integration, they would win the battle for public opinion and the federal government would have no choice but to mobilize the Justice Department to intervene on behalf of the movement. This strategy often proved successful, but it entailed serious consequences. The threat of violence assumed an ever-present reality in the daily lives of civil rights workers. During the 1961 Freedom Rides (organized by the Congress of Racial Equality), federal intervention tended to increase over the course of efforts to test compliance with Supreme Court–ordered desegregation of public facilities that served interstate travelers; yet only after Assistant Attorney General John Siegenthaler was clubbed with a baseball bat and hospitalized after trying to protect a white female protester in Montgomery, Alabama, did the Justice Department actively protect civil rights demonstrators from southern white mobs. This incident occurred after mobs set fire to the Freedom Riders' bus in Anniston, Alabama, and after the Ku Klux Klan had beaten the Riders with baseball bats, lead pipes, and chains in Birmingham, while FBI agents and Sheriff Eugene "Bull" Connor witnessed the violence but did not intervene.[41]

Singing helped civil rights workers to face such violence. First, it relieved the tension and pressure of potentially dangerous situations. Second, the words to many of the freedom songs were tailored to reflect the conditions of specific violent encounters, as new lyrics were adapted stressing the need for commitment to the struggle. Candie Anderson (later Carawan) commented that singing was "truly good for the spirit" and helped overcome apprehension during her stay at the Nashville city jail.[42] Albany Police Chief Prichett's practice of instituting mass arrests and jailings—attempting to minimize overt violence and its accompanying unfavorable publicity, harass the demonstrators, and diffuse their momentum—often entailed significant jail time for demonstrators, since SNCC's strategy was to refuse bail in order to pressure local authorities to capitulate to their demands in the face of clogged jails and continued direct action. Prichett avoided this scenario by getting wardens in as many adjoining communities as possible to mobilize their jails to house the Albany protesters, and consequently legions of Albany movement activists were neutralized in prison.[43] As a result, activists grew to recognize the "value of this singing in keeping the courage and morale of the students high." One student remarked that singing "helped to ease the knot in the pit of my stomach." Bernice Reagon remembered how those jailed during the Albany movement changed the verses of "This Little Light of Mine" to reflect the nature of the movement's struggle over public space—"All in the street / I'm going to let it shine"—and the need to persevere through the imprisonment experience—"All in the jailhouse / I'm going to let it shine."[44] Similarly, Julius Lester recalled how Nashville demonstrators responded to running the gauntlet on a street lined with a mob throwing rocks and bottles by singing "We Shall Overcome." Lester argued, "This was not a pretentious display of nonviolence. The song was simply their only recourse at a time when nothing else would have helped."[45]

Freedom songs bolstered civil rights workers' resolve when the threat of violent intimidation might otherwise have proved discouraging, as new adaptations of the songs served to reinforce their determination. This process often happened right on the front lines of protest. For example, Bob Zellner described a march on the mayor's office in Talladega, Alabama, to protest police brutality: "The march was stopped about a block and a half from the campus by 40 city, county, and state policemen with tear gas grenades, billy sticks and a fire truck. When ordered to return to the campus or be beaten back, the students, confronted individually by the police, chose not to move and quietly began singing 'We Shall Not Be Moved.' "[46] With its affirmation that "like a tree, planted by the water" the singers would not be moved, activists used this song to bolster their commitment to the protest. Similarly, "Ain't Gonna Let Nobody Turn Me 'Round" overtly declared the singers' intention to continue fighting for civil rights. Furthermore, the song featured a device that freedom singers wielded effectively, the songleader introducing new verses naming specific oppressors in local campaigns. In Albany, for instance, the singers called out the names of Chief Prichett and Mayor Asa Kelley, avowing their intention not to allow these two men to thwart their protest:

Ain't gonna let Chief Prichett turn me 'round
turn me 'round, turn me 'round

Ain't gonna let Chief Prichett turn me 'round
I'm gonna keep on a walkin', keep on a talkin'
Marching up to freedom land.

Ain't gonna let Mayor Kelley turn me 'round . . .

According to Hollis Watkins, naming local oppressors in freedom songs provided "a way of getting personal" and holding individuals in the southern segregationist power structure accountable for their actions. Watkins claims that this tactic made a powerful impression on local officials, since "they didn't know that you changed the names each time you came to a new town."[47]

Carrying the Story North: The SNCC Freedom Singers

In 1871 the Fisk Jubilee Singers traveled north from Nashville to try to raise $20,000 for the then-fledgling Fisk University. Despite some early struggles, this group, many of whom were ex-slaves, enjoyed monumental success, within three years earning over $100,000 and traveling overseas as well to England, Ireland, Holland, and Germany. Performing mainly for white audiences, the Jubilee Singers' musical trajectory anticipated the freedom singers'. The group started off with ballads and patriotic anthems, only later including slave spirituals, which, accounts suggest, moved audiences deeply, giving them a window into slave and African American culture.[48] The Jubilee Singers shared with the later SNCC Freedom Singers a fundraising purpose, the use of spirituals as the basis of their repertoire, and the aim of educating their predominantly white audiences about black life.

Cordell Reagon organized the SNCC Freedom Singers during the summer of 1962, capitalizing on the national recognition garnered by the music of the Albany movement. The initial group consisted of Reagon, Rutha Harris, and Bernice Johnson (later Reagon),[49] both veterans of the Albany movement, and Charles Neblett.[50] Though fundraising was the group's stated objective, its mission also involved moral and ideological suasion. "Our real purpose," Neblett explained, "is to carry the story of the student movement to the North. Newspapers and UPI often won't give the real story."[51] Regarding the coverage of the mainstream press skeptically, SNCC believed it necessary to find another way to communicate this story of the movement to people outside the South, and Neblett's observation indicates SNCC's conviction that singing could be a powerful instrument for shaping public perception.

The Freedom Singers mixed songs with spoken narrative to illustrate the struggles of blacks at marches and rallies and in jails around the South. Contending that in live performance the songs possessed a great emotional power, Bernice Reagon remarked that the songs "became a major way of making people who were not on the scene feel the intensity of what was happening in the south."[52] The SNCC Freedom Singers were designed to convey developments in the movement specifically to Northerners, with the implication that Southerners, black and white, already understood what Neblett referred to as the "real story" behind the student movement. In a sense, then, singing in the civil rights movement had already achieved a measure of success in fulfilling one of the main functions of public performance, establishing communion with its audience in order to arouse sympathy for the cause of civil rights. In doing so, the SNCC Freedom Singers were simply extending the practices of the larger, less formally organized legions of freedom singers in the movement, who had used singing as a kind of performance, broadcasting their commitment, to each other and to local southern authorities, and emphasizing their resolve in the face of intimidation.

The Freedom Singers debuted as a formal group in a concert with Pete Seeger on November 11, 1962. The following summer an audience of more than 2,000 New Yorkers attended a "Salute to Southern Freedom" benefit concert for SNCC at Carnegie Hall, featuring the Freedom Singers and Mahalia Jackson. Carnegie Hall epitomized northern elite high culture and society, attracting the kind of affluent patronage that often sympathized with liberal causes enough to offer financial support. Robert Shelton's *New York Times* review of this concert hints that the audience displayed a greater interest in the Freedom Singers than in the renowned Jackson, and he attributed this to the fact that the Freedom Singers' songs "echoed with the immediacy of today's headlines the integration battle in the South." This comment suggests that the Freedom Singers' performance re-enacted vividly for their audiences the public actions of the larger group of freedom singers in the South. Shelton's reference to "today's headlines" indicates the role of media coverage in paving the way for the Freedom Singers' favorable reception. Shelton added that the Freedom Singers' message was "delivered in a stirring fashion, musically and morally."[53]

Rather than reflecting a transition from public spaces to more conventional concert halls, the Freedom Singers' formal performances constituted an extension of the larger movement's public performances in the South. This extension, in making freedom songs and the "real story" of the civil rights movement available to a wider public, achieved considerable success, as representatives of northern high culture sometimes initiated their own benefit concerts for SNCC, such as the one the conductor Leonard Bernstein organized with the violinist Isaac Stern in Westport, Connecticut, during the summer of 1964.[54]

Bernice Reagon's discussion of the music at the March on Washington illustrates perfectly the various public functions of freedom singers. She shows how local songleaders from direct action campaigns in the South led the singing on the march itself, so that "the air was filled with the sounds of the jail-ins, Sit-ins, and street marches." Once the march reached the Lincoln Memorial and the official program of speakers began, only the formal group of Freedom Singers represented the music of the movement. The march aimed to convince Congress, then considering legislation that ultimately became the Civil Rights Act of 1964, that activists would continue to mount sustained public pressure for their cause. Reagon describes the contrast between the local songleaders who represented the essence of grassroots activism in the movement and the Freedom Singers. The local songleaders embodied SNCC's ethos of developing indigenous leaders to guide southern black communities in their struggles for voting rights and integration. The musical refinement of their singing was secondary to their passion, their commitment, and their ability to mobilize ordinary black southerners at the grassroots level. On the other hand, though the Freedom Singers individually were experienced veterans of local civil rights struggles, as a group they were already known and possessed a certain amount professional polish as entertainers. The Freedom Singers appeared at the march "as an afterthought through the grace" of the singer Harry Belafonte, who chartered a plane from their engagement in Los Angeles to Washington so that the group could appear on the formal program.

The contrast between freedom singers led by local songleaders and the SNCC Freedom Singers suggests that in the context of national and international attention, the broad coalition of civil rights, labor, and religious groups that organized the march wanted music that demonstrated movement unity performed in a professional and nonconfrontational manner. Putting a nonviolent and not overly militant face on the movement for a television audience in the millions was very important, as CBS aired continuous coverage of the event. The controversy over SNCC chairman John Lewis's speech epitomized this demand for unity. The speech had initially included such incendiary remarks as "The revolution is at hand, and we must free ourselves of the chains of political and economic slavery," and "We will march through the heart of the South, through the heart of Dixie, the way Sherman did. We shall pursue our own scorched earth policy and burn Jim Crow to the ground." At the eleventh hour, more moderate movement elements including the legendary

A. Philip Randolph, the march's original architect, persuaded Lewis to tone down his speech in the name of unity. In a similar vein, the march's leaders viewed the rank-and-file freedom singers led by local songleaders as too un-polished and potentially too militant to represent the movement. Thus the movement's moderate leadership highlighted freedom songs' ability to create unity rather than their value as a tool of direct action oppositional politics.[55] The two songs the Freedom Singers performed, "This Little Light of Mine" and "I Woke Up This Morning with My Mind on Freedom," both appealed to unity and declared the singers' intentions to persevere in the quest for freedom even as the more militant voices of grassroots activism suffused the earlier part of the march. Yet it is possible to overstate the contrast between the SNCC Freedom Singers and the larger grassroots masses who sang at the march. Both were engaged in public performance, and the formal group would not have existed had it not been inspired by singing at the grassroots level. Thus the Freedom Singers' performance should be seen as a more polished, more professional version of the larger group of freedom singers' performances of unity, resolve, and commitment through song at the local level.

Aside from fundraising and the suasion of public opinion, the Freedom Singers' work generated several other important consequences. For one thing, they received considerable critical acclaim for their musical merit. Specifically, the sense of conviction in the Freedom Singers' a cappella vocals sparked the imaginations of the predominantly white folksingers of the "folk revival," who relied primarily on guitar and banjo accompaniment. Folk notables such as Pete Seeger actively encouraged this influence, imploring would-be folksingers to "take up" some of the Freedom Singers' songs "if your heart is downcast or blue, if you feel discouraged and it seems as though the future is all darkness and uncertainty."[56] Such advice not only underlined the Freedom Singers' musical talents; it also implied that the songs themselves could be appropriated to address myriad issues. Unlike the often frivolous mainstream popular music of the early sixties, the music of the folk revival often was infused with serious political content. "Here was a way to make social comments about events in present-day America," Seeger explained, "comments they had been unable to make any other way."[57]

Songs weren't the only aspect of the civil rights movement that musicians of the folk revival were "taking up." Just as the SNCC Freedom Singers worked to spread sentiment for the movement outside the South, folk revival musicians adopted this effort as well. At his Carnegie Hall concert on June 8, 1963, Seeger included numerous freedom songs, opening with "If You Miss

Me at the Back of the Bus," and continuing with "Keep Your Eyes on the Prize," "I Ain't Scared of Your Jail(s)," and "Oh, Freedom!" He closed with "We Shall Overcome." Significantly, the recording of this concert indicates this northern audience's familiarity with freedom songs and their sympathy for the movement, which televised coverage of the violence in Birmingham earlier that spring had doubtless galvanized. The warm reception of Seeger's audience emerged clearly from the opening lines of "If You Miss Me at the Back of the Bus," as he sang, "If you miss me at the back of the bus / and you can't find me nowhere / Come on over to the front of the bus / I'll be ridin' up there," at which point the audience burst into applause. In his preface to the finale, Seeger implored the audience: "If you would like to get out of a pessimistic mood yourself, I got one sure remedy for you—help those people in Birmingham and Mississippi or Alabama." Again the audience cheered fervently as Seeger encouraged them: "All kinds of jobs that need to be done. It takes hands and hearts and heads to do it—human beings to do it—and then we'll see this song come true." Then he launched into "We Shall Overcome."[58] Seeger's concert highlights the interpenetration of the folk revival musicians and SNCC Freedom Singers in terms of both repertoire and political purpose, as both sought to arouse public sympathy for the cause of the civil rights movement at a national level.

Increasingly, the Freedom Singers came to share venues with performers in the folk revival, not only at the March on Washington but also at the 1963 Newport Folk Festival and the 1964 Mississippi Caravan of Music. Performers at the March on Washington included Seeger, Bob Dylan, Joan Baez, Odetta, and Peter, Paul and Mary. At the Newport festival, the Freedom Singers' influence permeated the occasion, as nearly every white folk performer included at least one a cappella selection and a freedom song in his or her repertoire. Seeger viewed the impressive attendance of forty thousand as evidence of a "revived" festival—indeed, though it had begun in 1959, it had not been held the previous two years—crediting the confluence of civil rights and folk music. During the Mississippi Caravan of Music it became clear that the benefits of folk music's alliance with the Freedom Singers worked both ways. Caravan musicians including Seeger, Guy Carawan, Phil Ochs, and Judy Collins encouraged voter registration by staying in Mississippi "for a week or two or sometimes more" and singing at meetings and freedom schools. True to both the oral tradition of folksinging and SNCC's agenda of developing indigenous leadership, the Caravan sessions at the freedom schools sparked young Mississippians to create their own freedom songs.[59]

Civil rights movement themes became common in the lyrics of the topical songwriters of the folk revival, including Dylan, Len Chandler, Phil Ochs, and others. Dylan's songs often examined specific incidents in the movement. For instance, "Oxford Town" dealt with James Meredith's attempt to become the first African American student to enter the University of Mississippi; "The Lonesome Death of Hattie Carroll" exposed the race and class biases of the southern legal system; and "Only a Pawn in Their Game" sought to extract meaning from the murder of Medgar Evers. Dylan typified the singers of the folk revival who generally embraced the cause of civil rights. As early as the summer of 1963, one year before Freedom Summer, Dylan performed with the SNCC Freedom Singers as part of a voter registration drive in Mississippi. The African American folksinger Len Chandler's "The Time of the Tiger" called for an awakening spirit of black militancy, and his pointed variation of the freedom song "Which Side Are You On?," which included the lyric "Come all you bourgeois black men / With all your excess fat / A few days in the county jail / Will sure get rid of that," exhorted the black middle class to redouble their commitment to the movement with direct action and financial support. The subject matter of the topical songwriters' songs mirrored both the themes and the fundraising imperative inherent in the Freedom Singers' mission.[60]

In addition to spreading the story of the movement outside the South, the SNCC Freedom Singers performed in the South itself. In July 1963 Seeger organized a folk festival in Greenwood, Mississippi, in the heart of the Delta, where white resistance to integration was particularly severe. The performers at this festival made up an interracial group, itself a provocation in the Deep South, with Seeger, Dylan, and the Freedom Singers among the notables. SNCC sponsored the event as part of its voter registration drive. The audience was predominantly black and estimated at nearly three hundred people, including about twenty young whites. This concert itself constituted a public direct action since it enacted the civil rights movement's vision of an integrated southern society. As in other direct actions in the Movement, the Freedom Singers and other activists played to a larger public, as the *New York Times* and a television crew from New York covered this event. Thus, freedom singers and the formal SNCC-sponsored singing group they launched not only broke through the taboo and self-censorship surrounding public political performance that existed during the fifties; their public performances garnered substantial national audiences.[61] Furthermore, though freedom songs and topical songwriters (with the exception of Bob Dylan) may never have reached mass audiences commercially (by topping record charts with hit singles, for instance), clearly the social transformations and injustices of which they sang marked an important point along the way in the transition to the more socially conscious popular music of the late sixties.

The freedom singers' awareness of a larger public became evident during the 1965 campaign for voting rights in Alabama. On the road from Selma to Montgomery, songs formed a "steady part of the day and evening activities," with freedom singers inventing new verses to reinforce their resolve and keep morale high. Singers reworked "Oh Prichett, Oh Kelley" from the Albany movement as a message to Alabama governor George Wallace: "Oh Wallace you can never jail us all / Oh Wallace segregation's bound to fall." Similarly, they amended "Ain't Gonna Let Nobody Turn Me 'Round" to include a verse that began, "Ain't gonna let Governor Wallace turn me round." The tone of the march reflected the militancy of SNCC and the movement vanguard— symbolized by the confrontational call-and-response chant of "What do we want? Freedom! When do we want it? NOW!"

Yet when the marchers arrived at the state capitol in Montgomery on March 26, the moderates' public projection of a movement that aspired merely to gain the vote and assimilate to mainstream American life replaced the militant rhetoric of the march. Professional entertainers such as Harry Belafonte, Joan Baez, and Peter, Paul and Mary signified this change and provided the singing, which included a rendition of "The Star Spangled Banner." The appeal to patriotism suggests the moderates' use of music to portray the movement as comfortably within the political mainstream.[62] To the militant SNCC veterans who risked their physical well-being on the movement's front lines, and who were beginning to articulate a political and social agenda whose goals reached beyond desegregation and voting rights to economic and cultural issues, such a musical program represented the co-optation of freedom singing, even as the public performances of the Alabama voting rights campaign had undeniably widened the music's audience.

The co-optation of music in the movement paralleled activists' fears about co-optation of the movement as a whole. By 1965 the radical element of the movement openly challenged integration and assimilation as the preeminent goals, affirming the greater importance of economic justice and cultural identity. These fears of co-optation were exemplified by President Lyndon Johnson's nationally televised speech announcing the legislation that ultimately became the Voting Rights Act of 1965, when Johnson concluded his speech by stating, "It is not just Negroes but all of us who must overcome the crippling legacy of bigotry and injustice. And we shall overcome."[63] From one perspective, that the country's highest-ranking politician cited the movement's theme song on national television in front of an estimated seven million viewers indicated the impact of the freedom singers' influence. Indeed, Martin Luther King reportedly cried as Johnson finished speaking. Yet from the radicals' perspective, Johnson's words amounted to a cynical attempt to "appropriate movement rhetoric in order to blunt protest."[64]

While Johnson attempted to claim his solidarity with civil rights advocates, his speech coincided with the waning of the influence of music in the movement. Bernice Reagon contended that Johnson's use of "We Shall Overcome" marked a "decline in the use of songs and singing" in the movement in general and "ended the effectiveness" of that song in particular.[65] This development occurred at the same time that activists who had been radicalized by confronting violent resistance to civil rights abandoned nonviolence both as a philosophy and a tactic, against a backdrop of urban unrest that began with the Watts riot, which erupted only five days after Johnson signed the Voting Rights Act. The changing course of Julius Lester's career exemplified the dramatic change in the movement and its music after 1965. In the early sixties, Lester stood among the leading enthusiasts of singing, serving as a songleader, writing articles for the seminal folk music publications *Broadside* and *Sing Out!*, and editing *We Shall Overcome!: Songs of the Southern Civil Rights Movement*, a book of freedom songs that Guy and Candie Carawan compiled and published to benefit SNCC. Though in early 1964 Lester had emphasized the importance of freedom singing in sustaining courage to "walk down the streets of Birmingham and face the dogs that are trained to kill on command," by 1966 his attitude toward the movement's earlier ideals of Christian and Gandhian nonviolence had reversed:

Now it is over. The days of singing freedom songs and the days of combating bullets and billy clubs with Love. . . . Love is fragile and gentle and seeks a like response. They used to sing "I Love Everybody" as they ducked bricks and bottles. Now they sing

Too much love,
Too much love,
Nothing kills a nigger like
Too much love.

Lester summarized the militant activists' abandonment of both singing and nonviolence during this period by citing the comment of a SNCC veteran appraising racial conflict in 1966: "Man, the people are too busy getting ready to fight to bother with singing anymore."[66]

Thus the influence of singing began to decline at precisely the same moment that the movement's goals began to shift from integration and voting rights to economic justice, black nationalism, and Black Power. This diminished role suggests that the freedom songs themselves became associated in radical activists' minds with those earlier goals, and appeared impotent in the context of a more militant phase of the movement which challenged the notion that integration and enfranchisement would solve fundamental problems facing African Americans. Yet to argue that "the singing stopped" once black people realized that nonviolent tactics and ideologies offered only limited answers to institutionalized racism is somewhat misleading—in many ways the music continued, only in a transformed state. [67] This transformation had begun as early as December 1964, when the SNCC Freedom Singers performed at a rally for Malcolm X at the Audubon Ballroom in Harlem, singing a tribute to Vice President Oginga Odinga of the newly formed Republic of Kenya. Not only did the Freedom Singers lend their performance to Malcolm X, who had long rejected nonviolence in favor of more militant means of racial empowerment, but one of their members, Matthew Jones, had written the song "Oginga Odinga" after being inspired by Odinga's stories of Kenya's successful struggle for independence, the forces of which had been set in motion by the armed Mau Mau rebellion.[68] Thus the Freedom Singers's performance at the Audubon Ballroom celebrated two figures who symbolized a type of resistance willing to embrace violence if necessary. This episode represented a departure even from the most militant SNCC rhetoric of the early 1960s, such as the original version of John Lewis's speech at the March on Washington, which had vowed, "We shall pursue our own scorched earth policy and burn Jim Crow to the ground."[69] After SNCC's disappointment at the 1964 Democratic convention, when the Mississippi Freedom Democratic Party tried to unseat the regular all-white Mississippi delegation and were offered only a token compromise, SNCC increasingly questioned the efficacy of racial progress via mainstream politics and nonviolent tactics. The SNCC Freedom Singers' performance at the Audubon Ballroom anticipated this ideological sea change within the radical wing of the civil rights movement.

This changing attitude found musical expression elsewhere in the movement and in popular music as well. For instance, responding to the racially charged upheavals in Watts, Chicago, and Detroit, the SCLC organizer Jimmy Collier wrote a song that linked black urban poverty and discontent with the impulse to riot—much as the Kerner Commission Report was to argue—and which ended with the notorious contribution to the lexicon, "Burn, Baby, Burn." In a less dramatic but probably more pervasive way, this more militant tone entered popular music, as the "raw, basic, almost angry" soul and R&B

sounds of the Stax-Volt and Muscle Shoals studios replaced the "cleaner, brighter" Motown aesthetic. The rise of James Brown epitomized this "Africanization" of popular music, and his 1968 hit single "Say It Loud—I'm Black and I'm Proud" explicitly brought the new cultural focus of African American activism to the forefront of public discourse. Furthermore, more closely corresponding to early freedom singing, during the 1968 SCLC-sponsored Poor People's Campaign in Washington, D.C., the organizer Frederick Douglass Kirkpatrick wrote a song that affirmed, "Everybody's got a right to live / Everybody's got a right to live / And before this campaign fail / We'll all go down in jail." This lyric referenced the couplet from "Oh, Freedom," "And before I'll be a slave / I'll be buried in my grave."[70] In this case, the tactic of freedom singing was deployed toward a different end, reflecting the movement's post-1965 emphasis on urban and economic issues rather than social or political conditions in the South.

Clearly the freedom singers left a rich body of work to adapt, transform, and redeploy, a valuable legacy for any cultural group engaged in social contestation. As the civil rights movement successfully entered public spaces in the early sixties, signaling the end of the McCarthy-era stranglehold on political dissent, the freedom singers emerged as a valuable resource in the fight against racial oppression, opening up the public space as a cultural forum and eroding the prohibition on mixing art and politics. The social realities of the segregated South during the early sixties made public spaces the logical sites at which to contest the system. In the spirit of what Students for a Democratic Society later memorably called "participatory democracy," so evident both in the New Left and the civil rights movement, black people at the local level tried to liberate themselves from oppression. Singing became a galvanizing force in achieving unity and an effective way for demonstrators to overcome their fears about the violence they hoped to provoke to dramatize their cause. Perhaps the greatest testimony to the efficacy of singing was the fact that subsequent mass movements of the sixties and seventies, notably the antiwar movement and the women's liberation movement, self-consciously attempted to create and utilize in their own struggles bodies of songs similar to the freedom songs.[71]

With its emphasis on public performance, freedom singing occupied a central place in the movement. Along with a handful of avant-garde innovations in the art and theater worlds, freedom singing helped to create cultural space for several artistic and cultural groups with oppositional and alternative political agendas. In many cases, the agendas of these groups had little to do with civil rights, although most endorsed the freedoms and the equality for which civil rights activists fought. As the sixties progressed, various artistic and theatrical groups struggled to combine their creative sensibilities with their political beliefs and ultimately found public performance crucial to this quest. Though the Living Theatre, a predominantly white New York avant-garde theater company, initially appears to possess little in common with the freedom singers, the two groups shared several crucial characteristics, such as the commitment to an expansive vision of freedom, the pursuit of a nonauthoritarian mode of conducting their everyday affairs, and the desire to make their cultural expressions available to wider audiences through public performance.

CHAPTER TWO

The Living Theatre:
Paradise and Politics in the Streets

"The theatre is in the street. The street belongs to the people. Free the theatre. Free the street. Begin."[1] These final words of the Living Theatre's landmark theatrical production *Paradise Now*, which the company performed from 1968 to 1970, encouraged audiences to begin a nonviolent revolution by moving from the theater into the street; they also encapsulated most of the salient themes of the group's career. The idea that "the theatre is in the street" underscored the cultural currency of public performance, and it was a revelation that came after nearly two decades of struggle to create new ways of making theater that incorporated audiences as more than passive spectators. The claim that "the street belongs to the people" invoked the affinity of the Living Theatre's anarchist and pacifist ideologies with the worldwide flowering of youth activism for democracy and liberation, led by the New Left in the United States. The appeal to "free the theatre" and "free the street" reflected the company's belief that cultural life, represented by "the theatre," and political, public life, by "the street," intertwined inextricably. Finally, these comments also demonstrated a growing awareness of a broad agenda of personal freedoms—such as liberalized sexuality, freedom to experiment with drugs, and freedom from authoritarian control—that characterized the sixties counterculture.

During the Living Theatre's 1968–69 American tour, and to an even greater extent in the seventies, the company embraced public performance as a means of meshing its political, artistic, and personal concerns. Its move to the streets resulted from the convergence of political beliefs and artistic concerns dating back to the late forties and early fifties, yet the company only escaped the confines of traditional paid admission theaters in the late sixties. The Living Theatre benefited from the civil rights movement's expansion of cultural expression in public spaces, and represented a growing number of artistic and theatrical groups who used public spaces as venues for spectacles of oppositional politics.

One of the world's leading experimental theater companies, the Living Theatre mounted its first formal production in New York City in 1951. The company contributed decisively to contemporary theater by challenging popular conceptions of what constitutes a theatrical event, by exploring ways to operate outside the financial constraints of conventional theater, by pioneering techniques for involving the audience, and by infusing its theatrical innovations with the politics of anarchism and pacifism. Along the way, the company angered and frustrated its audiences, inspired the hostility of theater critics and academicians, and encountered the wrath of police and other government authorities. Charles Mee Jr., a contributing editor for *Tulane Drama Review*, once described the Living Theatre as "the brat-child we love to see hit by a car—until we realize that for all its damnable qualities, it had life; for all its silliness and irresponsibility and selfishness and egotism, it was so often right."[2] Despite such visceral reactions, the Living Theatre has enjoyed the greatest longevity of any American theater company.

At a 1986 panel entitled "The Significance and Legacy of the Living Theatre" at New York's Cooper Union, moderator Michael Smith summarized the company's contributions: "Its persistence, the range of its repertory, its marriage of politics and art, its dual function as both a community and a repertory theatre, both in New York and on the road, its extension into five continents, its journeys, its movement from the theatre into the street and back into the theatre . . . make it more than a theatre and yet a theatre par excellence, opening up the concept of what theatre can be and mean." The dramaturge William Coco concurred, pointing out that few theater companies prove capable of sustaining themselves for even a decade. Coco compared the Living Theatre with the seminal Russian theaters of the early twentieth century, led by Vsevolod Meyerhold and Konstantin Stanislavski, arguing that the commonality linking the Russian theaters and the Living Theatre is their dedication to the "pursuit of an Idea."[3] Specifically, the company's dedication to dramatizing ideas of anarchism and pacifism have allowed the group to survive for five decades, most recently remaining active with a residency in Genoa, Italy, part of the year, and in New York for the remainder.

Infusing theater with serious political thought constitutes the Living Theatre's most significant achievement. Though a tradition of political commentary existed in American drama, epitomized by the Group Theatre in the thirties, the Living Theatre along with a handful of other collectives that emerged during the sixties, such as the San Francisco Mime Troupe, El Teatro Campesino, Bread and Puppet Theater, and the Open Theater (founded by former Living Theatre member Joseph Chaiken), revitalized theater's capacity to address political issues directly after the eclipse of obviously topical material during the McCarthy era. Among these groups, the Living Theatre particularly incorporated audiences into performances as a device to broach political issues. By the late sixties, the Living Theatre's notion of politics had expanded from its original emphasis on anarchism and pacifism to include matters previously regarded as lifestyle choices, such as diet, sexuality, and drug use. The Living Theatre shared this expansive conception of politics with the New Left, the counterculture, and the women's liberation movement.

As an anarchist company, the Living Theatre proposes initiatives to combat social problems that reside outside of electoral politics. "Don't vote for the next king," remains a favorite company motto. A strong strain of anticapitalism underlies the company's work, and avoiding the "money system" and the "strictures of Mammon" recur among its themes.[4] Although the Living Theatre's anticapitalism appears to contrast with the aims of the freedom singers, whose songs merely called for blacks' integration and inclusion as first-class citizens rather than for dismantling the society's economic system, it is important to remember that the individuals who were freedom singers and the civil rights movement itself were not static in their development, and that in the mid-sixties the movement's radical wing began to call for more fundamental change in American society, including economic justice, black nationalism, and cultural pluralism. Many individuals who were freedom singers were moving toward increasingly radical positions by the mid-1960s. By the same token, although individual members of the Living Theatre may have subscribed to radical political positions as early as the fifties, it wasn't until the mid-sixties that their theatrical work began to reflect an overt critique of capitalism. This progression suggests an expanding climate of radicalism and experimentation in the cultural realm during the mid-sixties. Like the Diggers, the Living Theatre agitated for radical social change in both personal behavior and political institutions, pointing out the many connections between the two. Both groups objected to the role of the "money system" in supporting a range of authoritarian social and cultural controls.

The Living Theatre shared with the Art Workers Coalition and the Guerrilla Art Action Group, as well as with the New Left, critical ideas about how corporate interests shaped both government policy and American cultural life. This commonality became evident in the way all three groups adamantly opposed the Vietnam War. Yet the Living Theatre's opposition represented only one instance of a deeply held commitment to pacifism that dated back to the fifties. Though the AWC and GAAG may have included individual members who were pacifists, their collective work usually voiced opposition to the Vietnam War specifically. The Living Theatre's work has always articulated general themes of pacifism and nonviolence, before (*Faustina*, 1955, *The Brig*, 1963), during (*Mysteries and Smaller Pieces*, 1965, *Antigone*, 1967, *The Legacy of Cain* 1970–78), and after (*Masse Mensch*, 1980, *Tumult*, 1989) American mobilization in Vietnam. Prior to addressing politics overtly, however, the Living Theatre spent its early career struggling to revitalize the form of theatrical events.

The Living Theatre Begins: A Revolution of Form in McCarthyite America

The Living Theatre's artistic and political vision stemmed from two individuals, Julian Beck and Judith Malina. The two met in New York in 1943; Beck was eighteen, Malina seventeen. During the close friendship that developed, Beck and Malina immersed themselves in the New York cultural scene, especially the theater, which they attended several times each week. In 1948 the couple married, with plans for starting a theater already under way.[5] Until his death in 1985, Beck designed most of the sets for the Living Theatre's productions and exerted the most profound influence on its visual aesthetics. Beck also played leading roles in many of the company's most important productions and wrote and directed several others. Malina directed most of the productions from the early fifties until the mid-sixties, when the company began to employ "collective creation." Even after the company had established collective creation to eliminate the authoritarian position of director, Beck and Malina functioned as the preeminent figures among putative equals.

Beck and Malina founded the Living Theatre in opposition to contemporary Broadway theater, which featured banal star vehicles, high ticket prices, and the stylized realism of modern drama. Expressing a distaste for modern realistic drama with its naturalistic, yet stylized, acting and scenic elements, Malina wrote in her diary, "Broadway buries itself under a sugary realism."[6] In an era when no significant off-Broadway theater movement existed, Beck and Malina sought a larger, more epic, nonnaturalistic style without the "plush seats" and inflated admission prices of Broadway theaters.[7] They planned to create a theater emphasizing contemporary poetic drama performed in repertory for reduced prices. Malina's work with the German director Erwin Piscator, with whom she studied in the New School for Social Research's Dramatic Workshop, shaped this guiding aesthetic. Piscator had emigrated from Germany, where he was renowned for his innovative stagings of classical plays set against the background of the disintegrating Weimar Republic. In 1940 Piscator came to New York and founded the Dramatic Workshop to train actors, directors, playwrights, and designers, and to stimulate an avant-garde theater movement. The Living Theatre emerged as the most significant product of this effort, and Beck and Malina took to heart Piscator's conviction that theater should not serve as mere entertainment but should rather convey a social message.[8] "I have learned to believe in what you believe in, to strive in my way for what you strive for," Malina wrote Piscator, underlining the depth of his influence. "All that I ever hope to be I owe to you."[9]

The Living Theatre's initial work, however, did not address political issues; rather it concentrated on reinventing the form of the theatrical event. This process centered on transforming the audience's experience of theatrical performances. From its inception, the Living Theatre actively subverted theatrical convention. For instance, before they found a theater in which to perform, Beck and Malina took a cue from the early days of the Provincetown Players, staging plays in their West End Avenue apartment in the summer of 1951, and calling their creation "Theater in the Room." Publicity was entirely by word of mouth, so that the audience consisted primarily of a circle of New York artists and intellectuals, Beck's and Malina's friends and colleagues. Responding to inflated Broadway ticket prices which they found so repugnant, Beck and Malina charged no admission, opting to pass a hat among the audience for donations.[10] By doing away with the idea of paying for one's seat, indeed by doing away with the seats themselves—some of the audience sat on a bench, while others sat on cushions—they hoped to involve the audience in an experience of greater intimacy than that of conventional theater. Born of necessity, a result of Beck and Malina's inability to find a suitable home for the Living Theatre, "Theater in the Room" demonstrated a willingness to stage theatrical events outside the theater proper, anticipating the company's move to the streets in the late sixties and seventies. Though radical politics was not yet a part of the Living Theatre's program, "Theater in the Room" represented the first of many attempts to transform the audience's expectations of theater.

According to Beck, "total experience" in theater demanded attention to "three imperatives." In addition to audience participation, Beck cited the need for "narrative," and "transcendence."[11] From the Living Theatre's creation until its watershed production of *The Connection* in 1959, which signified a new theatrical path, poetic drama was the vehicle by which the company pursued these objectives. The company's first performance in an actual theater, a production of Gertrude Stein's *Doctor Faustus Lights the Lights*, opened in December 1951. Beck noted the appeal of Stein's play in terms that prefigured the radical politics of the company's sixties work, calling it part of the "revolution of the word" and pointing to Stein's experimentations with "erasing the platitudes and exploring and pushing at the boundaries of meaning in writing." The connection to Stein reflects a pattern; the Living Theatre's poetic dramas harked back more to literary-oriented American theater innovators, such as the Provincetown Players, than to the radical theater of the thirties, which attempted to voice working-class interests in the conflict between labor and capital.

Poetic dramas such as William Carlos Williams's *Many Loves*, Kenneth Rexroth's *Beyond the Mountains*, Paul Goodman's *The Young Disciple*, and Jean Cocteau's *Orpheus* were among the company's notable productions during the fifties. Beck described the goal of the Living Theatre's poetic dramas as trying to "revivify language" to prevent it from becoming "outmoded" and thus to "enlarge the limits of consciousness."[12] This effort to revitalize theatrical language centered on its effect on the audience. Beck and the Living Theatre wanted language to affect the audience not just in the sentimental way that modern realistic drama attempted to elicit tears or laughter, but rather on a spiritual, transcendental level.

The Living Theatre's experiments with form during the fifties had their counterparts in the contemporary art and music worlds, with which its members were conversant. Beck and Malina commingled with many of the leading figures in these worlds both artistically and socially. Beck himself was an abstract expressionist painter, whose work had been displayed along with that of Jackson Pollock, Robert Motherwell, William Baziotes, and Willem de Kooning at Peggy Guggenheim's Art of This Century Gallery in New York. Beck managed to parlay this connection to the New York art world into financial support from Motherwell and de Kooning for early productions. The Living Theatre also developed a reciprocal relationship with major figures in the literary avant-garde. It hosted readings by Beat luminaries such as Allen Ginsberg and Lawrence Ferlinghetti and book publishing celebrations for several other writers. In turn, these writers furnished the poetic dramas that were the staples of the Living Theatre's early work. The company also worked with composers such as John Cage, Alan Hovhaness, and Lou Harrison on the music for its productions, and collaborated with figures from the modern dance world such as Merce Cunningham, Tei Ko, and Remy Charlip. These people mixed socially as well, from summer retreats in Provincetown, to such watering holes as the San Remo and the White Horse Tavern.[13]

One striking aspect of New York's cultural scene in the fifties was the extent to which artistically inclined individuals reached out to one another across media. "There was a cross-pollination of music, painting, writing," remembered the jazz musician David Amram, "an incredible world of painters, sculptors, musicians, writers, and actors, enough so we could be each other's fans. When I had concerts, painters would come, and I'd go play jazz at their art gallery openings, and I played piano while beats read their poetry." Yet though this cultural hybridity continued throughout the fifties, it did not remain isolated from political influences. Many fifties artists adhered to a political neutrality that a prominent editor referred to as "a dogged kind of centrism," but a number of leftist crosscurrents suffused the New York scene.[14] One of these, the Catholic Worker movement, which ran "hospitality houses" and a newspaper dedicated to alleviating the plight of the poor and homeless, exercised particular influence on the Living Theatre. The Catholic Worker's cofounder, Dorothy Day, a participant in New York's bohemian literary scene in the twenties and in the IWW in the thirties, furnished a powerful example of political and moral commitment for Malina particularly, who once wrote a poem referring to Day as "St. Dorothy of the Streets." Beck and Malina also made the acquaintance of Michael Harrington, an editor of the *Catholic Worker* newspaper and another representative of New York's emerging political left. Harrington ultimately achieved fame with his influential book *The Other America* (1962), which is widely credited with inspiring John F. Kennedy to call for federal antipoverty action, ultimately leading to Lyndon Johnson's "war on poverty." Malina's diaries record scattered contacts with Harrington throughout the mid-fifties: Harrington drank and discussed Ukranian anarchism with Malina at the White Horse; he attended Malina's court hearing, stemming from a 1955 protest of civil defense drills in which Day was also involved; Beck and Malina attended a Harrington lecture about the unequal distribution of wealth among the world's population. While the Living Theatre's founders' relationship with Harrington was never as close or personal as with Day or the writer and philosopher Paul Goodman, of whom Harrington was also a friend, Malina was sufficiently impressed to refer to Harrington as "brilliant," "heroic," to observe that "his approbation is highly valued," and to revere the way in which "his whole energy" was "devoted to his politics." Another key figure on the Left in fifties New York was the radical sociologist C. Wright Mills. A member of the Columbia University faculty, Mills authored several pivotal works, including *White Collar* (1951) and *The Power Elite* (1956), which articulated acute critiques of the contemporary American middle and upper classes.[15] Mills's work powerfully informed New Left organizations in the sixties, such as Students for a Democratic Society, whose Port Huron Statement (1962) resounds with his intellectual arguments.

Despite the presence of such icons of the embryonic New Left, the artistic work of New York's avant-garde was limited by contemporary American politics, which stifled dissent through the House Un-American Activities Committee and the anticommunist McCarthy hearings in the Senate. Not surprisingly, an atmosphere of fear permeated American cultural life. HUAC, after all, had consistently targeted the cultural sphere. Beginning in 1947, HUAC investigated the film industry's leading writers and directors for their involvement, whether fictitious or actual, with the Communist Party in the thirties. In this climate, much of the artistic output of the late forties and the fifties eschewed overt politics and social issues in favor of experiments with form. As Beck put it, "There was a peculiar kind of aesthetic law which dominated at least American art at that time . . . that you cannot mix art and political thought, that one despoils the other."[16] This ideology produced inherently conservative consequences. That is, if the arts were not seen as a fit medium for social and political commentary, a major forum for dissent was eliminated. So the artistic revolutions that took place in the fifties, from Jackson Pollock's splattered paintings to John Cage's atonal musical compositions, focused on expanding the boundaries of expression in art forms themselves rather than employing art as a vehicle for social and political expression.

Yet although the Living Theatre confined its fifties experiments to form rather than content, its founders were developing the political views that animated the company's work throughout its history. The two most salient political influences were the anarchism of Paul Goodman and the pacifism of Dorothy Day. Summarizing the pair's influence in a 1982 poem dedicated to them, Malina wrote, "Blessed be the Holy One who has sent me good teachers."[17] Beck and Malina not only enjoyed close personal relationships with Goodman and Day, they produced several of Goodman's plays and Malina participated in psychotherapeutic counseling sessions with Goodman. In 1955 Beck and Malina had willingly gotten themselves arrested with Day and served jail terms for protesting civil defense drills. Malina served much of her time sharing a cell with Day. As with many civil rights activists, jail radicalized Beck and Malina, leading to two of their most renowned productions, *The Connection*, a sympathetic portrait of heroin addicts whom they had first encountered in jail, and *The Brig*, a scathing indictment of life in a Marine Corps prison.[18] During the air-raid drills, Day, Beck, Malina, and the other protesters remained above ground on the streets waiting to be arrested by the police, consciously violating the injunction to practice civil defense by hastening to the nearest shelter. The staged nature of these protests anticipated Beck and Malina's ventures into public performance with the Living Theatre, setting a precedent for actions which publicly broadcast their moral and political beliefs.

The Connection and *The Brig*: Heightened Realism, Heightened Politics

The Living Theatre's production of Jack Gelber's *The Connection* (1959), inspired by the Beat literary movement and improvisational jazz, represented a turning point in the company's combining of formal experiments with its political and social vision. The play's title referred to heroin addicts' slang for their dealers, and the main characters were junkies and jazz musicians. *The Connection* offers little plot beyond chronicling a day in the life of a group of addicts waiting for a fix in the ramshackle tenement of a junkie named Leach. *The Connection* uses the device of a play within a play, forcing spectators to penetrate multiple levels of theatrical representation. *The Connection*'s characters include a producer named Jaybird and a writer who addresses the audience directly—he has supposedly convened a group of addicts to improvise dialogue he scripted previously. A two-man camera crew records the results. On stage, *The Connection* also features a jazz quartet "in the tradition of Charlie Parker," whose members periodically improvise for as long as ten minutes, while the dialogue ceases. Junkies are depicted going about their daily business. Leach slices a pineapple which nobody eats, they smoke cigarettes, go to the bathroom, sleep, and intermittently tell their stories to the film crew's camera. Finally, Cowboy, the dope pusher who is the "connection" of the play's title, arrives, and the junkies get their fixes. Leach, who has been addicted to heroin for so long that he can no longer get high, fixes in front of the audience and overdoses in an attempt to get enough of the drug into his bloodstream to calm himself. Though the overdose is nearly fatal, Leach ultimately recovers, and the play ends with Jaybird admitting that his concept got out of hand in its effort to convey the addicts' reality.[19]

    The Connection departed radically from the Living Theatre's previous work. Though most of the company's early career consisted of poetic dramas in which innovative language and writing were foregrounded, its productions of

Luigi Pirandello's *Tonight We Improvise* and William Carlos Williams's *Many Loves* explored the possibilities of improvisation through the device of a play-within-a-play, forcing the audience to become more active and work harder to decipher the plays' multiple realities. Yet Beck and Malina found these two plays unsatisfactory because their improvisatory techniques rested on disingenuous premises, as both plays used scripted dialogue that alluded to actors rehearsing rather than actual improvisation during performances.[20] With *The Connection*, the Living Theatre attempted to build on its experiences with *Tonight We Improvise* and *Many Loves* to create a more honest form of theater, which engaged the audience on a more immediate level.

The Connection combined scripted dialogue, representing junkies' everyday speech, with improvisational action to heighten the production's realism. The graphic realism of *The Connection* differed vastly from the "modern realistic drama" of Tennessee Williams or Arthur Miller, for instance, whose plays dominated the New York theater of that era. Williams and Miller employed a stylized realism that consisted of many dramatic scenes arranged to compress "real time," thus distorting the temporal integrity of everyday life. *The Connection* more literally represented the often tedious way time passes in daily life, in what Beck called "the scrutiny of actuality."[21] Rather than performing, or using the "illusionist acting techniques prevalent at that time," "actors" in *The Connection* simply behaved as they would in their own homes, "murmuring together conspiratorially" and consciously refusing their roles as performers.[22] Beck explained:

> A resurgence of realism was needed, what had been passing for realism was not real. There had to be pauses. Directors had to learn to let the actors sit for a long time in one place as in life. . . . If there was to be real speech, then there had to be real profanity; the word "shit" would have to be said, not once but again and again until audience ears got used to it. . . . There had to be honesty, as much honesty as we could pull out. We had to risk embarrassment, we had to risk boring the audience, but it had to be done.[23]

Malina directed *The Connection* to maximize the theatrical "honesty" Beck described, inserting graphic language, jazz improvisations, and long pauses in dialogue. Beck's scene design emphasized his philosophy that "there had to be real dirt, not simulations" on the play's set. The cumulative effect made *The Connection* a theatrical event that depicted more than two hours of "real time" in the lives of junkies waiting for a fix.

This staging not only convinced; at times it reflected a desire to frustrate and even shock the audience. The pauses often seemed interminable. Even critics with a positive predisposition toward theater that addressed social issues, such as Harold Clurman, who had founded the Group Theatre in the thirties, complained that a "terrible languor" suffused the production's pace. The *New York Times* critic Louis Calta typified the reaction of mainstream theatrical reviewers, referring to *The Connection* as "a farrago of dirt, small-time philosophy, empty talk and extended runs of cool music." Calta pinpointed the improvisatory staging as particularly distasteful, calling the performance's "periods of improvisation as frustrating as looking through a peephole into a darkened room." He also deplored the actors' treatment of the audience: "When someone in the cast rhetorically screams at the audience and asks, 'Why are you here, stupid? You want to watch people suffer?' Well, Mr. Gelber is not exactly going to influence people and make friends."[24] While Calta identified aspects of Gelber's play and the Living Theatre's staging that audiences found frustrating, he ignored the possibility that *The Connection* might be intended for social purposes, such as undermining middle-class complacency and mobilizing sympathy for a previously ignored and degraded junkie subculture, rather than solely for entertainment.

For New York theater in the late fifties, *The Connection* broached transgressive subject matter. Casual profanity and actors "shooting up" onstage challenged standards of mainstream propriety. The British theater critic Kenneth Tynan underscored *The Connection*'s unconventionality, observing that "starkly yet unsensationally, compassionately yet unsentimentally," the play "deals with a subject that theatre (or the cinema, or television) hardly even approaches except as a pretext for pathetic melodrama."[25] Yet in producing a play that assaulted middle-class sensibilities, Beck and Malina did not merely wish to shock; they envisioned their project in humanistic terms which anticipated the New Left's concern with poverty and other social ills: "We had to talk about heroin and addicts. It was important to show that these people who, in 1959, were considered the lowest of the low . . . were human . . . and that what the addicts had come to was not the result of an indigenous personality evil, but was symptomatic of the errors of the whole world."[26] For Malina, the inclination to put a human face on heroin addiction resulted from her recent prison term in New York City's Women's House of Detention. Malina's *Diaries* contain a poignant, protracted description of the "anguish" of a young twenty-year-old addict named Sherry, who had been driven to prostitution to support her habit and had her infant child taken from her and placed in foster care.[27] Malina implies that addicts are society's victims and therefore should not incur blame, and she cites examples of police brutality and the media's complicity in ignoring such episodes. Malina dedicated *The Connec-*

tion to Thelma Gadsden, an addict with whom she had served who had recently died of an overdose, "and to all other junkies, dead and alive, in the Women's House of Detention."[28] The Living Theatre's staging of *The Connection* reflected this goal of demystifying heroin addiction, representing junkies as an illegal version of the foibles and suffering that typified the human condition. *The Connection* established the precedent, continued by subsequent Living Theatre productions—including *The Brig*, *Mysteries and Smaller Pieces*, and *Frankenstein*—of making theater that operated under the premise that depicting human suffering as realistically as possible could inspire the audience to alleviate that suffering.

The final scene of *The Connection* asserts a pointed critique of American society as one character remarks, "Everything that's illegal is illegal because it makes more money for people that way." This observation follows a discussion between two junkies, which compares the addicts' lives with those of average "squares" who do not use drugs. "I used to think," reflects one addict, "that the people who walk the streets, the people who work every day, the people who worry so much about the next dollar, the next new coat, the next vitamin, the chlorophyll addicts, the aspirin addicts, those people are hooked worse than me." "They are," the second junkie responds, "Man, they sure are. You happen to have a vice that is illegal."[29] The junkies' exchange, which compared the social mainstream's quest for pleasure to the addicts' single-minded pursuit of heroin and occurred at the end of a decade noted for its conformity, situated *The Connection* and the Living Theatre among a small number of dissenting voices. With this play, the Living Theatre's critique of capitalist society's preoccupation with "getting and spending" began to emerge.

Though some middle-class theatergoers might have been drawn to *The Connection* through a vicarious interest in the drug scene, most would not have been sympathetic to this anticapitalist position.[30] Based on the initial negative reviews in the daily press, audiences at the early performances lagged, leaving the company in precarious financial straits. Fortunately a few sympathetic reviewers, including Robert Brustein of the *New Republic* and Jerry Tallmer of the *Village Voice*, championed the value of the play's rejection of stylized realism in favor of a more honest, heightened realism.[31] This handful of positive reviews and word of mouth sustained *The Connection* for a run of two and a half years, over seven hundred performances, and led to several Obie awards for Off-Broadway theater. Audiences for *The Connection* were remarkably diverse, including the emerging Off-Broadway movement's usual mix of artists and intellectuals, "'tourists' from uptown," and surprisingly strong working-class representation. Moreover, after the play became "a cultural must" and a *"succès de scandale,"* a "long procession of the celebrated" attended, including Leonard Bernstein, Lillian Hellman, John Gielgud, Tennessee Williams, Lauren Bacall, Salvador Dali, and Dag Hammarskjöld. Some theatergoers returned on multiple occasions as the company created an atmosphere that Tynan compared to Moscow Art Theatre productions of Anton Chekhov's *The Three Sisters*; the play, he wrote, "exuded a sense of life" to such an extent that "it was not like going to the theatre, it was like paying a call on old acquaintances."[32] After *The Connection* garnered such praise for its realism, the Living Theatre believed it could push the quest for realism further. The play's unflinching portrayal of the ravages of heroin addiction set within a seemingly improvisational framework had actually allowed only a fairly small opportunity for departures from the script. In the aftermath of *The Connection*, the Living Theatre realized that the key to fusing its social, political, and moral beliefs with artistic expression was to continue its efforts to involve the audience more immediately through a heightened realism based on maximizing improvisation in the theatrical event. The company began searching for a vehicle to take improvisatory techniques further, finding an appropriate script in Kenneth Brown's *The Brig* (1963).

The Brig takes place in a United States Marine Corps penal facility, where prisoners are disciplined by harsh methods of depersonalization. Prisoners are called by numbers rather than names, expected to be silent except when spoken to by guards, and must ask permission to cross over the white lines that separate various areas of the brig. The play's action consists of a day in the life of these prisoners, which includes reveille, washing, gymnastics, clean-up, and other activities, all of which are carried out in strict observance of prison rules. When a prisoner breaks any of the rules, the guards subject him to physical punishment. This usually consists of a punch to the solar plexus, staged realistically by having the actor open his fist at the last possible instant so the punch becomes a slap. The prisoners are also punished by psychological humiliation, such as being forced to shout their transgression at full volume to a toilet seat. Theatrically, *The Brig* allowed greater possibilities for improvisation than *The Connection*, because, although it used scripted dialogue, at any moment when a prisoner broke a rule the guards could alter the course of the action by changing their orders, by dealing out punishment for infractions, or by ordering the prisoners to prepare for frisks and shakedowns.

Thematically, *The Brig*, in its representation of military cruelty, marked the infusion of Beck and Malina's pacifist politics into the company's artistic work. Just as Day's pacifism and Goodman's anarchism shaped the Living Theatre's politics, the ideas of the French director and theoretician Antonin

Artaud decisively influenced the theatrical style of its productions. Artaud envisioned a "Theatre of Cruelty" in which the actors would become "victims burnt at the stake, signaling through the flames."[33] By this, Artaud meant that theater should renounce artifice, "talking heads," and intellectualism. He called instead for theater in which the actors' physicality and emotion affected the audience on a visceral level. The Living Theatre began to explore Artaud's concepts with *The Brig*.

The philosophy behind the company's portrayal of the Marine Corps prison was that by representing violent acts on stage as graphically and "cruelly" as possible, spectators would be purged of the impulse to commit violent acts in everyday life. Malina based her approach to directing *The Brig* on a passage from Artaud: "I defy any spectator to whom such violent scenes will have transferred their blood—the violence of blood having been placed at the service of the violence of thought—I defy that spectator to give himself up, once outside the theatre, to ideas of war, riot, and blatant murder."[34] Malina envisioned this effect in her staging of *The Brig*: "When the first blow is delivered in the darkened brig . . . [and] the prisoner winces and topples from his superbly rigid attention position, the contraction of his body is repeated inside the body of the spectator."[35] *The Brig*'s "cruel" improvisations heightened the reality of violence that the text depicted as characteristic of military prison. Malina staged *The Brig* to provoke a physical or psychophysical effect on the audience that would render them unable to perform violent acts such as the ones they had witnessed. Simply put, the paradoxical idea that informed *The Brig* was to eradicate violence by representing it.[36] In this way, *The Brig* joined the Living Theatre's pacifist political goals to its aesthetic goals of honesty and reality in the theater. Since this production, the company's art and its politics have been largely inseparable.

The Living Theatre's approach of eradicating violence by representing it emerges as noteworthy, since it essentially represents a strategy opposite to pursuing social change through representation, which was employed by early civil rights demonstrators and by the Diggers, and which the historian and former SDS activist Todd Gitlin calls the "as-if" idea.[37] In the sit-ins, for instance, black civil rights activists dramatized the injustice, absurdity, and oppression of the segregation of lunch counters and other public accommodations by acting as if they were free to use them. They did so with the understanding that their protest would likely draw a hostile reaction from local whites, and that the conflict this produced would prompt media coverage, generating sympathy for the movement. The Diggers, too, in their street theater actions, public performances, and community work adopted this strategy of living as though their social and political goals already existed. Yet the Living Theatre applied the opposite logic in *The Brig*, representing the repression and depersonalization of the Marine Corps Prison as vividly as possible. One explanation for the company's contrasting approach to the "as-if" idea is that, unlike many activists in the civil rights movement as well as in the white New Left, the Living Theatre had not yet come to think of itself as an oppressed group. Unlike the sit-in activists or the Berkeley free speech movement participants, the Living Theatre was not yet focusing its efforts on rooting out injustices which its members felt directly. By the mid-1960s, however, this began to change to the extent that the company's 1968 production of *Paradise Now* represented an archetypal example of the "as-if" approach, mobilizing theatrical art to critique the everyday repressions of the dominant society, assume freedom, transform social relations, and enact an alternative utopian society.

The Living Theatre's precarious financial situation at the time of *The Brig* precipitated an episode that ultimately helped articulate the company's aesthetic and political sensibilities. On October 18, 1963, Internal Revenue Service agents seized the troupe's theater, claiming it owed $28,435 in back taxes. The Living Theatre responded by using the sit-in tactics of the civil rights movement and harking back to the radical theater of the 1930s. The company refused to leave the building until its actors received a chance to earn their wages and—echoing Orson Welles's Federal Theatre's unauthorized performances of *The Cradle Will Rock* in 1937—staged renegade performances of *The Brig* inside the theater. This tactic integrated some forty audience members into the protest, since viewing the performances required climbing over rooftops and through a fire door to enter the seized property. As a result of these actions, twenty-five people including cast and audience members were arrested for "impeding a federal officer in the performance of his duties."[38]

Beck and Malina used the ensuing trial in May 1964 as another opportunity to mix politics and art, turning the courtroom into a theatrical forum to air their political views. Opting to conduct their own defense, Beck and Malina portrayed themselves as "the standard-bearers of beleaguered beauty and art" while characterizing the IRS agents as "the anonymous instruments of oppression of the military-industrial complex."[39] As to the charges of failure to pay back taxes, they virtually conceded the point, choosing instead to transform the trial into a public statement on behalf of anarchist politics. For instance, despite having studied legal procedure and witnessed the recent obscenity trial of comedian Lenny Bruce to familiarize herself with courtroom protocol, Malina consistently referred to witnesses and company members by their first names. Company members disturbed the courtroom with chants on several occasions, one persisting until she was forcibly removed. As the prosecutor asked for the jury to find the defendants guilty on each count, Malina clearly affirmed, "Innocent," after each charge was read. When the judge ordered her to stop, she reaffirmed her right to claim her innocence and rejected the judge's authority to restrict such a declaration. The Living Theatre's defense consisted of Beck's contention that if the company had paid taxes, it would not have had the money to pay its actors, and *The Brig* and *The Connection* would have had to close prematurely. "It was a matter," Beck asserted, "of insisting on art before money." Malina insisted on the company's moral right to resist the theater's seizure by the IRS and questioned the "rigidity of the law." An unsympathetic jury found the Living Theatre guilty, fining the company $2,500, and the judge sentenced Beck to sixty days and Malina to thirty days in prison for contempt of court.[40]

The Living Theatre tax trial received copious publicity in the New York press and within the theater world. Tennessee Williams and Edward Albee, perhaps the two most widely respected contemporary playrights in mainstream American theater, were out of the country at the time, yet both wrote depositions testifying to the character of Beck and Malina, which were read in court. Three New York daily newspapers and the *Village Voice* all ran stories covering the trial's final day. Within the world of serious contemporary theater, many found the issues raised by the trial, albeit in circus fashion, cause for reflection and debate. Representatives from several experimental regional theaters, responding in a spring 1964 *Tulane Drama Review* forum on the closing of the Living Theatre, found Beck's reasoning specious. Peter Zeisler of the Minnesota Theatre Company and John Caldwell of the Manitoba Theatre Center criticized the Living Theatre's lack of fiscal responsibility and inability to forecast its budgetary expenses accurately. Disagreeing with Beck's "art before money" formula for making theater, Caldwell addressed the distance between that philosophy and the standard operating procedure of most theaters, experimental or otherwise. "I think it is important, however," Caldwell explained, contrasting his own theater with the Living Theatre, "that the point be made that we raise the money to pay for those experiments prior to spending the money." The Living Theatre functioned differently, deciding what plays to produce, what artistic visions to express, and then finding a way to fund them. Most of the *Tulane Drama Review* respondents compared their own ability to formulate budgets and cover expenses, including taxes, favorably to that of the Living Theatre.

In the forum's most eloquent letter, Herbert Blau and Jules Irving of the

Actor's Workshop of San Francisco rejected Robert Brustein's suggestion in the *New Republic* that the closing of the Living Theatre resulted from *The Brig*'s criticism of the military, and that the IRS's actions constituted repression of civil liberties and "a definite narrowing in the range of free expression" in American theater. Arguing that "the closing of the Living Theatre seems to us an open-and-shut legal case," Blau and Irving debunked Brustein's interpretation and chastised the Living Theatre for its extralegal response to the government's actions. "When we first heard of the secret performance after the Internal Revenue Service had barred the doors," Blau and Irving remarked, "we were not inspired to Genetic ecstasies, for it all sounded like a comic soap opera of sentimental anarchy, an inexplicably dumb show—not civil disobedience but the most adolescent kind of law-breaking." Despite such criticism, Blau and Irving affirmed the Living Theatre's value, citing its "guts" and "conviction" as a theatrical innovator.[41] While generally deploring what they viewed as the Living Theatre's irresponsible fiscal mismanagement, the forum respondents uniformly praised its creativity.

The Living Theatre's innovation was linked to its critique of society's privileging money over humanistic concerns. This theme echoed throughout the company's work, most notably in the "Rite of Guerrilla Theatre" section of *Paradise Now* in which performers chanted, "You can't live if you don't have money," and in street theater performances of *The Money Tower* during the 1970s.[42] In the mid-sixties the Living Theatre responded to the challenge that the closing of its theater represented by unifying its political beliefs and artistic work, reflecting the New Left's examination of the public dimensions of personal experience and the counterculture's ethos of personal liberation.

Making Art and Politics One: *Paradise Now* and the "Beautiful Nonviolent Anarchist Revolution"

The psychic and legal fallout from the closing of its theater compelled the Living Theatre to confront philosophical and practical issues concerning economic viability. The company had always attempted to find strategies, such as building sets out of scavenged wood, making costumes out of discarded rags, and playing for donations rather than charging admission, to prevent financial considerations from dominating artistic endeavors. Yet in the aftermath of *The Brig* and the tax trial, Beck lamented that concern for actors' salaries motivated the Living Theatre to spend considerable time and effort financing productions, only to have these efforts fall short, ultimately necessitating its raising ticket prices. Though Beck and Malina undoubtedly had sincere concerns for the economic well-being of their performers, in point of fact the company has tended to formulate concepts for productions, find funding to cover sets, administrative costs, and other expenses relating to these productions, and then finally turn to the problem of paying actors' salaries.[43] Although this modus operandi is fairly typical of experimental theater ventures, which often rely on shoestring financing, it starkly contrasts with that of higher-budget mainstream theatrical productions that use paid peformers contracted as union labor under the Actors Equity Association. Ultimately, both the company's ability to finance production and administrative costs and its ability to pay actors' salaries has always proved precarious, a problem exacerbated by the Living Theatre's political rhetoric and actions. As Elenore Lester suggested in the *New York Times Magazine*, "Sit-downs and general strikes—anti-Bomb, anti-air-raid shelter, pro-integration—and the resulting busts and jail terms" constitued an "annoyance" for a company that had "launched an ambitious theater project dependent on private sponsorship."[44] Thus, courting potential funders often ended fruitlessly, leaving the company little recourse but to raise ticket prices.

For a company honing an increasingly incisive critique of capitalist society, raising ticket prices engendered contradictions. Julian Beck remarked that with *The Brig*, the Living Theatre's ticket prices had reached the point where the company was forced to appeal to exactly the same kind of "middle-income theatregoer" whose political sensibilities they were trying to shock.[45] His comment reveals that the Living Theatre was worried about "pricing out" politically sympathetic artists and intellectuals while becoming increasingly dependent on the support of a more conservative, or centrist, clientele, whom they were potentially only one radical idea away from alienating. In a 1962 prose poem Beck parodies this situation, as the narrator goes through the process of booking reservations for a Living Theatre performance for a typical theatergoer, settles the arrangements, and then concludes by asking the patron, "How about a revolution?"[46] Beck claimed that the company spent as much as 85 percent of its time fundraising, soliciting, among others, quintessential capitalist institutions such as the Ford and Rockefeller foundations. For the Living Theatre, contradictions abounded in producing art with a dissenting political view, while depending on middle-class audiences' ticket revenues, hoping for favorable reviews in establishment publications such as the *New York Times*, and courting funding from major foundations. Two prominent theater producers asked, "As anarchists and pacifists, could they in conscience have accepted blood money even from a benevolent agency of a permanent war economy?"[47] Ultimately, the moral ambiguities of trying to sustain politically challenging theater and economic viablity caused the Living Theatre to reformulate its approach. During the summer of 1964, following the tax trial, the company began to rethink the relationships among art, commerce, and politics, embarking on a voluntary European "exile."

The Living Theatre stayed in Europe from 1964 until the fall of 1968, touring extensively, living communally, and creating several new productions. The most significant development during this period was the emergence of a process called "collective creation." This technique encouraged company members to offer their individual suggestions, during rehearsal, on how productions should be staged rather than relying solely on a director's vision. Julian Beck describes how collective creation evolved in the company's work "naturally" and "organically" while creating an original improvisatory play called *Mysteries and Smaller Pieces* in Paris during October 1964. "In Paris we were almost not quite aware of what we were doing," Beck remembered. "We stumbled into it."[48] Collective creation had some theatrical precedent, most notably with the Provincetown Players during the 1910s, who rotated theatrical responsibilities so that those members whose plays were being staged served as directors.[49] The Provincetown Players were founded by a group of writers who were admitted theatrical amateurs, and they used this technique both as part of a romantic anarchist philosophy and to realize their playwrights' artistic visions. Similarly, the Living Theatre's anarchist political sensibility clearly motivated its decision to adopt collective creation as its primary mode of creating theater in the mid-sixties. The language with which the company discussed collective creation indicated its political dimensions. "Collective creation is an example of Anarcho-Communist Autogestive Process which is of more value to the people than a play," Julian Beck argued. "Collective creation is a secret weapon of the people."[50] Beck's remarks hinted that collective creation represented a way of working that itself contained intrinsic politically and culturally transformative value.

In a trend widely embraced by other sixties radicals such as those in the New Left, the black student activists in SNCC, and the women's liberation movement, the Living Theatre sought to find a way of working that embodied nonauthoritarian, egalitarian principles. Yet this quest was complicated by the intersection of a couple of salient factors. First, like the Provincetown Players, the Living Theatre's performing personnel included a number of actors with no formal theatrical training, as the company had come to view political commitment as more essential than theatrical technique. Along with this embrace of amateurism, collective creation, attempting to eliminate elitism and minimize "the authoritarian position of the director," typified the cultural politics of the sixties.[51] The varying levels of theatrical training and the diverse educational background of company members, coupled with the commitment to egalitarian consensus-based decision-making, often produced a lengthy, cumbersome, and even exhausting rehearsal process. "There had to be a general agreement about every given aspect of the production before it could go on to the next step," one company member recalled. "The struggle to realize any basic point in the production was monumental."[52] Beck concurred, remarking that after the initial experience with *Mysteries* "all our subsequent experiences were long grinding efforts."[53] This sense of the often frustrating tedium of collective creation parallels the New Left's experiences with consensus-based decision-making in trying to institute a process of working that reflected the egalitarian sentiments of participatory democracy. The New Left maxim "democracy is an endless meeting" summarized this idea, and Living Theatre rehearsals frequently appeared endless.[54]

Collective creation resembled the New Left ethos of participatory democracy also in its attempt to return decision-making power to ordinary individuals, as well as SNCC's attempts to function as a leaderless, grassroots organization, and freedom singing's capacity to foster an equality of musical opportunity. "We sit around for months talking, absorbing, discarding, making an atmosphere in which we not only inspire each other, but in which each feels free to say whatever she or he wants to say," Julian Beck observed of collective creation. "The person who talks least may be the one who inspires the one who talks most," Beck continued. "At the end, no one knows who was really responsible for what, the individual ego drifts into darkness, everyone has satisfaction."[55] The tendency of collective creation to incorporate individual creativity resembles the openness of freedom singing to individual input in adapting and creating new songs out of old ones in order to fit specific circumstances of grassroots struggles in the civil rights movement. Both reflect an impulse to live out a politics of equality in everyday life. Beck's remarks also illustrate the Living Theatre's concern with two concepts, preoccupation with authority, and intensification and loss of self, that the intellectual historian Lawrence Veysey has identified as recurring themes in American cultural radicalism.[56] The Living Theatre rejected authority by instituting a theoretically egalitarian creative process, yet Beck's remark that "the individual ego drifts into darkness," following his remark that collective creation was designed to value the contributions of individuals, epitomizes the ambivalence surrounding the role of individuals in an anarchist artistic collective. Notably, the Diggers reflected this same ambivalence, on the one hand eschewing publicity and maintaining a code of public anonymity, while at the same time urging young counterculturalists in San Francisco's Haight-Ashbury district to "do your thing."

For the Living Theatre, collective creation offered a practical experiment with the type of anarchist society the company envisioned politically. While in Europe, the company used this method to generate the entire text of an adaptation of Mary Shelley's *Frankenstein*, which emphasized the novel's "anarchist" elements. Collective creation and "nonfictional acting," in which actors played themselves rather than characters, represented two formal innovations that enabled the company to create *Mysteries and Smaller Pieces*, which has persisted as a staple of the company's repertoire and is often adapted for street theater.[57] In addition to its improvisational "ritual games," such as "The Chord," "Sound and Movement," and "Tableaux Vivants," which remain habitual company warm-up exercises before performances and rehearsals, the play's final scene, "The Plague," referenced Vietnam with Artaudian reenactments of fitful death and prefigured the Guerrilla Art Action Group's "Blood Bath" piece.

Collective creation catalyzed the Living Theatre's artistic output during this period, and the company waxed optimistic about its potential. "Judith and I are in the process of withering away," Beck commented, echoing Marx's utopian visions. "We are doing it deliberately and with effort."[58] Beck's remark illustrates the company's self-conscious attention to instituting a creative process consistent with its anarchist and egalitarian political sensibilities, yet in practice collective creation fell short of utopia. Not only was the rehearsal process often tedious; deciding on the political viewpoint that productions should express also proved a particularly thorny problem. "The whole company has thirty political ideologies," company member Henry Howard remarked, ". . . and there has to come out of it one front—not one mind because the thirty of us are never going to agree."[59]

The realities of mounting theatrical productions, where the pressures of meeting opening night deadlines predominated, made this difficult. In such situations, Beck's and Malina's preeminence did not just wither away, as Beck concluded (in regard to *Frankenstein*): "The problem was that during the last five or six weeks before Venice it was no longer possible to have twenty-five directors on stage. "The pieces of the puzzle had to be assembled." Beck continued. "Judith and I were holed up in a room. . . . We put the pieces together."[60] Although collective creation entailed numerous practical problems, at its best the technique demonstrated the company's commitment to establishing a creative process consistent with its politics. It is difficult to imagine that any process other than collective creation could have generated the Living Theatre's most famous and important work, *Paradise Now*.

The Living Theatre created *Paradise Now* in Cefalu, Sicily, during the winter and spring of 1968. The production combined the troupe's anarchist/pacifist politics with theatrical spectacle and made the audience an indispensable part of the event. The "Preparation" section of the play's production notes makes this political intent clear by introducing the play as "steps which culminate in the Revolution of Action, marking the beginning of Anarchist social-restructure and the end of Capitalism and the State." Certain elements of *Paradise Now*'s political outlook embodied Beck and Malina's longstanding concerns such as embracing nonviolence and highlighting and criticizing the myriad ways in which the capitalist state exercises coercive power over the lives of its people. The company's brand of anarchism rejected the associations of anarchism with violence, chaos, and tumult from the late nineteenth and early twentieth centuries, marrying the concept instead to the pacifist beliefs Beck and Malina first publicly displayed in the civil defense protests during the fifties. To reinforce this pacifist sensibility "Preparation" emphasized that the actors should seek to demonstrate the "futility of violence" and to expose "the joyous quality" of nonviolent action. These key elements of *Paradise Now* represented continuity with the company's past political inclinations, but the interior, personal aspect of the revolution for which the play called reflected the political and cultural dynamics of the sixties specifically. The Living Theatre viewed *Paradise Now* as a direct action aimed at beginning a nonviolent anarchist revolution that would provide a blueprint for an alternative society, and it construed that revolution to contain elements of both the anachist/pacifist political transformation and an interior personal transformation for both the actors and the audience. The play's text states that "the actors take as a premise that no revolutionary action can be fulfilled externally (socially/econonomically/politically) without a parallel change within the revolutionary himself."[61] This statement reflects the sixties counterculture's concern with personal, psychic, often spiritual, development as a prerequisite for achieving social change (which often informed the Diggers' work as well). To the end of synthesizing this interior, personal journey toward change with its political goals, the company drew from the I Ching, the Kabbalah, and Hindu sacred texts to create the structure of the play's action.

With *Paradise Now*, the company sought to build on the revolutionary spirit of the late sixties, which they experienced firsthand as participants in the May 1968 student riots in Paris. *Paradise Now* premiered at the Avignon Festival in France that July. After a handful of performances, the city's mayor banned the play, worried about the presence of more than two hundred spectators and company members in the streets, chanting for revolution at the performance's conclusion. Rather than substitute another play, the Living Theatre left the festival, citing an unwillingness to compromise its commitment to freedom amid an atmosphere of censorship. In August, the company gave free performances of *Paradise Now* and *Mysteries* in Olliules and Geneva, after which an organization called the Radical Theatre Repertory coordinated a U.S. tour for the group beginning in September.[62]

The structure of *Paradise Now* consisted of a map of steps, or "rungs," on a ladder leading toward paradise, culminating with the performers leading the audience into the street to begin the "Beautiful Non-violent Anarchist Revolution." The eight rungs of the ladder each contained a "Rite," a "Vision," and an "Action," each of which attempted to achieve a specific aspect of the revolution. The Rites were "physical/spiritual rituals/ceremonies" performed by the actors. The Visions, also performed by the actors, were "intellectual images, symbols, dreams." The Actions were "enactments of political conditions," and demanded active participation by the audience. These conditions were geographically specific to particular places and designed to "lead to revolutionary action in the here and now."[63] For instance, during a New York performance the Action of the First Rung urged the audience to participate by calling out phrases, including the following:

New York City.

How The Rite of Guerrilla Theatre and The Vision of the Death and Resurrection of the American Indian lead to The Revolution of Cultures.

Free theatre. The theatre is yours. Act. Speak. Do whatever you want.

Free theatre. Feel free. You, the public, can choose your role and act it out.
New York City. Eight million people are living in a state of emergency and don't know it.

Manhattan island is shaped like a foot.

At the foot of New York is Wall Street.

Free theatre. In which the actors and the public can do anything they like.

Free theatre. Do whatever you want with the capitalist culture of New York . . .

Act . . .

Be the police.

Be a foot . . .

Show the violence. Show the anti-violence. Be the Statue of Liberty . . .

Be the forces of repression.

Be the students at Columbia.

Undo the culture . . .

Enact the culture of New York. Change it.[64]

The actions of *Paradise Now* reflected the company's long-standing concern with actively incorporating audiences into theatrical events. Audiences responded to these actions in diverse ways. In the "Rite of Universal Intercourse," sympathetic audience members often stripped completely naked and joined in caressing that stopped short of actual sexual acts, to symbolize the sexual liberation the Living Theatre believed was an integral part of revolutionary action, though other audience reaction ranged from shock to caustic wise-cracking.[65] The phrase "Free Theatre" described not admission to the performance (which audiences were required to pay on the 1968–69 tour) but rather the audience's freedom to act however they wished. As such, "Free Theatre" can be included in an array of personal freedoms endemic to the larger counterculture. The Living Theatre shared this use of "free" with Digger initiatives such as Free Stores and Free Food (discussed in the following chapter) although the Diggers asked for no payment for their services. In the next few years, the Living Theatre took this step as well, mounting street theater productions for which it charged no admission. Yet during the 1968–69 tour, it was only just dawning on the Living Theatre that the key to unifying its political and theatrical sensibilities lay in street theater.

Paradise Now laid the foundation for The Living Theatre's growing involvement with street theater. Through the play's Actions, the Living Theatre sought to transform audience members into "a state of being in which nonviolent revolutionary action is possible."[66] In the play's final Action, at the end of performances that lasted as long as four and a half hours, the company led the audience out of the theater to begin the revolution, imploring, "The theatre is in the street" (fig. 2).[67] Thus *Paradise Now* synthesized the company's foremost theatrical concern, audience involvement, with the political goal of nonviolent anarchist revolution. The idea that "the theater is in the street" represented a revelation that the end of each performance reinforced. After seventeen years of theatrical experimentation, the company finally brought its aesthetic and political sensibilities outside the traditional proscenium theater and into full public view in the streets. The logic of the company's development to this point dictated further experimentation with public performance, and, accordingly, street theater figured prominently in the Living Theatre's work from *Paradise Now* onward.

FIG. 2. With epic performances that involved audiences as an active part of the spectacle and sometimes lasted as long as four and a half hours, *Paradise Now* became the Living Theatre's signature production. *Paradise*'s concluding idea that "the theater is in the street" inspired the course of the company's subsequent work. Courtesy Gianfranco Mantegna/Living Theatre Archives.

The company performed the American premiere of *Paradise Now* in New Haven, Connecticut. Robert Brustein, dean of the Yale School of Drama, had arranged the visit. The production was well received by students sympathetic to the Living Theatre's message, and several hundred audience members followed the cast into the streets at the end of the evening. Five audience members and three company members were arrested and charged with indecent exposure. In "The Rite of Guerrilla Theatre," the play's most biting indictment of the repressions of capitalist society, cast members chanted phrases such as "I am not allowed to travel without a passport," "I don't know how to stop the wars," "You can't live if you don't have money," "I'm not allowed to smoke marijuana," and finally, "I'm not allowed to take my clothes off." With this, company members stripped to the legal limit, the men in loincloths, the women in bikinis, and entreated the audience to do the same. Accounts vary, but after this New Haven performance police alleged that several individuals were completely naked and arrested several performers and audience members. The New Haven Police chief remarked, explaining the arrests: "As far as we're concerned, art stops at the door of the theater, and then we apply community standards."[68] This comment highlights the cultural and political gulf between "straight society" and the countercultural sensibilities that flourished in the late 1960s. For the Living Theatre, the goal was to eradicate precisely the separation between art and everyday life that the chief delineated.

From these beginnings in New Haven throughout the remainder of its 1968–69 tour, the company encountered widespread resistence to *Paradise Now* from various forces of cultural traditionalism. In Philadelphia, for instance, members of the company were arrested for indecent exposure and inciting a riot. The Massachusetts Institute of Technology and the University of Southern California banned performances of the production amid the negative press preceding the Living Theatre's scheduled visits. Malina lamented:

Poor *Paradise!* It has been busted for so many different reasons:
for making noise in the streets
for indecent exposure
for breach of the peace
for too many people outside
for too many people inside

"None of the officials will say they don't want a play that advocates anarchism," Malina continued, ". . . or perhaps they are saying they don't want a play that demonstrates the conditions of anarchism."[69] Malina's comments reflected more than paranoid suspicion of authority. During the U.S. tour, *Paradise Now* benefited, in terms of audience enthusiasm, from a climate of campus upheaval in which students were primed for the play's revolutionary exhortations. Accordingly, local authorities often tried to pre-empt any rebellions the production might arouse.

The Living Theatre encountered abundant and expected hostility from the establishment, but elements of the radical Left also criticized the troupe's politics. In New Haven, company members disputed the issue of revolutionary violence with members of a black militant group called the Hill Parents Association. As the company defended pacifist principles, the spokesman for the Hill Parents group argued that nonviolent revolution was no longer possible in the United States: "That nonviolent shit died when King was shot.

. . . We ain't talking non-violence anymore. . . . You cats better get your shit together and find out what's happening here . . . you lay that shit down in Brooklyn [the next stop on the tour was the Brooklyn Academy of Music] and some of those Bedford-Stuyvesant cats'll bust your head open."[70] Malina conceded the merit to Hill Parents' leader Ronnie Johnson's criticism that *Paradise Now* and the Living Theatre dealt with revolution without fully understanding that concept's implications in the black community.[71] The *Oakland Tribune*'s John Rockwell criticized *Paradise Now* as insufficiently flexible to address audiences that were already radicalized, such as the one the Living Theatre encountered in Berkeley, California, in February 1969. *Paradise Now* "is, really, an exhortation to the straight world," Rockwell argued. "when they are confronted with an audience that is both personally free and committed, more or less consciously to violent revolution, they lack the flexibility and theatrical skill to adapt their performance."[72] Malina's diary entry corroborates this, noting how actors returned to their dressing rooms after the Berkeley performance musing, "We can't get through to them," and "They don't hear us."[73] Rockwell's comments exposed the tension between the Living Theatre's commitment to pacifism and the growing willingness of the radical Left to endorse violent means of revolutionary change.

This criticism highlighted a problem the Living Theatre confronted regularly on its 1968–69 American tour. *Paradise Now* conflicted with the prevailing spirit of revolutionary fervor in the United States at that historical moment. The company created *Paradise Now* in Europe early in 1968 and participated in the May student protests in Paris, including the liberation of the Odeon theater, which included a marathon of public political discourse that resembled a Parisian version of the Berkeley free speech movement. At the Odeon, led by a group of artists, students, workers, and actors, a crowd took over the building and instituted an open forum for politically, socially, and culturally transformative ideas. "It was pure theatrical forum and it was pure revolutionary," Beck recalled. "It was hardly ever boring."[74] Though the May 1968 demonstrations were fraught with violence, especially the counterrevolutionary violence of France's special paramilitary units (the *Compagnies republicans de securité*), Beck and the Living Theatre emerged from their European experience inspired by the combination of theater and politics at the Odeon. Returning to the United States in the fall of 1968, the Living Theatre encountered the radicals' disillusionment with nonviolence in the wake of the assassinations of Martin Luther King Jr. and Robert Kennedy and the violence of Mayor Richard Daley's police at the Democratic National Convention in Chicago. In her diary Malina expressed her disappointment with a revolutionary impulse increasingly dominated by radicals who advocated the use of violence. She took specific exception to those who considered themselves pacifists, a sprinkling of Living Theatre company members included, yet who sympathized with revolutionary groups such as the Black Panthers, the White Panthers, and the Motherfuckers. "The myth of the broad base is a bitch goddess," Malina wrote, "Of course we will all overcome tyranny together. Of course we know the Black Panthers are our soul brothers in the fight for liberation," conceding the appeal of these groups. "But the revolution is beyond that," Malina continued, "the revolution has come to the point where we have to say: 'Here, my brother, I differ with you.'" In rejecting affinity with militant groups on the Left who advocated either violence or armed self-defense, the Living Theatre diverged significantly from the mainstream of New Left sentiment after 1968, maintaining a steadfast adherence to pacifism that was a hallmark of the company's work and philosophy.[75]

In addition to criticism from the radical Left, *Paradise Now* also incurred the wrath of the critical establishment. Many critics opposed the play on political rather than artistic grounds. Under particular fire were the company's methods for engaging the audience, which many critics viewed as aggressive and hostile. For instance, at one performance, the actor Steven Ben Israel screamed at an audience member: "If you think violence is good for anything, I think you are an asshole." For Eric Bentley of the *New York Times*, such belligerent behavior contradicted the Living Theatre's pacifist politics: "The comedy here is black . . . and suggests just what is hateful in the Living Theatre's arch enemy, the Establishment, the habit of praising nonviolence while bringing more and more violence into being." Company members themselves grew concerned about the tension between the Living Theatre's pacifist ideology and its confrontational theatrical style. Judith Malina commented: "We ask the audience to say whatever they want, but we don't warn them they are going to be beleaguered for what they say."[76] The seeming contradiction between the company's pacifist ideology and a passionate, sometimes even aggressive, performance style was widely noted in reviews of the 1968–69 tour and applied not just to *Paradise Now* but to its other work as well. For instance, in what was otherwise a fairly positive review of *Mysteries and Smaller Pieces*, *Time* magazine noted of the Living Theatre, "It preaches love, but it would rather rape an audience than woo it."[77] In an example of the quest for consistency between political beliefs and artistic expression, the company reflected on these criticisms and sought strategies to "adapt our theatre to be better able to facilitate revolutionary change."[78] This soul-searching culminated in the Living Theatre's January 1970 decision to divide the company into four groups, or "cells," each of which planned to focus on a different aspect of revolutionary change.

After *Paradise:* The Living Theatre and Public Performance

The most prominent and enduring of these Living Theatre "cells," the "action" cell, which included Beck and Malina, focused on making political street theater.[79] The logic of *Paradise Now*, with its concluding words that "the theatre is in the street," compelled the company throughout the 1970s to experiment with fusing its political and theatrical concerns in public performances. Moreover, the January 1970 "Living Theatre Action Declaration," which announced the company's division into cells, pointed to its desire to reach new audiences who would not ordinarily venture into a theater. Referring to theaters as an "architectural trap," and observing that "the man in the street will never enter such a building," the statement declared, "The Living Theatre doesn't want to perform for the privileged elite anymore. . . . The Living Theatre doesn't want to perform in theatre buildings anymore."[80] The company used this reasoning to embark on its next phase of theatrical work, creating topical street theater that engaged a broader audience than the "privileged elite" of which the "Declaration" spoke.

The Living Theatre came relatively late to public performance. R. G. Davis's San Francisco Mime Troupe and Peter Schumann's Bread and Puppet Theater, to take two examples, had been creating Left-oriented street theater or, as Davis called it after 1965, "guerrilla theater," since the early sixties.[81] The Living Theatre's late entry into public performance reflects the company's roots in New York City's avant-garde scene and its strong ties to a conventional avant-garde audience of artists and intellectuals rather than the broader cross-section of the public that street performers typically encounter. Nevertheless, this did not prevent the company from making its own unique imprint on public performance in the seventies and beyond.

The Living Theatre street performances began tentatively in February 1970, when the company devised a brief scene for the Paris Metro protesting rate increases, but police intervention prevented its execution.[82] Shortly after this aborted attempt, the company received overtures to bring the action cell to Brazil. Attracted by the possibility of bringing theater to a new constituency, the company relocated to Brazil in the summer of 1970. "We were concerned with bringing theater to people who don't ordinarily experience it," company member Tom Walker recalled, "workers and the poorest of the poor."[83] This objective of using the theater to serve the poor demonstrated Dorothy Day's continuing influence on the company. Indeed, "Stop all the killing, feed all the people" became a favorite mantra of Malina and the rest of the company and remains one today.[84] In Brazil, the Living Theatre began work on *The Legacy of Cain*, a projected cycle of 150 plays. The introductory play, which became known as *Seven Meditations on Political Sado Masochism*, focused on how the "tyrannical" and "sadistic" power of leaders depends on people's subconscious complicity and "masochism."[85]

The theme of *Seven Meditations* responded to the contemporary social and political moment in Brazil, during which the Médici government, a repressive military dictatorship, ruled the country. A majority of the inhabitants belonged to the two categories the company hoped to reach: workers and the poor. The company traveled to Brazilian *favelas* (ghettoes) creating street plays that articulated exploitative working conditions using laborers' own words, and performed a "Mother's Day Play" in the recreation hall of an aluminum foundry, which used working-class junior high school students' dreams about their mothers to create a dramatic piece examining the possibilities of resisting authority. The company's antiauthoritarian politics and members' marijuana use and sexual liaisons with members of the community in Ouro Preto, Brazil, all contributed to the arrest of several of the company by Brazil's Department of Political and Social Order on July 1, 1971. They remained imprisoned until the end of August, where several of them were subjected to torture. Recalling the freedom singers' use of singing to perservere through prison experiences, the company passed nights in jail singing, "We Shall Overcome" and other songs and even performed a version of *Mysteries* for the prisoners. Ultimately, during a trial for possession of marijuana and suspicion of subversion, which lacked compelling evidence, and amid an international publicity campaign by Living Theatre sympathizers, including such luminaries as Jean-Paul Sartre, Bob Dylan, John Lennon, Allen Ginsberg, Arthur Miller, Susan Sontag, Jean-Luc Godard, and Bernardo Bertolucci, the Brazilian government decided not to risk damage to its reputation and tourist industry income. Rather than further pursuing the charges, President Emilio Garrastazu Médici expelled the company from Brazil.[86]

While using anarchist/pacifist ideas to create street theater and flaunting cultural rebellion in a country operated by a military dictatorship predictably resulted in an abrupt end to the Living Theatre's stay in Brazil, the company derived valuable street theater experience from its time there. One company member commented, "It was an extreme experience, it was a real experience," since "prison reduces things to their essence" and the company bonded very closely. On the other hand, the company returned to the United

States "psychologically beat-up" and "disorganized financially." From a political standpoint as well, "in the atmosphere of armed groups like the Weathermen and the Black Panthers, all this utopian thought was challenged, and the group was forced to react." Again, as during the *Paradise Now* tour, the contemporary climate of American radicalism compelled the company to engage in soul-searching, and what followed was a period of "retrenchment," while living communally in Brooklyn, that one member recalled as "two years of meetings." Yet both the Brazil experience and the inward period in Brooklyn convinced the Living Theatre to continue performing outside of theater buildings, which the company saw as "hopelessly controlled by a bourgeois sensibility."[87]

Thus in the early and mid-seventies street theater, with its capacity to address political issues flexibly and directly, became the company's preferred performance mode. The company performed the "Plague" scene from *Mysteries and Smaller Pieces* at the ITT building in New York, as a street theater piece protesting President Richard Nixon's May 1972 order to re-escalate the Vietnam War by mining Haiphong harbor. In the summer of 1973 the company performed a weekly street theater in front of the national Chilean airline's New York headquarters, protesting the overthrow of Salvador Allende's democratically elected government by a U.S.-supported military coup. During this time the company developed a number of street theater forms that were capable of adaptation to a variety of issues, such as the *Strike Support Oratorium*, which was originally created to show solidarity with the Cesaer Chavez–led United Farm Workers' nationwide boycott of grapes and lettuce. The *Strike Support Oratorium* has remained a part of the company's repertoire, adapted, for instance in Kraców, Poland in 1980 to show support with the workers' Solidarity movement, and in New York City in 1991 to protest the Persian Gulf War. By the mid-seventies the Living Theatre had developed an ease with street theater in a variety of situations, usually without provoking unwanted interference from local authorities.[88] The company's skills with this performance idiom received further refinement during its year-long residency in Pittsburgh, Pennsylvania, in 1974–75.

The experience in Pittsburgh highlighted the internal tensions of making oppositional street theater. Though the company had abandoned fundraising from major foundations after *The Brig* closed, citing the contradictions of courting capitalist institutions while striving to create theater that undermined their existence, the economic pressures of sustaining a collective of over thirty people necessitated long-term support. In 1974, thanks largely to the brokering of Leon Katz, then a Carnegie Mellon University faculty member, the

Living Theatre received a grant of $22,000 from the Mellon Foundation for a one-year residency.[89] Viewed against the backdrop of the company's work in Pittsburgh, accepting the Mellon Foundation's grant amounted to using corporate resources to create oppositional art, an effort in which the Living Theatre enjoyed a least a modicum of success.

As in Brazil, members of the Living Theatre not only performed plays in Pittsburgh, they enmeshed themselves in the community as well. The company interviewed workers in the slumping steel and coal industries to incorporate their concerns into street theater. "The idea was to confront the problems of the American working class," Walker remembered. At times, however, the lines between theater, politics, and everyday life appeared murky. "We don't want to do plays anymore," Beck mused in his workbook, "and yet we don't know how else to proceed."[90] As they deepened their involvement in the community, members of the company questioned how theater could achieve the social transformation they envisioned. Some of this community involvement was with black activists who "weren't necessarily nonviolent," and this caused conflict within the group. An internal rivalry developed between two of the company's cells, the militant "Lucha" cell, which espoused a social realist approach to theatrical work and openly criticized pacifism in the wake of the violence of the late sixties; and the "Joy" cell, which included Malina and Beck, who remained committed to achieving social and political change nonviolently. Led by longtime Living Theatre performer Jimmy Anderson, the Lucha cell broke off from the company, renouncing theater for more direct action and creating a food cooperative to serve the black ghetto where its Bidwell Street house was located.[91] The Joy cell continued the Living Theatre's effort to use theater as a catalyst for transforming people's lives.

The company designed its two most significant productions of the Pittsburgh years, *The Money Tower* and *Six Public Acts*, for public performance. It had begun work on *The Money Tower* while living collectively in Brooklyn after returning from Brazil. The production's outstanding feature, a five-story, forty-foot tower of scaffolding, constructed by Beck and Bill Shari, included a moving elevator topped with an enormous neon green dollar sign to symbolize the class conflict the performers played out in scenes at the tower's various levels, which represented different tiers of the social structure. When the banking class, positioned near the top, announces a plan to cut wages and a fatal industrial accident occurs, performers on the lower tiers realize their common interests, unite, strike, and ultimately "dismantle" the money tower. During its residence in Pittsburgh, the company staged performances of *The Money Tower* near steel plants, hoping to reach an audience of workers. They also performed *The Money Tower* in front of U.S. Steel headquarters and were arrested when police said one of the actors was using a real gun during one of the play's more frenetic sequences.[92]

Six Public Acts, also created in Pittsburgh, further explored the theme of society's corruption through the money system, along with the relationships between freedom and enslavement, and pacifism and violence. Conceived as a traveling outdoor play along the lines of a medieval mystery play, *Six Public Acts* consisted of a "Preamble" and six scenarios, which the company performed with audience interaction at six different locations: "The House of Death," "The House of the State," "The House of Money," "The House of Property," "The House of War," and "The House of Love." Company members presented spectators with mimeographed maps to follow the performance to its different locations, strategically selected to symbolize the theme of each scenario. For instance, at a performance of *Six Public Acts* at the University of Michigan, the company selected a site in front of the Engineering building to stage the "House of Death" scenario, invoking the familiar New Left critique of scientific research on American campuses as inextricably linked with military applications and defense contracts. The "House of Death" reprised a version of the "Plague" sequence from *Mysteries and Smaller Pieces*, as performers adopted various attitudes of death and dying during a reading of a text based on the Cain and Abel story. The company usually performed "The House of Money" in front of a bank, randomly chanting, shouting, singing, or speaking the words printed on a one-dollar bill, and, in a gesture that echoed the Diggers and the Yippies, burning bills around a "golden calf." The company then distributed bills to the audience, on which were printed phrases such as "Whoever accepts money is the slave of the government who prints it," and "This note legalizes the exploitation of labor," which underscored the Living Theatre's critique of capitalism and political philosophy of anarchism. Burning the bills was the obvious audience response that this scenario suggested, and several spectators obliged.[93]

The most striking opportunity for audience interaction in *Six Public Acts* occurred in the "House of Love" scenario, which focused on the personal and political ways in which individuals and society repress the expression of love. In "Love Enslaved," which was the scenario's theme, the actors recited:

This is the House of Love.
This park where love is illegal, or a series of games
in which we become bound to each other in the end in matrimony
Where love is a struggle for possession
For Power

> Where the way we make love is a fundamental
> image of a master and a slave
> Of one who forces and one who yields
> Of one who strikes and one who is struck
> Of Abel and Cain.[94]

Created during the heady days of the women's liberation movement in the mid-seventies, the "House of Love" with its characterization of matrimony as a "struggle for possession" in a master-slave relationship, illustrated the Living Theatre's desire to enter the discourse on sexual politics, arguing that true personal freedom included the realm of sexual expression. The performers dramatized the spoken text by creating various tableaux of "Love Enslaved" in pairs over a period of approximately fifteen minutes, concluding with one member of each pair tying up the other with rope. The actors continued to tie each other up until only one was untied. This last untied actor moved through the audience offering a black rope to various spectators until one of them tied him up. Following this, a pause ensued until audience members untied the actors. If the delay was particularly protracted, the company used audience "plants" to begin this process. After the audience freed all the performers, spectators and company members gathered in a circle to participate in "The Chord," which originally was part of *Mysteries and Smaller Pieces* but had become a favorite group warm-up exercise for relaxation and communion with other cast members. The performance ended with company members asking, "Are you free yet?" to which spectators responded with the words printed on their programs, "Not yet."[95]

The Living Theatre's 1970s productions, such as *The Money Tower* and *Six Public Acts,* synthesized the company's long-standing aims to involve the audience, revitalize the form of theatrical events, and express political ideas through theater. Public performance was the glue that facilitated this synthesis. "Everything we learned from the *Paradise Now* trip, brought us to this moment," Julian Beck remarked. "In *Paradise Now* had we not brought the audience to the doors of the theatre and said, 'The Theatre Is In The Street!'? It was there at the doors of The Theatres, that we knew the street was where we had to go."[96] Street theater represented the logical next step developmentally for an avant-garde company that for twenty years had explored ways of engaging the audience in order to transform them politically. In many respects, the Living Theatre's less-publicized street theater, created after the *Paradise Now* era, came closest to meshing its artistic and political goals (fig. 3).

After the Pittsburgh residency the Living Theatre returned in the fall of 1975 to Europe with *Seven Meditations on Political Sado-Masochism, The*

FIG. 3. Fulfilling *Paradise*'s promise. Performance of "The Love Procession," a street theater piece derived from *Six Public Acts*, in Stockholm, 1982. Courtesy Living Theatre Archives.

Money Tower, *Six Public Acts*, and other pieces, performing these productions in the streets, in festivals, and in psychiatric hospitals. In addition to the need to seek new economic sustenance once the Mellon grant expired, the company's traditionally favorable reputation in Europe motivated the decision to return. The Living Theatre found that European audiences were more open to ideas that seemed radical to Americans and sometimes inspired their hostility. "You can talk about anarchism and communism," one company member observed, "and the workers say 'Thank you.'" Despite the Living Theatre's later return to proscenium theaters because of economic hardship, street theater performances remain a frequent element of its repertoire.[97]

Indeed, street theater has survived as a vital part of the Living Theatre's work even through the politically conservative Reagan/Bush years and into the twenty-first century. *Body of God*, a street theater play dramatizing the plight of New York City's homeless population and the question of the right to public space, employed both company members and homeless people previously unaffiliated with the company. *Waste*, a street theater piece examining environmental issues and attitudes, dramatized the cultural tendency to waste natural resources and suggested alternatives.[98] Several company members performed street theater actions using the *Strike Support Oratorium*, which protested the Persian Gulf War. These protests included "Operation Storm the Media," which protested media coverage of the war and was organized by the alternative media collective Paper Tiger Television, just one of several contemporary groups that owe a debt to the Living Theatre's model for mixing art and politics in the public space. Most recently, in Italy and New York the company has performed and held workshops teaching students to create performances of *Not in My Name*, an anti–capital punishment street theater play that calls for "an end to state killing." This play is designed for performance on nights when executions are scheduled to occur, adapting the specific names of victims and circumstances of actual executions into the play's text.

Though the Living Theatre pioneered techniques of politically oriented public performance, it also demonstrated the limitations of theater's capacity to transform society. The confluence of the Living Theatre's politics and art rested on the notion that theater could make the audience feel human suffering, and that the audience would be inspired to alleviate the pain of others. The idea that a play, even a street theater play, could produce such compassion in its audience, converting them to a politics of anarchism and pacifism, was unrealistically optimistic. At the end of the Living Theatre's plays, the audiences still faced their same everyday problems, from the Carnegie Mellon University student who saw *Paradise Now* but was still required by his father to take part in the Reserve Officer Training Corps, to the workers in Brazilian *favelas* who still faced exploitation after the Living Theatre's deportation. Even Julian Beck conceded that this approach rested on "naive" hopes.[99]

The Living Theatre's greatest transformative effect occurred among the numerous individuals who joined the company after first experiencing it as audience members. Rain House, originally Leroy House, who became involved with the Living Theatre while laundering the guards' and prisoners' uniforms for *The Brig* in the early sixties, ultimately developed into a featured actor and remains with the company. Tom Walker first encountered the Living Theatre during the 1968–69 tour, carrying Judith Malina into the street on his shoulders at the end of *Paradise Now*. Walker later joined the company in Brazil, where he was incarcerated in the DOPS prison. "I saw *Paradise Now*, and it changed my life," remarked Walker, now one of the company's veteran performers.[100] Ilion Troya, a young student in Brazil when he encountered the Living Theatre, joined the company in the early seventies and remained with it. After Beck's death in 1985, Troya became the company's preeminent scene designer. The homeless men and women who collectively created *Body of God* with the company, using their own stories as texts, found a public forum for their voices in the Living Theatre. The countless participants in Living Theatre workshops on three continents, who studied physical performance techniques and strategies for incorporating contemporary political and social issues into theater, have reaped profound benefits from the company's work, a fact suggested by its enduring following and name recognition in diverse parts of the world. At times, the Living Theatre also involved itself more directly with affecting change in the community, such as establishing food cooperatives during its residency in Pittsburgh, conducting theater workshops for patients in Italian psychiatric hospitals, publicizing the cause of unemployed workers in Naples, and housing homeless individuals in its Third Street theater in New York City from 1989 to 1993.

These efforts toward improving the actual lives of individuals in the community represented the type of action that the Diggers initiated from the outset. Both the Living Theatre and the Diggers described themselves as anarchists and sought to explore the new frontiers of personal freedom that the countercultural movement promised. As "anarchists of the deed,"[101] the Diggers demonstrated a genius for putting their philosophical beliefs into action, briefly energizing San Francisco's Haight-Ashbury district with their combination of street theater and community services.

CHAPTER THREE

The Diggers:
Politicizing the Counterculture

Unlike the Living Theatre, which evolved into a community-oriented street theater group only after twenty years of experiments that mixed creative and political impulses, the Diggers articulated their countercultural ideas through public performance from their inception in the mid sixties. "We were doing a piece of theater called the Diggers," Peter Berg remarked, "and it involved the audience," emphasizing the collapsing of boundaries between art and everyday life, between performer and spectator that typified this aesthetic. The Diggers performed their street theater mainly in San Francisco's Haight-Ashbury neighborhood, distributed free food in the Panhandle of Golden Gate Park, and made free clothes available in their "Free Store." For the Diggers, theatricality went hand-in-hand with their community-minded efforts to better Haight-Ashbury, the home of a burgeoning counterculture.

Former members of the San Francisco Mime Troupe, a politically oriented theater company, started the Diggers. Their work with the SFMT provided practical theater experience (including public performance), but the Diggers' work was primarily driven by their relationship to the burgeoning Haight-Ashbury counterculture. Like the Living Theatre, the Diggers focused on marrying countercultural lifestyles to a more transformative and oppositional political vision. Their most important work created street theater that illustrated the counterculture's ethos of personal liberation, infused with a dose of leftist politics. In the process, the Diggers' public performances and free services—from the "Intersection Game," which tied up traffic at a busy intersection to dramatize pedestrians' right to the streets, to their appropriation of abandoned buildings to provide housing to indigent young hippie migrants—challenged conventional conceptions of public space.

Specifically, the Diggers sought to create an anarchist community that circumvented the money system, which they believed caused American society's most pernicious evils. The group's numerous broadsides and manifestos proclaimed that the free food and free clothes they offered were "free because it's yours."[1] The Diggers' communal understanding of property, which contrasted markedly with mainstream America's emphasis on personal material aspirations, reflected the influence of the seventeenth-century English utopian group who were the Diggers' namesake. The English Diggers believed property should be held communally rather than only by the privileged classes. In 1649 the group took direct action to construct the kind of society they envisioned when they began digging and planting upon the commons in Surrey. The original Diggers, who based their society on ideals of peace, love, and mutual sharing, lasted only a short time, but their principles were revived three hundred years later in Haight-Ashbury.[2] The modern Diggers undertook numerous initiatives to subvert the prevailing capitalist economy, actively committing themselves to implementing practical means for people in their community to live without money and publicizing their work with events such as the "Death of Money" parade.

The Diggers tried to act as a political conscience for the Haight-Ashbury counterculture. Their rhetoric and public actions underscored certain moral contradictions in the hippie way of life, which, they argued, were more materialist than many adherents professed. Their October 1967 "Death of Hippie" parade tried to reclaim the counterculture's spirit of personal freedom from the commodified and "stereotyped hippie artifacts" that many young people donned as a superficial badge of a media-generated phenomenon. The parade attempted to retire the word "hippie," which the Diggers believed the media overused, rendering a potentially powerful countercultural movement devoid of its idealistic significance and authenticity.[3] Though the Diggers experienced mixed results in sparking political sensibilities among hippies—mainstream journalists noted that Digger politics often eluded the grasp of younger, less sophisticated hippies in particular[4]—the group initiated several free services in the community and dramatized the possibility of radical personal liberation.

In doing so, the Diggers in public performances such as the "Intersection Game," "Death of Money," "Death of Hippie," and "Invisible Circus" further eroded the boundaries between art and life in a process the art world Happenings had catalyzed earlier. Drawing from many of the same influences—Beat poetry, improvisational jazz, and the musical experiments of John Cage—that spurred the Living Theatre's work at the time, Happenings, which began in 1959, set a precedent for performance in nontraditional venues, for applying artistic practice to everyday-life events, and for participatory experience by an audience who became increasingly indistinguishable from the artists. The Diggers' public, participatory events, however, expressed sensibilities unique to the sixties counterculture, most notably the imperative of radical personal freedom epitomized by the Digger phrase "do your thing." In addition to bringing art and life closer, Digger street theater integrated specific artistic and political ideas. "Our attention was to 'assume freedom'" Peter Coyote contended, "as opposed to winning it."[5] This distinction indicates a convergence of Digger ideas with New Left philosophy, while highlighting the difference between the two. The New Left, the civil rights movement, and the antiwar movement, as well as the Diggers, all pursued the general goal of freedom, whether freedom from externally imposed bureaucratic authority, Jim Crow, imperialistic foreign policy, or the counterculture's ideal of individual "pursuit of absolute freedom." Yet the means by which the Diggers implemented their vision of freedom contrasted markedly with the New Left's approach. Whereas the New Left formulated ideological platforms and made demands in the style of an orthodox political organization, the Diggers repudiated the notion of demands, opting for often playfully theatrical community-based innovations that attempted to provide a framework for the utopian life they imagined. Although the Diggers' concept of assuming freedom might seem naive when activists in the civil rights movement, for instance, fought protracted struggles for freedom involving considerable personal sacrifice, nevertheless, assuming freedom paralleled the strategies of the sit-in movement and the Freedom Rides. In those campaigns, civil rights activists attempted to dramatize racial injustice in the segregated South by behaving as though segregation did not exist, assuming the freedom to sit at the segregated lunch counters or to integrate bus terminals as a tactic to provoke white racist reactions and possibly violence that would illustrate the brutality that enforced segregation as custom. Though the consequences that civil rights activists faced were far greater, the Diggers' strategy of assuming freedom resonated with the direct-action tactics of the civil rights movement and also appealed to countercultural notions of spontaneity, authenticity, and personal liberation.

Haight-Ashbury ultimately degenerated under the population pressure generated by the massive influx of young people in the 1967 "Summer of Love" and the rise of hard drugs and violent crime. At the same time, the Diggers experienced population pressure of their own, evolving into "a loose confederation of several hundred people."[6] The Diggers' communal existence necessitated transformation to ensure survival. Even before the Summer of Love and the "Death of Hippie" parade, the Diggers forged relationships with like-minded groups and individuals in San Francisco's hinterlands, securing land to farm from Lou Gottlieb, who owned the communal Morning Star Ranch in Sonoma County, California. Later many Diggers emigrated from San Francisco to rural communes, establishing informally related living communities that they called the "free family." Thus the Diggers did not implode after 1967; a critical mass of the group rechanneled its effort to mesh politics with the counterculture's "back to the land" movement.

Digger Origins: The San Francisco Mime Troupe, the Artists' Liberation Front, and the Hunter's Point Riots

The Diggers germinated in the mid-sixties, while several key members still served in the company of Ronnie Davis's San Francisco Mime Troupe. Emmett Grogan, the most renowned Digger, had come to the SFMT as an actor, and Peter Berg, another influential Digger, joined the SFMT as a playwright. Peter Coyote and Kent Minault continued to work with the SFMT even after the Diggers formed, leading a number of Mime Troupe workshops. During their time with the SFMT, many future Diggers learned a way of looking at the world that connected their artistic and political sensibilities. Coyote, who wrote, acted in, and directed SFMT productions, noted:

> It was in the Mime Troupe that I first really got introduced to a comprehensive world view, a way of looking at the world and analyzing it according to inherently Marxist principles. Not necessarily doctrinaire, but analysis: class, capital, who owned what, who did what, who worked for what. And it was like speed for the imagination. . . . Suddenly, everything came together, your intellectual life correlated with your artistic life.

The SFMT helped in molding the political consciousness of several key Diggers, in Coyote's words, "closing that gap between my politics and what I do as an artist." In 1968–69, as the Diggers continued their transformation to "Free Men" and shifted their activities to rural communes, Minault wrote a play for the Mime Troupe based on the life of Che Guevara, and other Diggers continued to contribute their talents to the SFMT.[7] The two groups enjoyed consistent, though not always harmonious, personal, intellectual, and creative exchange.

Well before the Diggers originated, the Mime Troupe had established a tradition of public performance in the Bay Area. Davis, the troupe's founder and artistic director, started the company in 1959. By 1962 the SFMT started playing outdoors in Golden Gate Park and North Beach's Washington Square Park among other public venues. These outdoor performances used commedia dell'arte, the theatrical style of sixteenth-and seventeenth-century Italian pantomime, to create highly original spectacles. Although the Mime Troupe mounted some productions in traditional theaters for set fees, Davis and the SFMT supported themselves in part by soliciting donations from their audiences.[8] In the summer of 1966 Davis called together a group of "avant-garde, more-or-less politically active" writers, actors, artists, and musicians, who united as the Artists Liberation Front for mutual aid. The ALF reacted against the role of major national foundations in the arts and their funding of "cement mausoleums," such as New York's newly built Lincoln Center complex. For Davis and the ALF, the foundations construed the arts too narrowly, funding only antidemocratic high arts initiatives that ignored the majority of San Franciscans' tastes. Future Diggers figured prominently in the ALF, as Grogan and others planned a series of free neighborhood street fairs for the group. The free fairs featured street art and rock-and-roll bands; some observed that they served as a "participatory event model" for the January 1967 "Human Be-In" in Golden Gate Park that brought national media attention to the hippie phenomenon.[9]

The ALF meetings considered allowing booths to sell food and other goods at the fairs, which irritated the emerging Digger vision of a world "free because it's yours." Participation in commercialism contradicted the Diggers' idea that the counterculture should do things for love rather than for money. As a Digger-authored *Berkeley Barb* piece argued, love "isn't an Artists Liberation Front 'Free' Fair with concessions for food and pseudo psychedelia." In a series of informal discussions, Grogan, Berg, Billy Murcott, Coyote, and other soon-to-be Diggers articulated a perspective toward the money system which became a hallmark of the group's philosophy. "They agreed that the ultimate goal of the Haight community seemed to be freedom and a chance to do your thing," Grogan wrote of these discussions in his autobiography (typically using the third person), "but they felt one could only be free by drawing the line and living outside the profit, private property, and power premises of Western culture." Thus, even before the group adopted the name "Diggers," they combined countercultural freedoms with a quest to circumvent conventional capitalist social and cultural practices. In early October 1966, the Diggers broke away from the ALF, calling for a "renewal of purpose."[10]

In addition to the debate over vendors' booths at the free fairs, another development during the fall of 1966 encouraged the Diggers to coalesce. On September 27, less than a week after the Diggers circulated their earliest broadsides, a white police officer shot and killed Matthew Johnson, a sixteen-year-old black youth, touching off six days of rioting. The rioting began in Johnson's Hunter's Point neighborhood but spread to other black neighborhoods in San Francisco. To quell the riot, Mayor John Shelley deployed local police thickly, requested that Governor Edmund "Pat" Brown mobilize the National Guard, and instituted a dusk-to-dawn curfew for neighborhoods with significant black populations. This curfew included Haight-Ashbury. Students for a Democratic Society urged neighborhood residents to violate the curfew to show solidarity with black San Franciscans; Haight-Ashbury merchants counseled people to stay indoors and refrain from causing trouble. The Diggers charted a third response that reflected the hippie community's emerging ethos of liberation. Rather than recommend civil disobedience, a paradigmatic New Left response, the Diggers challenged the curfew by advising residents either to go outdoors or to remain inside according to their desires at the moment. When police arrested 124 people who followed this advice, the Diggers posted another broadside publicizing the attempts of the "hippie merchants," who ran shops purveying the stylistic trappings of the counterculture, to fraternize with the police in order to protect themselves.[11]

The Diggers' response to the Hunter's Point riots typified the group's thinking, and it raises larger issues about the extent to which sixties-style public performance functions on a symbolic level. The injunction to violate the curfew only if one truly wished to may appear frivolous, whimsical, and even trivializing by post-sixties-generation standards. Yet at the time, this response to the curfew along with other, more elaborately staged Digger public actions embodied a desire to confront authority with the emerging counterculture's new code of conduct based on authentic feeling rather than on socially constructed constraints. The Diggers' often outrageous theatrics were conceived primarily with live audiences and person-to-person intimacy in mind, an element that distinguishes the Diggers from, say, the Yippies, who explicitly adapted various Digger tactics yet used them to concoct media stunts designed to garner maximum exposure to large audiences through electronic and print media.[12] Yippie initiatives such as levitating the Pentagon were purely symbolic, whereas the Diggers' actions more often than not attempted to prompt individuals in Haight-Ashbury to question their values and actions and broaden their conceptions of the possible, and often included practical benefits for the community.

Distinguishing themselves from "straight" New Left activists and the media-oriented Yippies, the Diggers also exposed "the gap between psychedelica and radical political thought," criticizing the counterculture's apolitical tendencies.[13] "FORGET the war in vietnam. Flowers are lovely," proclaimed "Time to Forget," a Digger broadside satirizing countercultural sensibilities. "FORGET America's 3300 military bases. Make music."[14] This early Digger paper sarcastically excoriated hippie apathy, calling attention to issues with ramifications too pervasive to ignore. Aside from implying that the counterculture should take an interest in the U.S. military presence in Vietnam, the Diggers criticized hippie merchants and other "marketers of expanded consciousness," arguing that hippie alternatives, from macrobiotic diets to hallucinogens to Eastern religion, represented only temporary forms of escape from competitive American society. The Diggers repudiated the idea that purchasing the accoutrements of a countercultural lifestyle could achieve meaningful social transformation. Instead, they stressed the need to "manage the world with love" as an alternative to American consumer society with its capacity to "incorporate and market anyone."[15] The key to the Diggers' injunction to "manage the world with love" was the radical vision of personal liberation embodied in their idea of "free."

"Free Because It's Yours": Digger Broadsides and the Idea of "Free"

A week before the Hunter's Point riots, the Diggers started circulating their broadsides, or "Digger Papers," around Haight-Ashbury. Murcott and Grogan, who grew up as childhood friends in Brooklyn, coauthored several of the earliest; one of these, "Money Is an Unnecessary Evil," which Digger archivist Eric Noble called "the quintessential Digger manifesto," illustrates the Diggers' critique of the money system. "Money Is an Unnecessary Evil" assails money as "addicting" and a "temptation to the weak," and notes its connection to violent crime. Identifying money as the source of criminal activity did not constitute any new insight into the pecuniary nature of society; rather, the Diggers' claim that money blocked "the free flow of energy" emphasized the counterculture's rejection of traditional middle-class goals and its embrace of alternative values and spirituality.

The Digger Papers raise the issue of the extent to which the Diggers engaged in "putting on" their audience. Their prescription in "Money Is an Unnecessary Evil" reflects this kind of "putting on" and illustrates the creativity and humor with which the Diggers confronted both the establishment and Haight-Ashbury. "As part of the city's campaign to stem the causes of violence the San Francisco Diggers announce a 30 day period . . . during which all responsible citizens are asked to turn in their money," the broadside announced. "No questions will be asked." The broadside linked the Diggers' critique of money with the wave of racial violence plaguing the city, mobilizing wry humor to emphasize its point. "Bring your money to your local Digger for free distribution to all," the document continued. "The Diggers will then liberate its energy according to the style of whoever receives it."[16] To Haight-Ashbury denizens, such levity offered a refreshing counterpoint to the earnest New Left's moral and intellectual critique of capitalism, and spoke in a language that echoed countercultural sensibilities.

Though humor and irony abounded in the Digger Papers, the broadsides also unleashed an incisive critique of the prevailing economic system. The Digger paper "A-Political Or, Criminal Or Victim . . ." asserted that American citizens live in a "nation of rulers who legislate rules commanding you to be free" and mocked among other freedoms the freedom to "pay sixty percent of your taxes to the military budget," "work for a minimum wage," and "buy clothes, food, and property from the 200 corporations which account for 45% of the total U.S. manufacturing."[17] In addition to such insights about the distribution of wealth, the Digger Papers promulgated the "economic idea of Free," which as much as any insight emblematized the Diggers. For the Diggers, "free" contained a double meaning, implying not just a lack of economic motive, but that people acted through their own conscious volition, or "freely."

"In Search of a Frame," which the *Berkeley Barb* reprinted from a Digger broadside in November 1966, criticized materialistic impulses of the hippie community and of those who appropriated the hippie phenomenon for commercial benefit. The broadside explained the significance of the appearance of San Francisco rock band Big Brother and the Holding Company (which achieved fame as Janis Joplin's backup band) in the purportedly "mod" magazine *ID*, noting the position of the band's photograph next to ads for Bally shoes and Town Squire:

> There are tribes of natives that will not be photographed because they believe that the photographer then possesses their spirit. One might laugh, but they are correct. Big Brother had his image lifted while he wasn't looking. Whatever the revolutionary implications of his band are, none threaten Town Squire and Bally and all they stand for. By sponsoring the magazine the merchants simply attached the rock-revolution image to their product.[18]

Several important aspects of Digger philosophy appear in this critique. First, unlike other countercultural groups that used guerrilla theater tactics, most notably the Yippies, the Diggers did not believe that any publicity amounted to good publicity. In fact, the Diggers remained anonymous as individuals when confronting the media. "In Search of a Frame" shows the Diggers' realization of the potential for countercultural ideas and images to be co-opted by corporate culture. Furthermore, this passage exemplifies the Diggers' views concerning advertising, which they lambasted as dangerous to the ideals that fueled hippie community. Finally, the passage links hippies to the "tribes of natives that will not be photographed," and praises this as the correct response. The Diggers consistently emphasized tribal, communal, less technologically oriented behavior as countercultural ideals.

"In Search of a Frame" chastised rock groups in particular for behavior that diverged from the countercultural ideal, criticizing the Charlatans for filming a hair tonic commercial. The Diggers attacked the band's participation as "contributing to an unlovely and crumby state of mind" and questioned the Charlatans' motives. They concluded that whether the Charlatans sought money or publicity, neither of these activities was "central to making music or beads or flutes or any disinterested act of involvement, of worship." The Diggers implied that for countercultural rock musicians, ethical action involved making music for its spiritual value rather than for personal gain, fame, or career advancement. The Diggers adhered to this idealistic perspective firmly, since they believed the integrity of the countercultural movement was at stake. "Where will Jefferson Airplane, Grateful Dead et al go but up to bigger gigs, better publicity, managers—etc. until they are ***STARS***," the broadside continued. "Where's the revolution? Long-hair? Beautiful clothes? Would our soldiers be substantially different if we dressed them in mod?"[19] By suggesting the discontinuity between rock bands' "hip" countercultural image and their conventional pursuit of fame and fortune, the Diggers lay the intellectual groundwork for their most important goal: mobilizing the counterculture for anarchist and utopian political and social transformation.

The Diggers reserved their most potent venom for the hip merchants. By the mid-sixties, as Haight-Ashbury solidified a reputation as the nexus of hippie culture, various retail venues sought to capitalize on its new popularity. Brothers Ron and Jay Thelin owned the most notable of these stores, the Psychedelic Shop. Phoenix, Far Fetched Foods, and In Gear joined the Psychedelic Shop as other new Haight-Ashbury businesses that either catered to the hippie community or benefited from the hippie phenomenon's ability to draw curious potential customers to the neighborhood. Older neighborhood merchants, represented by the Haight Street Merchants' Association, rejected a bid by the newer stores to join their group. Shortly thereafter, in November

1966, the Thelins led the newer merchants to form their own organization, the Haight Independent Proprietors (HIP), who quickly became a target of the Diggers' efforts to agitate the counterculture into living up to a set of ideals that challenged mainstream American consumer culture.[20]

Three days after HIP's formation, the Diggers blasted the group for supporting efforts to remove loiterers and panhandlers from Haight Street. The burgeoning numbers of young people without gainful employment entering the neighborhood resulted in pressure on the hip merchants. For instance, in October 1966 the Psychedelic Shop received a notice threatening eviction for tolerating "shabbily dressed clientele" and "unkempt loiterers." The hip merchants displayed some inclination toward responsibility for this problem, meeting to formulate plans for a job co-op for unemployed hippies, but for the Diggers this response was insufficient, and they circulated a painted picture of shop owners expelling panhandlers from their boutiques. The Diggers argued that the hip merchants treated panhandlers as a nuisance with little discretionary income and therefore irrelevant to their businesses, observing that young hippies "made the scene" that the hip merchants "are there to capitalize on."[21] This comment resembled the ideology of the People's Park Movement in Berkeley and of later urban homesteading; namely, that groups and individuals who improve abandoned or unused land should enjoy legitimacy and protection as its rightful occupants. The original English Diggers, who sought reforms in elitist land policies and established homesteads on unoccupied land, most likely influenced the Diggers on this point, whose cultural currency increased in the late sixties and early seventies.[22]

The hip merchants' overtures toward neighborhood police especially provoked the Diggers. Rapidly increasing drug busts in Haight-Ashbury prompted neighborhood residents to initiate a series of biweekly discussions with the police Community Relations Unit at the I/Thou coffee shop. Ron Thelin believed miscommunication underlay the problem and posted a sign in his Psychedelic Shop urging Haight residents to "Take a Cop to Dinner" in order to improve relations with the police. When several other shop owners followed suit, the Diggers responded with a vitriolic broadside equating the merchants' actions with bribery. The broadside compared the merchants' intentions with the ways that racketeers, pimps, drug dealers, business leaders, labor unions, the federal government, and media and entertainment figures all courted favor with the police, offering gifts and services in exchange for reduced police scrutiny and increased police loyalty. The Diggers lampooned the hip merchants directly, citing their proffering of "discounts and gifts" and "free discussions offering discriminating insights into hipsterism, black militancy and the drug culture." While the first part of the broadside simply observed the ways various individuals and groups curried the police's favor, the italicized closing of what Grogan called "probably the most famous Digger Paper" underlined the Diggers' scorn for the hip merchants' initiative: "And so, if you own anything or you don't, take a cop to dinner this week and feed his power to judge, prosecute and brutalize the streets of your city."[23] For the Diggers, the police's role as protectors of the same private property system they sought to eradicate made fraternizing with police morally reprehensible. The eruption of the Hunter's Point riots within a week of the "Take a Cop to Dinner" broadside seemed to vindicate the Diggers' comments about police brutality.

The Diggers' critique of the hip merchants was aimed at the merchants' unwillingness to renounce values of competition and success embodied in mainstream society. The Diggers extended this criticism to the counterculture as a whole. "The Hipster . . . invites the indignation of his allies with a mockery of 'straightness' and his alienation from the social norms of morality and dress," the Diggers commented in the *Berkeley Barb*. Yet they also contended that despite this departure from the mainstream, hippies represented the "perfection of success—liberated from the inhibitive life of bourgeois conformity and established in a packed class of happiness which combines the highest material pleasure with a total lack of commitment to middle-class humanism." Several salient points emerge from this remark. First, by noting that hippies represented the "perfection of success" and enjoyed the "highest material pleasure," the Diggers questioned the counterculture's alleged repudiation of mainstream values. "Hip and middle-class . . . values, goals, reactions, and attitudes offer different styles, but amount to the same end," the article pointed out, identifying the pursuit of personal success and material pleasures as common threads among hip and mainstream culture. Recent scholarship echoes this observation, suggesting that "the counterculture was not a blot on the American creed but its apotheosis" and stressing that the sheer numbers of baby boomers within the counterculture made them a force as "dynamic consumers."[24]

Such comments attempt to undermine the serious political, ideological, and spiritual content in sixties movements, including the counterculture. But the counterculture was a more complex phenomenon than this formulation suggests; it was neither a "blot" on the American creed nor its apotheosis. Rather, the counterculture contained both materialist and antimaterialist strains that were manifest or submerged depending on time, place, and situation. The Diggers themselves offer proof of this more nuanced interpretation. Digger broadsides and rhetoric repeatedly criticized materialistic impulses within the counterculture. "Where's the revolution? Long hair? Beautiful clothes?," a Digger-authored article asked. "Would our soldiers be substantially different if we dressed them in mod?" This attack suggests that a critical mass of hippies placed vital importance on consumer and lifestyle choices. Yet the presence of groups such as the Diggers, who were clearly enmeshed in the counterculture, attempting to infuse it with a "frame of reference" that transcended mere lifestyle choices so that it could "operate freely, harmoniously and generously," indicates that the movement amounted to more than crass consumerism.[25]

In "The Ideology of Failure," the Diggers attempted to provide an antidote to the success ethic that promoted community—group-oriented rather than individual—welfare. If the drive for personal success led to the exploitation of the "unequipped children" of Haight-Ashbury, then they needed an ethic of failure to counteract that exploitation. The Diggers identified the solution through the following advice: "Refuse to consume." This advice equated freedom with "failure," or refusal, to participate in the consumer economy. "Everything we do is free because we are failures," the article opined. They advocated finding ways to circumvent consumer capitalism and "do our thing for nothing." Through abandoning the success ethic and avoiding the money system, the Diggers believed that the counterculture could forge a community based on the positive value of love: "To Show Love is to fail. To love to fail is the Ideology of Failure. Show Love. Do your thing. Do it for FREE. Do it for Love."[26] The phrase "Do your thing" symbolized the counterculture's quest for personal freedom and became recognized as the Diggers' contribution to the American lexicon. Yet the passage also reveals how the Diggers rooted personal freedom in the community goal of love for others and in operating outside the money system, or, for "free." Remarkably, the Diggers' ideology of "failure," "love," and "free" did not remain merely a part of their writings. "We live our protest," the Diggers asserted in "The Ideology of Failure." Through community initiatives and public performances, the Diggers proved this claim.

"Create the Condition You Describe": Digger Public Actions as Cultural Revolution

The historian David Farber argues that the Diggers were the counterculture's "visionary core." The Diggers' public acts demonstrated how the group grappled for means to implement its visions. Even their detractors conceded the significance of the group's greatest accomplishment: each day at 4 p.m., for several months, the Diggers fed a free stew to a gathering of fifty to a hundred people, and as many as four hundred people on weekends, in the Panhandle of Golden Gate Park. This "Free Food" ritual provided Haight-Ashbury's young hippies with much-needed nourishment, fostered community, and initiated a social practice that served as an alternative to participation in the money system.

The sentiment that motivated this initiative paralleled other contemporary impulses within the political and cultural rebellions of the sixties. The Black Panthers, for instance, coordinated a free community breakfast program. Like the Panthers' program, the Diggers' Free Food started in response to an immediate community need. In October 1966, after Emmett Grogan stopped performing with the SFMT, and after his unemployment checks ran out, he and Billy Murcott found themselves among the numerous panhandlers in the neighborhood. They decided "not only to relieve their individual strapped conditions" but to help the "larger down-and-out community." By this time, Haight-Ashbury, which had demonstrated a remarkable capacity to incorporate runaways into the community, showed signs that the swelling ranks of young migrants were outstripping its resources. Young hippies, eager to find like-minded community, arrived to find a dearth of jobs and housing. The neighborhood's new young indigents, including Grogan and Murcott, commonly panhandled for spare change, a practice derided by the hip merchants. Yet the sheer numbers of new arrivals mitigated against the long-term efficacy of panhandling, which motivated Grogan and Murcott to formulate a plan to distribute free food.[27]

The two Diggers visited the San Francisco Produce Market and procured donations of vegetables and fifty pounds of spare chicken and turkey parts. Since many of Haight-Ashbury's young people lived on the streets and lacked access to kitchen facilities, Grogan and Murcott concluded that cooking would be a necessary part of Free Food. They made a stew from the wholesalers' food donations and stole two twenty-gallon milk cans from a dairy plant for cooking the stew. The Diggers supplemented their stew with day-old bread donated by the Ukrainian Bakery. Perhaps not coincidentally, the Diggers' forerunners in San Franciscan counterculture, the Beats, had patronized the Ukrainian Bakery during the fifties for free bread. To announce the advent of Free Food, Murcott wrote and distributed the following leaflet in the Haight-Ashbury's streets:

FREE FOOD   GOOD HOT STEW
RIPE TOMATOES   FRESH FRUIT
BRING A BOWL AND A SPOON TO
THE PANHANDLE AT ASHBURY STREET
4PM   4PM   4PM   4PM   4PM
FREE FOOD   *EVERYDAY*   FREE FOOD
IT'S FREE BECAUSE IT'S YOURS!
the diggers[28]

While on one level this leaflet simply announced a new community event, it also contained several key aspects of Digger philosophy. Free Food addressed the imperative of feeding what the journalist Hunter S. Thompson called the "penniless heads" of "Hashbury," and it took place in a highly visible venue. The Diggers designed Free Food as a public act, specifically to foster "collective interaction."[29] Though they appreciated that most hippies did not have kitchens, they demanded that participants "bring a bowl and a spoon." On one hand, this demand could simply be read as the Diggers' unwillingness to take on the responsibility of providing hundreds of bowls and spoons, yet considered in theatrical terms, it amounted to giving the audience some small part in creating the spectacle of Free Food. The Diggers' quest for collective interaction with their public paralleled the Living Theatre's efforts to create communion between performers and the audience.

The Diggers created Free Food as a communal ritual that enacted their vision of a moneyless society—"Why do kids panhandle for dimes instead of tomatoes?" a Digger-authored *Berkeley Barb* article asked. To highlight Free Food's ritual nature, the Diggers required those who ate their free stew to pass through "The Frame of Reference" before being served "as part of the general festivity and communality of things." Murcott constructed the Frame of Reference from four two-by-fours bolted together to form a thirteen foot doorway, which Grogan painted a golden orange.[30] Passing through the Frame of Reference symbolized abandoning conventional consumer-based society and fundamentally reconfiguring one's priorities, and it dramatized the countercultural notion of personal liberation as a prerequisite to transforming society.

The mechanics of sustaining Free Food offer a unique window into the Diggers' culture. The group served Haight-Ashbury's counterculture by skimming the excess of mainstream consumer culture, soliciting donations of meat, vegetables, and day-old bread, and they were not above stealing. Grogan habitually boosted sides of beef from meatpacking plants and stole milk cans for cooking the stew. Police once arrested him for possession of stolen property after he heisted a one-hundred-pound package of prime round steaks from the

Armour Meat Company. The group also pilfered much of the clothing for its Free Frame of Reference Store.[31] On one level the Diggers' willingness to use thievery reflected Grogan's and Murcott's backgrounds as street-wise youths from a working-class Brooklyn neighborhood, yet on another level stealing squared perfectly with the Diggers' ideological rejection of capitalism and repudiation of private property.

The Diggers served the free food well into the spring and summer of 1967, and they found ways of encouraging others to continue to provide these services. For instance, they circulated a leaflet entitled "Free Bread" with the recipe for the whole wheat bread they distributed as part of Free Food, detailing instructions for baking the bread in one- and two-pound coffee cans. The leaflet explained how to create the Digger bread inexpensively to feed quantities of people by listing various flour wholesalers who sold one-hundred-pound sacks cheaply. And they included the encouraging words: "Please take this recipe home and start making bread. The only stipulation is that you always give it away." The food historian Warren Belasco has documented how the Diggers' Free Food and Free Stores wielded a crucial influence on the food co-op movement and helped catalyze political activism on behalf of healthy, ecologically sound food production and consumption. The Diggers accomplished this through such measures as using food which might otherwise go to waste to feed the hungry and later by growing food in rural communes to feed urban hippies.[32]

Just as "Free Bread" encouraged others to perpetuate the bread bakes, the Diggers transferred responsibilities for Free Food. Charles Perry's history, *The Haight-Ashbury*, chronicles a gradual petering-out of the Diggers' Free Food service, beginning with the closing of their Free Frame of Reference Store on Frederick Street on February 5, 1967. After that, the Diggers' Free Food in the Panhandle ceased as an everyday event. According to Perry, Free Food "became irregular" long before the summer of 1967. By June 24, for instance, the *Berkeley Barb* had canceled the standing notice in its events column. As the numbers of young people in the neighborhood swelled, "the Haight came crashing to the ground under the weight of population pressure," Perry wrote.[33] Free Food was among the casualties of this overpopulation.

Though the Diggers realized the magnitude of the population pressure, their own accounts of dwindling involvement in Free Food cite other factors. For instance, Grogan claims his relapse into heroin use contributed to the demise of Free Food. More important, Grogan contends that in the spring of 1967 the Diggers turned their attention from providing free food in the Panhandle themselves to trying to ensure the service's continuance by others. To this end, Diggers and other concerned Haight-Ashbury denizens joined together as the Free City Collective and performed daily guerrilla theater skits, poetry readings, and songs during the lunch hour in front of City Hall in order to convince municipal authorities to assume responsibility for the Free Food services. These performances went on for several weeks, before police ultimately arrested forty Free City Collective members. Because newspapers gave coverage to these arrests and reprinted the Free City Collective's "not unreasonable proposal" that the city use its administrative capacities to provide and distribute free food, free housing, and free clothes, Grogan claimed that municipal authorities were retaliating against the collective for making these demands public in a way that embarrassed the newly elected administration of Joseph Alioto. Grogan argues that authorities ordered produce wholesalers to stop supplying the Diggers with fruit and vegetables and enacted a spate of new regulations on free food distribution to curtail the Diggers' ability to provide free food.[34]

But if overpopulation and authoritarian repression undermined the feasibility of Free Food, the Diggers' own philosophical predispositions about institutions also affected the group's will to continue. "The Diggers were not very good at institutions," Peter Coyote explained. "Things were based on what you felt like doing. After you'd hustled the food for a while and that got to be a drag . . . you would stop, and then other people would take it over."[35] Coyote's remark underlines the Diggers' optimistic commitment to personal liberation, but it also exposes a key problem of an approach to social change based on contingent, noncompulsory, personal commitment. The Diggers continued to offer free food when they "felt like it"—such as the barbecued lamb and fried hamburgers they provided for a summer solstice event in Golden Gate Park—and other groups initiated their own Digger-like free food activities. A group with some members who called themselves Diggers distributed about a thousand pounds of homemade whole-grain bread at All Saints Episcopal Church two to three times per week, while a group called Teddy Bear and the Thirteenth Tribe provided free public barbecues at intermittent concerts in the park. During the summer of 1967 the Digger-affiliated Community Affairs Office at All Saints served free pancake breakfasts three days a week. Long after the Diggers started calling themselves the Free Men and migrating out of the Haight-Ashbury, various groups and individuals periodically staged free food events and provided other free services. Free Food did not completely die out, though no other group managed the regularity of the Diggers' Panhandle feeds. "Other people took it over," Coyote explained in 1989. "There's still Free Food going on in San Francisco." Numerous anecdotal contributions to the Digger website suggest the veracity of Coyote's assertion. In San Francisco, as well as at over a hundred chapters in North

America and Europe, the group Food Not Bombs, founded in 1980, serves free food five days per week. Reflecting an obvious debt to the Diggers, Food Not Bombs uses food that would otherwise go to waste, "giving away free food in public spaces to dramatize the level of hunger . . . and the surplus of food being wasted."[36] The two sites where San Francisco Food Not Bombs distributes its free community meals reflect this agenda: the intersection of Haight and Stanyan Streets at Golden Gate Park, not far from where the original Digger feeds took place; and the United Nations Plaza, symbolizing the global nature of hunger. Just as SNCC and the New Left sought to foster indigenous leadership at the community level, the Diggers too, albeit much more casually and even haphazardly, attempted to inspire others to perpetuate the services they initiated.

Free Food represented the Diggers' paramount accomplishment in terms of service to the community and demonstrated the group's ability to activate its ethical and political philosophy by circumventing the money system. The Diggers launched other initiatives to avoid commercial exchange, such as their Free Frame of Reference Store, their involvement in developing the Haight-Ashbury Free Medical Clinic, and their sponsorship of free "crash pads" for new migrants to the neighborhood who lacked accommodations. Todd Gitlin argues that the Diggers' ability to conceive of tangible means to produce the society they envisioned represented an "as-if" principle, which he defines as "the idea of forcing the future by living in it, as if the obstacles, brought to a white heat, could be made to melt." Gitlin identifies the civil rights movement's influence on the Diggers in providing a model for "as-if."[37] That is, by acting as if a desegregated society already existed in sit-ins, Freedom Rides, and other direct action protests, civil rights workers provoked prosegregation violence, which focused sympathetic public attention on their cause. The Diggers invented their own expression for the "as-if" principle, urging fellow counterculturalists to "Create the Condition you describe." This phrase served as the group's "theory of action" or working philosophy, the idea that participatory events should "go beyond rhetoric," and actually "generate the conditions" that begin to redress the social problem or issue the event addresses.[38] In the case of Free Food, for instance, the Diggers created a daily public ritual that fulfilled a basic community need, providing a meal for cash-poor, hungry migrants to the neighborhood. Armed with "Create the Condition you describe" as a guiding principle, the Diggers' actions melded countercultural lifestyle, art and theater, and pragmatic community-oriented problem solving.

The Free Frame of Reference, a free store which the Diggers opened shortly after Free Food started, exemplified this philosophy. The store distributed clothing and household items with the assertion, "It's all free because it's yours."[39] Like Free Food, the store attempted to serve basic community needs, though the Diggers sought to avoid the aesthetic of a Salvation Army or similar charity operation. Grogan explained that just as the Diggers did not create Free Food to "prolong the economic usefulness of day-old bread or vegetables or bad cuts of meat," the free store aspired to do more than "prolong the economic usefulness of secondhand clothes and other items."[40] Indeed, far from simply attempting to fulfill the basic human need for clothing, Free Frame of Reference was the Diggers' response to the "hip merchants," providing clothing and other items while avoiding financial transactions. As with Free Food, the Diggers used theft along with donations to procure goods for the store. They thwarted police by answering all queries regarding who ran the free store with a response that embodied their nonauthoritarian, anarchist politics: "You're in charge. You wanna see someone in charge? You be in charge!" Vagabonds unaffiliated with the Diggers signed the the Diggers' leases so that no one in the group could be legally responsible for possession or receipt of stolen property.

Despite such subterfuge, the Diggers' free store in its various incarnations periodically encountered official interference and experienced shutdowns. In the wake of one such episode, Peter Berg seized the opportunity to modify the free store concept, creating The Trip Without a Ticket. This "store" featured not only an array of free clothing, but was also designed to "encourage reflection on the relationships among goods and roles—owner, employee, customer—implied by a store." In other words, not only was the merchandise in The Trip Without a Ticket up for grabs, so were the roles available to people who entered the store. Fully conscious of store's theatrical possibilities, Berg drafted a manifesto which advised: "If someone asks to see the manager tell him he's the manager." Coyote recounted that some customers found the open role-playing of The Trip Without a Ticket so disarming that they simply left, while others "got it" and played along. One anecdote particularly suggests the breadth of possible audience responses to the free store concept. Coyote recalled that while working as "manager" of the free store one day, he spotted an "obviously poor black woman" trying to stuff clothing in a bag surreptitiously. He explained to the woman: "You can't steal here," and the women denied that she was trying to steal. Coyote persisted, asserting that stealing was by definition impossible in a free store, since all the goods were free, and that furthermore the roles of customer and staff were up for grabs as well. The two reached an understanding; the woman proceeded to ask Coyote for recommendations on outfits, and ultimately she returned to the store with a tray of doughnuts, leaving them as a free donation for customers and staff to share.[41] The Trip Without a Ticket was the Diggers' object lesson in assuming personal freedom. It suggested that conventional notions of "store-ness," of what constitutes a store, lay open to transformation. The Diggers wanted their public to assume the freedom to change the store rather than demand freedom from external sources of oppression as the political Left might.

Anarchism and steadfast rejection of authority and institutions set the Diggers' projects apart from the political Left. For instance, whereas SNCC sponsored its freedom schools, and SDS launched its Economic Research and Action Project to assist the poor to create institutions to serve their own needs, the Diggers did not intend Free Food and the Free Frame of Reference to become institutions that would foster a redistributive politics whereby greater economic and political power accrued to poor people. Rather, their initiatives avoided traditional politics, institutions, and economic exchange altogether. "People find it safe to assume that we were the Salvation Army," Coyote remarked. "But what they don't understand is: the Free Store was done because some people wanted to do it. The Free Food was done because some people wanted to do it." The Diggers' guiding principle of "free" thus signified both that individuals should undertake activities voluntarily and that no monetary exchange should occur. Coyote remembered an anecdote that depicts the idea of "free": "The first time I was offered Free Food, I so completely missed it. I said, 'Oh no, I can afford to buy lunch. Let the people that can't afford it eat.'" He recalled that Grogan prodded him to rethink this position, and finally Coyote "got it," concluding that Digger activities were designed to "create the conditions they described."[42] In other words, Coyote realized that the Diggers sought less to redress conditions of poverty than to launch activities that circumvented the institutions that created poverty in the first place.

The Diggers attracted media attention for their practice of burning money, a ritual that inspired Abbie Hoffman and the Yippies to drop one-dollar bills on the floor of the New York Stock Exchange and burn money themselves while discussing the stunt with reporters. By the time Hoffman led the Stock Exchange action, Diggers had been burning money for several months. As early as November 1966, when *Realist* editor Paul Krassner compared the Diggers' Free Food and Free Store operations to social work, Grogan highlighted the group's uniqueness by burning a ten-dollar bill he had asked Krassner to produce.[43] Grogan illustrated the idea that whereas social work actually functioned to perpetuate the institutions of capitalist society by ministering to its most visible casualties, the Diggers' initiatives represented alternatives to commercial exchange. "The Diggers did not want to be a 'community service,'" Alex Forman wrote in the radical journal *Anarchy*. "They wanted the community itself to be based on the new morality."[44] The Diggers wanted to root this new morality in the ideas of love, the common treasury ("free because it's yours"), and personal liberation and freedom ("Do your thing," "Tomorrow is the first day of the rest of your life.") During the remainder of 1966 and in 1967 the Diggers burned money on numerous occasions, including one instance in New York City at a protest in front of the *East Village Other*, which had run an unflattering news story on the Diggers, portraying them as threatening the hip merchants with violence.[45]

Though burning money dramatized the Diggers' repudiation of the money system, it also exposed the group to criticism. "Is there no poor family in the area who might have managed an unaccustomed, proper supper with a ten dollar bill?," one columnist asked in the spring of 1967 after another had compared the Diggers to early Christian mendicants for the way they "joyously burn ten dollar bills."[46] The criticism this columnist raised, that money the Diggers burned to signify their anarchist politics could be better used to feed the indigent, resulted in part from the fact that the services the Diggers provided often mirrored those of social work. For example, the Free Store offered a series of classes called "How to Avoid Getting Busted, Gangbangs, VD, Rape, Pregnancy, Beatings, and Starvation."[47] Free Food and free clothes represented only the beginning of Digger services. The Diggers periodically made a free doctor available at their office, which served as a crude forerunner to the influential Haight-Ashbury Free Medical Clinic. In late November 1966 the Diggers also started to provide free "crash pads" for people who needed a place to sleep.[48]

Shortly after Free Frame of Reference opened in a garage on Page Street, the Diggers made the garage available to people who needed lodging. This arrangement promptly met interference from municipal authorities. In late December, building inspectors cited the Digger garage for violating city health and safety statutes that prohibited using a garage for living quarters, as well as for violations of lighting, ventilation, and sanitary regulations. Yet the Diggers continued to make living space available to those who needed it after the demise of the Page Street garage. From early January to late February 1967, the Diggers made the second Free Frame of Reference storefront on Frederick Street available as a "crash pad" for those who needed it, until it too was condemned and then padlocked. Shortly thereafter, the Diggers rented an apartment on Haight Street to house the homeless. As Perry remarked, "the Diggers did not burn every $10 bill that came their way."[49]

Though Free Food received greater media attention, the fact that the Diggers provided shelter to the Haight-Ashbury community did not go unnoticed. Loudon Wainwright's March 1967 *Life* article described the scene at a Digger crash pad:

> The house . . . was packed with people. In the living room there were perhaps 20 around on shabby furniture and on the floor, some talking, some writing in notebooks, some listening to softly played guitars. Throughout the rest of the house every available bit of space was covered with cushions, mattresses, sleeping bags. Makeshift walls of cardboard and sheets partitioned the bedrooms into still smaller spaces, and in most of these, whose walls were painted with splashes of color, psychedelic designs and slogans like "Love is the Trip," more young men and women sat and talked or were sleeping ("crashing").[50]

Wainwright's portrait of the Diggers' overcrowded crash pad exposes the gulf between the utopia that young hippies expected to find upon migrating to Haight-Ashbury and the daunting conditions they encountered when they arrived. Indeed, many of the Diggers' innovations addressed this gulf, which only worsened as the 1967 Summer of Love drew near. By May 1967, rumors and reliable reports indicated that anywhere from fifty thousand to two hundred thousand "indigent young people" would arrive in San Francisco at the end of the school year. "The Diggers will continue to receive the casualties of the love generation," one Digger woman responded.[51]

Though Wainwright's tableau captured the seamier side of the countercultural lifestyle, it also revealed the sense of collectivity and shared community that young hippies enjoyed. Hippies based this community on personal liberation—note, for instance, the variety of different activities Wainwright depicts in his description—and on an antimaterial lifestyle which eschewed middle-class comforts. The Diggers established a space that promoted personal liberation and offered partial relief from the practical housing problem for some individuals, reflecting their dual maxims "Do your thing" and "Create the condition you describe." Yet the longer-term realities of life in a Digger household suggest that the group's ethos of personal liberation did not necessarily result in utopia, particularly for women.

Life in the Digger Household: "Free Men" and Digger Women

Gender-based inequalities of experience prevailed in the Diggers' culture. These differences appeared in many areas, perhaps most obviously at the level of language. For instance, when Grogan authored a manifesto entitled "The Post-Competitive, Comparative Game of a Free City," outlining the inner workings of utopian, urban life for "Free Families," he detailed women's role in Free Stores and workshops in telling language. "Space should be available for chicks to sew dresses, make pants to order, recut garments to fit, etc." The document exemplified the gendered expectations of a cultural moment in which the women's liberation movement had not yet emerged.[52] Similarly, the "remembrance cards" distributed at the "Death of Hippie" parade bore inscriptions featuring unapologetically masculine language. "Once upon a time, a man put on his beads and became a hippie," the cards proclaimed. "Today the hippie takes off his beads and becomes a man—a freeman!"[53] Rejecting "hippie" as an insidious, media-generated term, this declaration tellingly defined the countercultural freedoms the Diggers endorsed as the realm of male prerogative. If "hippie" was the "son" of media as the cards affirmed, there was no indication that the term's retirement in favor of "Free Men" involved extending countercultural freedoms to women as well. At the least, the Diggers lacked the women's liberation movement's subsequent insights about the role of language in sustaining patriarchy, and their language reflected expectations of male privilege, which went beyond language.

Gender differences also suffused the Diggers' division of labor. The mechanics of Free Food provides an excellent example. Grogan procured ingredients by any nonmonetary means necessary, but only women's large-scale cooking efforts ensured the daily continuation of Free Food. Originally, a half dozen young women, including a group of Antioch College dropouts, volunteered to take over the cooking in their Clayton Street residence. Jane Lisch, whose husband Arthur worked for the American Friends Service Committee and attempted to get VISTA to institute a program in the Haight, also performed cooking duties for the Digger feed in the Panhandle. These women cooked two to three twenty-gallon containers of stew daily, which served approximately two hundred people. "If it hadn't been for those women there wouldn't have been 4 P.M. Free Food in the park everyday or any day," Grogan wrote. "They were the real strength in the Haight-Ashbury community, the real Diggers."[54]

Though Grogan retained sole claim to food procurement for himself, Coyote's memoir *Sleeping Where I Fall* suggests otherwise. Coyote praised women as the "mainstays" of Free Food and contended that the largely Italian-descended produce wholesalers at the Farmer's Market would not give food to "able-bodied guys," but they would give to the women.[55] Coyote called his competing account "closer to the truth" than Grogan's in his autobiography *Ringolevio*. Whether this disagreement reflects Grogan's sizable ego or the vagaries of memory, both Grogan and Coyote acknowledge women's primary role in the Diggers' most tangible accomplishment.

The division of labor suggests that within the Diggers, men tended to formulate ideas while women executed the myriad practical tasks involved in carrying them out. Nicole Wills, a veteran of several communal Digger households, corroborates this point: "There seemed to be a formula that many of the men used when explaining ideas . . . if he had an idea it was his . . . if you both shared an idea together, it was his . . . if you had an idea it was ours," suggesting the male Diggers' control over decision-making in the new community they were inventing. Yet Wills also suggests that though Digger women realized their own contributions were unrecognized, their shared sense of purpose militated against frustration boiling over into confrontation: "We learned to humor them. That's how I sometimes thought about it."[56] The Diggers' failure to examine the gendered division of labor typifies prefeminist-era radicalism in the sixties. Accounts of experienced women field-workers in the civil rights movement reduced to secretarial duties and the masculinist language of Students for a Democratic Society's Port Huron Statement constitute only a couple of the most obvious examples of sexism among sixties radicals.

In a 1989 interview Coyote addressed the gender-differentiated experiences of living in a Digger household. After praising Digger women as "the backbone of the whole deal," Coyote compared men's and women's roles:

> The guys held down a lot of the visionary, metaphysical end of things. You know, in an orthodox Hebrew community. The men are studying Talmud and they're looking at heaven. The women are taking care of the household and paying the bills and cooking the food. There's a joke, "My husband takes care of the important things in the world: balance of trade, international relationships, the national debt, draft policy, and our relationship to South Africa. And me, the wife, I take care of the unimportant things: the rent, the mortgage, the groceries, the children's education." You know it was that kind of deal.

Coyote underscored the inequality of this division of labor, which appears dramatic by post–women's liberation movement standards, conceding that "we were accused of being pretty chauvinistic by some." Yet he hastened to add his own perception that "the women had all the authority that we did." He explained this seemingly anomalous remark by pointing out that Digger women often furnished the main sources of income to Digger households by securing food stamps or welfare checks, and that this role gave women considerable authority over spending decisions. Coyote implies that conditions were not as chauvinistic as one might assume since the reality of communal living ensured that "accommodations always occurred." As he puts it, "It was no fun to live anywhere with an angry woman, or women."[57] Wills, on the other hand, argues that Coyote's description of accommodation "smacks a little of 'granting' us authority," implying that the presumption that distributing power was a "naturally" male prerogative was indicative of the problem. Still, Wills adds that she "always felt on equal footing with everyone" personally, citing an "incredible" level of "mutual respect" in the Digger community.[58] Taken together, Coyote's and Wills's comments suggest that the Digger household was neither a utopia of gender relations nor as sexist as mainstream culture. The philosophical commitment to individual freedom combined with the realities of communal living created a situation that often pitted men and women against each other, and in which authority was consistently subject to negotiation.

Coyote's account of the Diggers' "Free Bank," where household members pooled economic resources, illustrates the tedium of the negotiation process:

> There was a bank book. I don't know who has the original, but it's a great document. Because you'd see people were exactly who they were. People would sign out, you know, "$2.19, dental floss and tooth-paste," might be one thing, "Nina." And then underneath, it might say, "Emmett, $20, to fix truck, Monday. Tuesday, $20, to fix truck, Emmett. Wednesday, $20, to fix truck . . ." I mean people revealed who they were. The fact that it went on for as long as it did was amazing. You'd have these big meetings and the women would say, "No, the kids need shoes." And the men would say, "Well how are we going to get the shoes if we can't pick 'em up in a truck. We gotta keep the trucks running." And it was like the Pentagon budget fights on a smaller scale. But it was anarchic, it was cooperative, and it was collaborative.[59]

Coyote's vignette of Digger budget politics suggests that Grogan used the Free Bank to finance "fixing" more than just the truck; his well-known heroin dependency eventually led to his death in 1978. More important, Coyote's comments highlight women's role in securing basic necessities to sustain the men, women, and children who were part of the collective. Coyote applauds the courage these women displayed in raising children amid a community of adults committed to a philosophy of "do your thing," contending that they "knocked the bullshit out of the men and kept them honest."

Coyote's characterization of Digger women as "the real unsung back-bone . . . the audience that you'd want to impress, the people that you'd want to charm, the people that you'd want to win for,"[60] lends itself to competing interpretations. On one hand, his comments echo the sexist mainstream rationale for women's domesticity and resemble a justification for why women should remain "behind the scenes" at home. Sam, a woman Digger, corroborated this interpretation: "The guys thought They WERE what the '60's was all about. The women were just there as fan club and support to their vision for all the credit we got." Sam acknowledges women's complicity in creating the men's attitude, yet also insists that "women were really the glue" to the men's vision.[61] Consistent with this position, Coyote's remark acknowledges Digger women's critical contributions to the community and hints at the sexual power that women wielded within the communal life the Diggers created.

Nicole Wills echoes this same tension between gender-differentiated roles and mutual respect in an anecdote about her introduction to the Digger "family." "When I entered the house there was a huge oak table in the living room," Wills remembered, "Seated around it were about 8 men . . . taking turns reading aloud from a book called *Njal's Saga*, an Icelandic epic. In the other room, the fireplace room, were about 6 women and several children . . . it was 'get ready for bed time' for the kids." Just as Wills appears to have painted an obvious picture of male privilege to pursue esoteric intellectual endeavors and women's simultaneous exploitation through unpaid domestic labor, she resists this analysis, remarking that she "couldn't remember ever seeing an assemblage of that many beautiful women and strong men in one place ever." Wills continued that they were all "very serious . . . it was all about the work to be done . . . and everyone was committed to the chores at hand, be it an event or cleaning or gardening or discussing a notion . . . man and women alike."[62] Wills's focus on the "family's" physical attractiveness coincides with Coyote's account, suggesting the heightened sense of sexual possibility in a communal household based on personal freedom. More importantly, Wills's remarks portray the Digger household as contested terrain, in which a shared sense of purpose between Digger men and women on the one hand and gender-based exploitation on the other existed in a dynamic and complex relationship.

This tension was particularly acute after many Diggers relocated to rural areas, forming communal households as part of a larger "Free Family." Rural life enmeshed the Free Family in a set of daily tasks that were subsistence-oriented, and, as practiced at the time, that tended to reinforce a stereotyped gendered division of labor. Lynnie, a female participant in the Free Family, recalls her first thoughts about the Digger women on meeting them: "I thought they were the most perfect, gorgeous, and intimidating women I'd ever met. . . . I thought the women were from another century. How did they know how to do all that gardening, cooking for hundreds, embroidery?" But at the same time that women participated in these gendered activities, Lynnie asserted, their accomplishments enhanced their sense of individualism and competence. Ultimately, however, accounts of participants in the communal life of the Diggers and the Free Family suggest that the ethos of personal freedom helped erode rigidly defined gender roles. As Lynnie put it, "Roles were divided in the Diggers: the men fixed trucks, the women gardened. It worked for awhile, but we were all too idiosyncratic—the guys, too—for it to work very long."[63]

Digger Public Performances: Creating Model Participatory Events

The Diggers' idea to use Golden Gate Park's Panhandle for public spectacles such as Free Food reflected the legacy of the San Francisco Mime Troupe in shaping the intellectual, political, and artistic consciousness of among others Grogan, Berg, Coyote, and Minault. For example, the SFMT used setting up for shows as an integral part of the performance. Constructing the backdrop, unpacking trunks full of costumes and musical instruments, actors changing into costume, musicians playing recorder or tambourine, warm-up gymnastics, and joking with bystanders were activities the SFMT utilized to attract the largest crowd possible.[64] The Mime Troupe's loud, colorful, brash commedia dell'arte performance style engaged audiences in performances which radically critiqued the dominant politics and culture. Drawing from their Mime Troupe experiences, the Diggers' public performances made the group better known and publicized their community work. Grogan contended that these public performances merely represented "accessories" to the "fundamental reality" of Free Food, the free stores, and other "free services made available to the people."[65] In retrospect, however, the Diggers' public performances and "guerrilla theater" assume a larger significance. Inspired by the SFMT, the Diggers honed their own aesthetic of street theater which engaged countercultural sensibilities. Digger performances promoted convergence between the counterculture and the political left, lampooning the New Left as too serious and restrained and cautioning hippies about the dangers of political disengagement.[66] Digger street theater questioned authority, declared the idea of "free"— the combination of personal liberation and antimaterialism—and exposed hypocrisy within the counterculture by mounting public events to dramatize how hippie behavior often resembled the mainstream culture it purportedly sought to repudiate.

Shortly after Free Food started in October 1966, a broadside headed "Public Nonsense Nuisance Public Essence Newsense Public News" announced a "test match" of the "Intersection Game," the Diggers' first public spectacle. This document outlined what amounted to a recipe for public chaos and detailed guidelines for the game. "Game Board formed by intersection of public streets," the broadside asserted, hinting at the spectacle they would perpetrate in the Haight-Ashbury. Diagrams illustrated the game's "object," which consisted of inciting pedestrians to walk routes that described various geometric shapes at the intersection "that gives that hip district its name" during rush hour on Halloween night, 1966. The "Public Nonsense" flyer indicated that the Diggers sought to highlight competing claims to the public space: "PUBLIC STREETS CONVEY MACHINES—ONLY A FOOL WALKS IN TRAFFIC." Especially at 5:30 p.m., the intersection that the "game" targeted primarily accommodated automobile traffic. Not coincidentally, most of the young hippies in the Haight-Ashbury were pedestrians rather than motorists. "BRING A SQUARE TO DIG THE INTERSECTION GAME," the broadside advised, exemplifying the Diggers' project of imploring others to reinvestigate their "frames" of reality. The Diggers intended to expose the plight of pedestrians with a participatory theatrical event that tied up traffic.[67]

The Intersection Game represented only part of the spectacle the Diggers created on Halloween 1966. The weekend before Halloween they passed out fifteen hundred leaflets in Haight-Ashbury and Berkeley announcing a "Full Moon Public Celebration of Halloween," which one observer called "an experiment in psychedelico-political theater and provocation." At 5:30 p.m. on Halloween night the Diggers carried the gigantic Frame of Reference from the Panhandle, where it served as the backdrop for Free Food, to the appointed intersection. Next, they mobilized a pair of the Mime Troupe's eight-foot puppets to drum up a crowd. After accomplishing this, they distributed seventy-five 6-inch-high Frames of Reference to the audience and improvised a play called "Any Fool on the Street." This play featured the puppets and employed the Diggers' device of using the Frame as a symbol of reinterrogating reality. Furthermore, "Any Fool on the Street" questioned the purpose and ownership of the streets themselves. During the play, the Diggers passed out instructions for the Intersection Game. These instructions played on the "Don't Walk" traffic signal by imploring pedestrians to adopt alternative forms of mobility such as the "umbrella step, stroll, cake walk, sombersault, finger-crawl, squat-jump, pilgrimmage." "It was a translation of the civil rights sit-in technique directed against automobiles," Perry remarked.[68] Perry's comment and the Diggers' recruitment of Berkeley's politically oriented contingent for this event indicate that the Diggers desired to marry New Left ideals and direct action techniques to a countercultural aesthetic sensibility. Yet as the Intersection Game encountered resistance, it became clear that the Diggers intended to foster dialogue about more than pedestrians' rights.

By 6:00 p.m., approximately six hundred people filled the intersection, creating a considerable traffic jam. When police arrived to intervene they confronted the puppet operators as the most visible troublemakers. This episode complemented the Diggers' street theater piece since, to many in the crowd, it appeared as though the police were addressing the puppets directly. The *Berkeley Barb* reported the following dialogue:

> *Cop:* We warn you that if you don't remove yourselves from the area you'll be arrested for blocking a public thoroughfare.
>
> *Puppet:* Who is the public?
>
> *Cop:* I couldn't care less; I'll take you in. Now get a move on.
>
> *Puppet:* I declare myself public—I am a public. The streets are public. The streets are free.[69]

This dialogue underscores how the Diggers interrogated the right to use public streets, drawing on the civil rights movement's legacy of instilling awareness of public space. The historian Kenneth Cmiel argues that the "strategic dramas" of civil rights protests created necessary cultural space for the counterculture's "more raucous, incivil disobedience" in public spaces. Digger actions and rhetoric demonstrated the counterculture's ethos of authenticity, which Cmiel defines as "the expressive individualism of liberated human beings."[70] A Digger paper entitled "where is PUBLIC at?" lamented what they viewed as the restrictive nature of public space. "Where in the street can you take off your shoes and sing and dance without disturbing the death called peace," asked the broadside,[71] illustrating the group's desire for authentic self-expression in the streets.

The Intersection Game highlighted these issues. In response to the officer's intervention, the Digger puppeteers did not cease and desist but proceeded with their performance. Police arrested five Diggers. At its worst, the Intersection Game inconvenienced motorists and resembled a juvenile prank designed to provoke authority, yet it also provided a theatrical object lesson on the value of First Amendment rights. One measure of the Diggers' effect on their audience occurred when a spectator responded to the arrests by protesting to the police, "These are our streets." For this outburst police arrested the spectator.[72]

The Halloween Celebration, the Intersection Game, and other public events linked the Diggers with the New Left's rising insurgency in the streets, which started to crest after 1967, when the slogan "from protest to resistance" galvanized a more militant phase of antiwar activism that relied on public confrontation. In one sense, the Diggers engineered absurdist street theater, and they created a "public nuisance." Yet the group also challenged conventional notions of appropriate public behavior, claiming that what constituted a "nuisance" to the straights represented "new sense" to the counterculture.[73] The arrests resulting from the Intersection Game and the "Any Fool on the Street" puppet play raised the Diggers' public profile both within the counterculture and outside it. On November 30, 1966, the *San Francisco Chronicle* ran a front-page item reporting that the deputy district attorney urged the dismissal of charges against the Diggers, "in the interests of justice." A large photograph of the five released Diggers striking celebratory poses which mocked authority appeared next to the article.[74] The photo remains the most famous visual image of the Diggers, whose strategy regarding the media involved cultivating anonymity. After these arrests the Diggers received increased attention from Berkeley's political left. The Halloween Celebration received coverage in the *Berkeley Barb*, which began listing the Diggers' Free Food in its entertainment and events column.[75] Within the first two months of their existence, the Diggers had attracted a following among the radical left.

The Diggers staged their next public spectacle, "The Death of Money and Rebirth of the Haight Parade," on December 17, 1966 (fig. 4). Whereas the Intersection Game consisted of equal parts bizarre street theater and civil disobedience, "The Death of Money" added a new element by highlighting the Diggers' objections to the money system. Street theatrics again predominated as Mime Troupe members helped Diggers initiate the festivities by passing out pennywhistles, flowers, incense, candles, and signs reading "Now!" to an audience variously estimated at between one thousand and four thousand people. Like those of the Living Theatre, Digger theatrics promoted communion between the performers and an audience incorporated into the performance. To signify their connection to the onlookers, the Diggers scavenged approximately two hundred automobile rearview mirrors from junkyard wrecks and distributed these to bystanders "to symbolize that they were actually watching themselves." Perry describes other features of "The Death of Money":

> Three hooded figures carried a silver dollar sign on a stick. A black-clad modern Diogenes carrying a kerosene lamp preceded a black-draped coffin borne by six pallbearers wearing Egyptianesque animal masks. . . . Mime Troupe members . . .

Fig. 4. In the "Death of Money and Rebirth of the Haight" parade (December 17, 1966) the Diggers created an offbeat, participatory street spectacle that playfully welcomed the demise of the money system that they had criticized in their broadsides. Photo © Gene Anthony.

walked down the sidewalk in two groups on either side of the street, chanting "oooh," "aaah," "sssh" or "be cool" as people tootled on the pennywhistles.[76]

"The Death of Money" visually symbolized the demise of the money system through elements such the coffin and imagery of Egyptian mummification linked to dollar signs. Although the parade ended quickly, because of the arrests of two Hell's Angels who participated, "The Death of Money" won the Diggers a larger following.

Whereas the Halloween Celebration won the affection of the Berkeley Left, "The Death of Money" attracted an even broader cross section of the local counterculture. Prior to the arrests, the police attempted to halt the gathering on the grounds that it was unlawful because none of the participants had secured a permit. The Diggers and their followers responded to this intervention by chanting "The streets belong to the people!" "The streets belong to the people!" These words proclaimed the underlying message of "The Death of Money" as public street theater by invoking the participants' claim to the public space. Once police arrested the Hell's Angels, the Diggers solicited donations to raise their bail, using "The Death of Money" coffin as a collection box.[77] The Diggers' ability to redirect their parade toward the practical objective of raising funds for bail suggests their talents as street theater improvisers, capable of responding to the contingencies that can suddenly arise in public performance. This transformation also demonstrated the Diggers' complex relationship to money. On one hand, the Diggers wished to live free from monetary exchange, yet on the other hand, the group's ethos of personal freedom dictated that they use money in situations where no alternative existed in order to "liberate its energy." Thus, in the Digger notion of "free," personal freedom trumped the freedom of living without recourse to money.

Raising bail for their colleagues endeared the Diggers to Hell's Angels, who expressed their gratitude by throwing the Diggers a party in the Panhandle on New Year's Day. The participation of the Beat poet Michael McClure in "The Death of Money," leading the parade and supplying musical accompaniment on his autoharp, linked the Diggers to their countercultural predecessors in San Francisco. A month later at the Human Be-In, the event that conferred national media attention on the counterculture, McClure, Allen Ginsberg, Gary Snyder, and Lenore Kandel numbered among the Beat luminaries represented in the official onstage proceedings.[78] There were numerous ties among the Diggers, Beats, and Hell's Angels. Kandel was the longtime lover and companion of Digger and Hell's Angel Billy Fritsch. Snyder, Ginsberg, and other poets held a benefit for the Diggers' "philanthropic social work" at a North Beach bar, and were impressed when Grogan and Coyote refused to accept the proceeds, instead giving them to the bartender and instructing him to buy "free" rounds for the crowd. The Beat poet Gregory Corso performed a ceremony marrying a Hell's Angel at Coyote's Olema commune, where fellow Beats Snyder and Lew Welch visited frequently.[79]

While "The Death of Money" fostered countercultural community, the Diggers occasionally employed guerrilla theater as an alienating force. In June 1967, Grogan, Berg, Murcott, and Billy Fritsch invaded an SDS alumni conference in Denton, Michigan. The group disrupted the conference's proceedings and appropriated it as a forum for "calling the white radicals' bluff."[80] The Diggers meant to challenge the New Left to move beyond demanding social and political change from external authorities and toward initiating change themselves, à la the Free Food and Free Frame of Reference operations. Berg, Fritsch, and Grogan each commandeered the audience's attention, interrupting Tom Hayden's keynote address, and delivered speeches that provoked, insulted, and infuriated the SDS-ers. The Diggers' actions demonstrated coordinated planning and a theatrical sensibility. They "knew how to take over a crowd," commented Gitlin, who recalled that Grogan "held a flashlight under his face for horror-movie effect."

The Diggers perpetrated this piece of guerrilla theater to critique the New Left's approach to change. "Don't organize students, teachers, Negroes," Berg declaimed, "organize your head." Berg argued that the New Left needed to incorporate countercultural ideas of personal liberation and freedom, and he castigated the SDS-ers for focusing on issues external to their personal realities, such as Vietnam, the nuclear threat, and civil rights. Berg's argument represented the inverse of the Diggers' approach to the counterculture, whom they spurred to transcend esoteric self-involvement and to recognize that freedom necessitated engagement with the larger society. Class antagonism played a role in the Diggers' diatribe. Grogan, Murcott, and Fritsch all came from working-class backgrounds, and thus differed from the majority of SDS as well as the hippies. The Diggers challenged both predominantly white and middle-class groups to transcend an approach to social and cultural transformation based on sustaining their own privilege by "comforting themselves with plans for the future while supporting themselves with checks from Mommy."[81] This perspective suffused the Diggers' perception of the countercultural masses as well. "They billed the Human Be-in as a 'Gathering of Tribes,'" Grogan mused, "but it was more like a Gathering of Suburbs."[82] The pointed class analysis in such comments criticized the lack of racial and economic diversity in hippie culture.

The Diggers also criticized the Human Be-In for failing to encourage its audience to become active participants rather than "passive stargazers." In conjunction with the larger Artists Liberation Front, the Diggers formulated a response to the Human Be-In designed to provide a better model for a participatory event. They secured permission for a "happening" from the Methodist clergy of the Glide Memorial Church in the city's Tenderloin District, home to numerous prostitutes and transvestites. During the planning stages, this happening quickly metamorphosed into a "72 hour environmental community" known as The Invisible Circus. In a leaderless, consensus-based style comparable to the Living Theatre's process of collective creation, the Diggers and the ALF designated different individuals and groups to be responsible for transforming various areas of the Glide church into environments that motivated people into "assuming freedom."[83] The Diggers continued to engage the same issue that confronted the Living Theatre's creative work, namely, how to facilitate greater audience involvement in order to transform them.

The Invisible Circus reflected a preoccupation with melding art and everyday life that was prevalent in the visual arts in the sixties. Not coincidentally, the ALF and the Diggers billed the Invisible Circus as a "happening," replicating the terminology of the Happenings movement in the art world led by Allan Kaprow, Claes Oldenburg, Jim Dine, and others, which, with the Fluxus movement, exercised seminal influence on politicized groups of artists such as the Art Workers Coalition and Guerrilla Art Action Group.[84] Like Happenings, the Invisible Circus installations at the Glide church deployed everyday objects in unusual ways. For instance, Grogan crammed the entrance corridor to the church with a two-foot-high pile of shredded plastic. "Wading through this fill was like a dream sequence of being stuck in place while trying mightily to move," one observer recalled. Since merely entering the hall entailed a physical struggle, the Invisible Circus enmeshed visitors in its bizarre spectacle from the outset. Another room featured a discussion forum on pornography, including Berg, a lawyer, a minister, a police community relations officer, and a "free pulpit" for the audience to contribute their thoughts. When the police officer spoke, Minault inserted his penis through a glass display case behind the officer. "The audience broke apart in hilarity over the irony of these two juxtaposed images," the observer remarked, "the staid cop discussing in a quite serious tone the dangers of porn, while the anonymous flasher performed his silent interpretation of 'do your own thing' behind the podium. The cop never caught on."[85] The Diggers used such spectacles to affirm a point the Living Theatre also emphasized, that sexual liberation and the liberation of the body from social taboos were vital aspects of the cultural revolution.

The Invisible Circus introduced a device intended to reinforced the audience's sense of active participation. Chester Anderson and Claude Hayward, who together formed the Communications Company ("the public information arm of the Diggers," which conceived and printed Digger leaflets after Murcott's and Grogan's original Digger papers), transported their Gestetner mimeograph machine to the Glide Church and installed it in a church office. With the poet Richard Brautigan, Anderson and Hayward called themselves "The John Dillinger Computer Service," which they established to cover the events of the Invisible Circus as they unfolded. One anecdote that epitomizes the theatrical possibilities of this device concerns Anderson, who during the Invisible Circus visited a bar across the street and overheard a confrontational discussion between two patrons. Anderson took notes, went across the street and typed them up, and ran off an "instant news bulletin." He then returned to the bar and "astounded these very patrons with copies of their conversation memorialized in print."[86] The John Dillinger Computer Service's function of delivering immediate news to Invisible Circus attendees reinforced the idea that their actions carried weight, since at any moment an audience member might do something that could find its way into print. It also broadened the audience by extending its wacky scenarios out of the Glide Church and into the bar across the street.

The most striking and controversial images the Invisible Circus presented involved transgressive sexuality. Grogan's *Ringolevio* attempts to convey, no doubt hyperbolically, the scene at the Glide Church:

> The cathedral-like interior of the church itself was alive with hundreds of people actualizing their fantasies . . . Several couples were draped over the main altar, fucking . . . people stripped off each other's clothing in the candlelight, and clouds of smoke from a thousand burning incense sticks swirled aloft to the center of the cupola. A group of drag queens stood in the vestibule giving each other head in an orgy of mmm's and ahhh's and being looked at by a small band of teeny-boppers who were turning red in a flurry of giggles. Some Frisco Hell's Angels were in the back pews being entertained by a beautiful woman dressed in a Carmelite nun's habit who kept shouting for "More! More!" and they were giving it to her. . . . Some youngsters felt one another's recent pubescence, pantsying in the balcony, while a few naked bodies raced up and down the aisles, pedaling bicycles. Two hookers walked in off the street with a horny john and gave him some behind a statue of Christ.[87]

Grogan's glorification of exposing minors to unbridled sexual expression is a disturbing aspect of this event, and it epitomized Coyote's insight that the "failure to curb personal indulgence was a major collective error."[88] Though Grogan most likely embellished this account to promote the Diggers' legend, clearly the Invisible Circus combined aspects of the Diggers' most redeeming and least attractive traits. On one hand, it was a community event attended by over five thousand people which democratically welcomed all comers and provided a medium to "do your thing." Yet it set no responsible limits to the personal freedom it unleashed. The myriad indiscretions described by Grogan and others beg the question whether all the sex at the Invisible Circus was consensual. Participants in a candle-carrying procession spilled quantities of wax in the Glide Church and risked its incineration. For better and worse, however, the Invisible Circus established a new model for participatory events that became "legend in San Francisco's hip community."[89]

The massive migration of young people to Haight-Ashbury during the 1967 Summer of Love formed the backdrop for the Diggers' last major piece of street theater, the "Death of Hippie" parade. Perhaps in an attempt to galvanize the potential power for cultural transformation which the growing hippie movement represented, the Diggers themselves promoted the idea that legions of hip youngsters would descend on San Francisco during the summer of 1967. The author and journalist Joan Didion identified Berg as the person who "more or less invented and first introduced to the press the notion that there would be an influx . . . of 200,000 indigent adolescents." That spring, major publications including *Time*, *Life*, and the *New York Times Magazine* ran articles such as "The Strange New Love Land of the Hippies," sensationalizing the hippie phenomenon and forecasting its apotheosis that summer. In early June, the songwriter John Phillips and the singer Scott McKenzie seized on this prediction and spurred its momentum by releasing the single "San Francisco (Be Sure to Wear Flowers in Your Hair)," which heralded the arrival of flower children in the city.[90]

Yet the Diggers also understood that the Summer of Love promised to strain resources in the neighborhood, and this realization inspired many of the free services the Diggers initiated. The summer of 1967 marked a transitional period for Haight-Ashbury. As approximately three hundred new arrivals a day filtered into the neighborhood, an inadequate supply of housing forced many of them away. Many sought one of several rural outposts of hippie culture that started germinating earlier that year, such as the Digger farm Morning Star. Other hippie communes sprang up in the Bay Area, in Sonoma County, and in New Mexico. The Diggers themselves abandoned their name when a Digger named Billy Jahrmarkt, also known as "Billy Batman," named his newborn son "Digger" in early July. After the birth of Jahrmarkt's son, the Diggers referred to themselves variously as the "Free City Collective," the "Free Men," or the "Free Family." Another significant development that summer was that the Haight's drug culture became more ominous, with marijuana and LSD increasingly supplemented by potentially lethal amphetamines, STP, and heroin. The increased drug trade resulted in an upsurge of violent crime and police harassment of hippies.[91] Diggers and collaborators designed the "Death of Hippie" parade as a response to these developments.

The "Death of Hippie" protested what the historian Timothy Miller refers to as a "perversion" of the hippie "rhetoric of peace and love." Media sensationalism and the commercialization of hippie culture constituted the main sources of this perversion, and the "Death of Hippie" responded to the perceived malice of "media poisoners." From their inception, the Diggers maintained a complex attitude toward the media. They reveled, for instance, in "putting on" reporters. In one renowned episode, Berg convinced each of a pair of reporters from the *Saturday Evening Post* and *Time* (both "having dressed down for his foray into the wild and mysterious Haight") that the other was the manager of the Free Store.[92] (The Diggers preferred to function in anonymity to avoid any individual's vulnerability to arrest for infractions, such as stolen free food or clothing or violations resulting from providing free housing for indigents. Similarly, they let the name "Emmett Grogan" be used for a wide array of Digger deeds that the actual Grogan may or may not have perpetrated.) The Diggers periodically made use of the media for their own ends, such as the time Berg appeared on a local New York television talk show and turned the program into a pie-throwing mayhem of guerrilla theater, usurping the host Alan Burke and delivering the following exit soliloquy: "I am in a box looking at you through a box. And you are in a box watching me through a box. I am leaving my box and the things that make up my box. I've made my decision. What are you going to do about the box you are in?"[93] Berg mobilized television to challenge the audience's conception of reality, proselytizing for the Diggers' credo of pursuing whatever personal freedoms an individual desired at the moment. Gitlin's comment crystallizes the Diggers' relationship to the media: "Although the Diggers loathed the media for faking experience, they were willing to use them as public address systems."[94]

The "Death of Hippie" parade criticized the media for its disingenuous portrayals of the Haight-Ashbury scene and the counterculture, from its "discovery" of the Human Be-In to its hype of the Summer of Love. The press release for the parade said in part: "The media cast nets, create bags for the identity hungry to climb in. Your face on TV, your style immortalized without soul. . . . NBC says you exist, ergo I am." Organizers of the "Death of Hippie," including Diggers and others, proposed to replace "hippie," a media-created term, with "Free Man," which they viewed as a term that emphasized the positive essence of the counterculture. "The FREE MAN vomits his images and laughs in the clouds . . . he flexes his strong loins of FREE and is gone again from the nets."[95] Thus the organizers designed the "Death of Hippie" as a piece of street theater to purify Haight-Ashbury and reclaim its original essence, before "media poisoners" further domesticated it.

After a "Wake for Hippie" the previous day, the "Death of Hippie" parade started on the morning of October 6, 1967, the first anniversary of the California law criminalizing LSD. Mourners dressed in "death costumes à la Ingmar Bergman," lit candles, played "Taps," and began a funeral procession carrying a black fifteen-foot cardboard coffin which held stereotypical hippie paraphernalia such as beads, flowers, and hair, and which bore the inscription "Hippie, Son of Media" on its side. Inside the coffin a representative hippie maintained a "death-like" trance throughout the procession. During the procession, paraders sang and chanted while a bluegrass fiddler played and a drummer beat an "occasional dirge" on a trash can lid. As the parade reached the end of its route at the Panhandle, marchers burned the coffin ("without occupant") and the hippie litter while "whooping dancers" circled and leaped over the pyre. When firemen doused the flames, several self-proclaimed "Free Men" gathered ashes and painted their faces with them. During the entire event, which received extensive media coverage, the participants performed a ritual exorcism of the "hippie" label.[96]

Predictably, the mainstream media generated a spate of articles trumpeting the death of the "hippie movement" and pointed to the inevitable demise of a counterculture that defined freedom as "the end of the need to produce." "The hippie movement is over," Earl Shorris remarked in a *New York Times* account. "The alternative to the 'computerized society' has proved to be as unsatisfactory to its adherents as the society that gave birth to it."[97] The columnist Russell Baker satirized the exodus of hippies from Haight-Ashbury, inventing a scenario in which the few remaining hippies prove inadequate to respond to the deluge of media attention, and in which "every hippie on Haight Street is now being subjected to a minimum of eleven interviews a day."[98] The rush to report the hippies' demise, combined with the Diggers' point that hippies were a media-driven phenomenon from the outset, suggests that the mainstream media orchestrated a view of the counterculture as a fad with a finite life expectancy rather than as a lasting, legitimate alternative to the status quo.

The Diggers argued that efforts to build an alternative social structure were under way. Throughout 1967, Diggers and other Haight-Ashbury residents began moving out of the city to rural communes, first to Morning Star Ranch in Sonoma County, where Lou Gottlieb welcomed newcomers nonexclusively, then to the adjoining Wheeler Ranch. These two communes served as a meeting ground for like-minded individuals who in turn opened their own communes, both in northern California and in New Mexico. The most important of these from the Digger point of view was the ranch in Olema, California, in which Coyote played a leadership role. In part, what motivated this exodus to the country was the opportunity to pursue the ideals of "free," which Grogan expounded in his "Post-Competitive Game of a Free City" manifesto, away from the population pressure, deteriorating drug culture, and police harassment.[99] Since the Diggers had already lived in communal dwellings in San Francisco, the collective aspect of this new life was not completely new—but the rural setting represented a substantial change.

Several of these communal experiments collapsed quickly because of tensions between the ideal of absolute personal freedom and the reality of sustaining an interdependent household with limited resources, a generally low level of competence in rural living skills, and an increase in drug abuse. "I nick-named Olema 'the Fool's School,'" mused Coyote, regarding his fellow com-munards' lack of knowledge concerning "group life, hygiene, and labor." Yet despite such shortcomings, Coyote added that people usually stayed long enough to manage the rudimentary skills of gardening, machine maintenance, and communal cooking to present themselves as "seasoned communards" to outsiders.[100] One commune with Digger roots, Turkey Ridge in northeastern Pennsylvania, persisted until 1973.

Though the Diggers' shift from urban "cultural terrorists" (as R. G. Davis called them) to rural communards did not endure long enough to reverse the usual sixties declension narrative that the historian Allen Matusow referred to as "The Rise and Fall of a Counterculture," it certainly represents a case study that challenges the notion that the impact of the cultural rebellion of the sixties was minimal. Cultural shifts such as the emergence of the countercul-ture are difficult to gauge by quantitative means. "Our victories occurred in the deep waters of culture and not in the frothy white water of current events," Coyote remarked, citeing the transformation of a complex of attitudes about health, the environment, human rights, spirituality, and agriculture as the counterculture's primary accomplishments.[101] Contemporary phenomena that testify to the staying power of Digger visions include the annual counter-cultural festival known as the Rainbow Gathering; the now-institutionalized popularity of whole, organic, and natural foods; and the Digger website itself, a nexus of information about free goods and services.

The Diggers furnished the counterculture with a vocabulary ("do your thing") and an idea ("free because it's yours"), and imbued public life with a distinct style which one observer called "participatory theater." The Diggers' Free Food and Free Store, the Intersection Game, the Invisible Circus, the Death of Money, and the "Death of Hippie" all involved public encounters with audiences going about their daily business in the Haight during the years 1966–67. These participatory events questioned ordinary reality and percep-tion, challenging spectators to assume personal freedom. Though Digger street theater failed to address the long-term needs of those uninterested in street theater, who longed only to escape "from under the heel of an oppressive system,"[102] to hold the Diggers accountable for failing to solve deep-seated, structural social and economic problems ignores their context and intent. At their most effective, the Diggers staged guerrilla theater events that injected the counterculture with a dose of anarchist politics and created alternative institutions that made an impact on their community.

The Diggers' attempts to forge alternatives within a countercultural constituency resemble the efforts of the Art Workers Coalition to reshape art world institutions. The AWC served as a focal point for rethinking power relationships in the art world, as well as the artist's role in society. Unlike the Diggers, however, the AWC demanded change from external authorities, most notably art institutions and U.S. foreign policy apparatus. Yet the AWC, along with their fellow political artists, the Guerrilla Art Action Group, shared with the Diggers an impulse to collapse the space between art, politics, and everyday life, which propelled these groups to publicize their protests and ideas through performance in the streets.

CHAPTER FOUR

The Art Workers Coalition and the Guerrilla Art Action Group: Politicizing the Art World

Arts and cultural groups of the sixties used performance in public spaces to dramatize a vision of social transformation. Public performances such as the freedom singers' accompaniment of civil rights demonstrations, the Living Theatre's procession to the streets at the end of *Paradise Now*, and the Diggers' "Death of Money" and "Death of Hippie" street parades, emerged as the groups' political and creative sensibilities converged. It was especially appropriate for the freedom singers to be singing in public, as desegregating public accommodations was one of the fundamental goals of the early civil rights movement. Though the Living Theatre existed for almost twenty years before street theater became their preferred form, certain events in the company's history anticipated this development, such as Julian Beck's and Judith Malina's participation in the protests of civil defense drills, the "Theater in the Room" experiments, and the trial following the closing of the 14th Street theater during *The Brig*. Finally, leading the audience into the street at the end of *Paradise Now* in the context of late-sixties political activism committed the company to follow the logic of its own development and begin to create politically oriented street theater in the seventies. The Diggers incorporated public performance from the outset of their formation as a community group. For these groups, mixing performance and politics in a public setting did not constitute a "stretch" in their creative development. The path of the Art Workers Coalition to politicized art and protest in public spaces on the other hand, followed a more tortuous route. For the AWC, and the Guerrilla Art Action Group, a related but separate group, politicized performances developed only when the political and social crises of the late sixties intersected with a decade of art world trends that deployed everyday life as subject matter.

The Art Workers Coalition, a New York City–based group active in the visual arts, formed in 1969 as an umbrella organization to lobby and protest on behalf of the artistic rights of visual artists. Eventually its concerns broadened to include the politics of race, class, and gender in the art world, and opposition to the Vietnam War. Whereas the Living Theatre and the Diggers cultivated a collective identity, the AWC tellingly adopted the word "coalition" in its name, implying a more tentative alliance than "collective" or "union." AWC members could thus coalesce in small groups on discrete issues rather than creating a more formal, traditional organization. Though "everyone was poor and did a lot of sharing," at no point did AWC artists live together communally as did the Living Theatre and the Diggers.[1]

A variety of factors inhibited visual artists from undertaking collective political activity. First and foremost, the nature of artistic creation itself tended to be more individual than group-oriented; visual artists were less likely to engage in collaborative artistic enterprises than, for example, theater artists. According to the art critic and AWC member Lucy Lippard, the artist, "is by nature unequipped for group thinking or action."[2] Moreover, the mid-twentieth-century art world venerated individual artists, most notably the abstract expressionists, and such veneration works against impulses toward collective action, even as it encourages innovation. Unlike theater artists, visual artists were not represented by an organized labor union such as the Actors' Equity Association. Thus, a constellation of circumstances discouraged collective political activity by visual artists, a set of cultural and institutional barriers that made the careers of the AWC and the GAAG all the more remarkable, and accounts for the groups' relatively late emergence.

The cultural conservatism of the postwar era held sway over the content of American art well into the sixties. In the late forties and the fifties, abstract expressionist painting emerged as the dominant artistic form and became the leading edge of innovation in contemporary art. Jackson Pollock's paint splatterings, Willem de Kooning's jagged forms, and Mark Rothko's blurred abstractions were visual arts parallels of the Living Theatre's poetic dramas, revolutions in form rather than content. Many of the most important individual artists within the New York school of abstract expressionism possessed political sentiments that aligned them with the Left, as evidenced by their sponsorship of the socialist journal *Dissent*.[3] Despite personal status as *engagés*, the abstract expressionists refrained from introducing overt social or political commentary into their work, reflecting what the art historian Patricia Hills refers to as "the shift of many artists away from politics and towards subjectivity and aesthetics at a time of world crisis."[4] This avoidance of overt political content left fifties abstract art vulnerable to appropriation for ends which sometimes ran counter to the political sentiments of its creators. The historian and art critic Serge Guilbaut has shown how abstract expressionism, while a formal rebellion, seemed so "neutral" and devoid of politics that politicians easily deployed it as cold war propaganda symbolizing the "freedom" of the individual artist under American capitalism.[5] This co-optation occurred despite the intent of many artists in the New York school to communicate through their painting, often by a strategy of negation, a critique of dominant, mainstream American values in the fifties: conformity, materialism, automation. The art historian David Craven argues that many abstract expressionists shared "a keen sense of the failings of U.S. society, which was related to the bleak political terrain of the McCarthy years."[6] Yet if abstract expressionism functioned as a cultural critique of dominant American values, it did so more at the level of the artist's intellectual inspiration rather than that of the artwork's overt content.

The hegemony of abstract expressionism yielded to pop art, minimalism, and conceptualism in the sixties, yet the atmosphere of caution about overt political content persisted, as these forms addressed politics subtly or ambiguously if at all. Though the Happenings and Fluxus events of the early sixties utilized public space directly, their political content remained oblique. Considering the individualistic nature of visual artists and the conservative political tendencies of the art world, it is a considerable accomplishment that a group of artists banded together to agitate for a broad spectrum of changes. The AWC's and GAAG's careers demonstrate that by the late sixties artists with political sensibilities could not help being swept into the vortex of activism. For these artists, combining spectacle and direct action in the streets proved essential to the struggle.

Art World Awakenings: Seeds of the AWC

In the years before the AWC's January 1969 formation, sixties artists seeking social and political change initiated a number of forays into activist politics. In June 1962, the group Artists and Writers Protest, which included several future AWC members, published an open letter in the *New York Times* protesting nuclear testing, requesting a test ban treaty, and calling for "tangible disarmament agreements." The letter, signed by hundreds of artists, began: "We artists of the United States are divided in many ways, artistically and ideologically, but we are as one in our concern for humanity."[7] This statement echoed the concern with nuclear annihilation expressed in the founding state-ment of the preeminent New Left organization, Students for a Democratic Society, which was issued the same year. Indeed, several of the artists respon-sible for this letter, who later played key roles in the AWC, had published a 1968 letter protesting racism and the Vietnam War in the SDS magazine *Caw*. Though with few exceptions art was not politicized until after 1967, the Artists and Writers Protest and the AWC shared the New Left's critique of United States imperialism, the Vietnam War, and the military-industrial com-plex that underwrote American intervention globally. This letter acknowl-edged aesthetic and political divisions among artists, which highlighted the letter's significance as a public statement of condemnation for nuclear testing. That such a diverse group of artists took the unusual step of coalescing to speak out against the war heightened the letter's efficacy and foreshadowed the approach of the AWC, which consistently maintained that they did not share a set of aesthetics, but rather united around salient political and artistic issues. Subsequently, in the spring of 1965, Artists and Writers Protest pub-lished two more statements in the *New York Times* protesting the United States's role in Vietnam.[8]

The Los Angeles–based Artists Protest Committee (APC) similarly antici-pated the AWC. In June 1965, this group, which included future AWC mem-bers such as Irving Petlin, Leon Golub, and Max Kozloff, picketed the Rand Corporation, which held major contracts for government defense research. The APC persuaded Rand to hold a "public dialogue" at the Warner Play-house, where members of the Committee traded barbs with Rand staff, South-east Asia specialists, and political scientists in a four-hour debate, which ap-proximately eight hundred spectators witnessed. "To many it appeared that the small but intense and extremely well-informed artists' group came out on top," Lippard wrote. "Rand executives were reportedly instructed never to get into such a spot again." Petlin concurred: "From all accounts we wiped the floor with them on every issue—they were amazed at artists' knowledge of the war." In 1966, the APC organized construction of a sixty-foot sculpture called *Peace Tower* on a rented vacant lot at the corner of Sunset and La Cienega Boulevards. *Peace Tower* was designed by Mark di Suvero and covered with four hundred small panels by artists including Robert Motherwell, Louise Nevelson, Ad Reinhardt, Eva Hesse, Mark Rothko, Roy Lichtenstein, Larry Rivers, and Frank Stella. Petlin remarked that *Peace Tower* showed that "artists were among the cutting edge" of the antiwar movement, as these artists were engaged well before a critical mass of U.S. public opinion turned against the Vietnam War. The location of *Peace Tower* at a highly visible Los Angeles intersection demonstrated artists' willingness to move beyond museums and go on record publicly with their artistically expressed political sentiments. "Fairly early on," Petlin continued, "these activities galvanized previously apolitical artists who rallied around a series of direct action events." Not only did artists unite around antiwar activities, they started using the mass media, taking out an advertisement in the *New York Times* to announce *Peace Tower*'s opening.

The career of *Peace Tower* illustrates the struggle for political expression in the public space that the freedom singers, the Living Theatre, and the Diggers all encountered in their work. The APC intended *Peace Tower* to stand "from February 26 until the End of War in Vietnam," but the owner of the lot where the sculpture stood reneged on the agreement when local publicity attracted a contingent of pro-war forces who wanted to tear the sculpture down. Fights ensued (one APC member suffered a punctured eardrum), and the landlord, who "saw disaster looming," asked the group to dismantle the sculpture.[9] Although the Vietnam War outlived *Peace Tower*, this episode signified how opposition to the war energized artists to shrug off McCarthy-era prohibitions against mixing politics and culture that had limited the abstract expressionists. The *Peace Tower* collaboration symbolized that, by the mid-1960s, as Petlin asserted, "the old saw of artists as not able to organize, or not verbal, was simply not true."[10]

Though most artists kept this growing political consciousness separate from their art, a significant minority started to incorporate topical themes. In February 1967 several artists created unflattering paintings, drawings, and sculptures of President Lyndon Johnson for a one-week show at the Richard Gray Gallery in Chicago. One of the sculptures, a wooden figure six feet three inches tall "with a gaily colored, long wooden nose," highlighted the growing "credibility gap" between official government body counts designed to show "progress" in the Vietnam War and the actual stalemate that existed.

At the same time, in New York, Artists and Writers Protest organized a week of "Angry Arts Against the War in Vietnam," a series of dance, music, film, art, poetry, and photography events in which over six hundred artists took part. As part of the festival, painters and sculptors collaborated on a single large project, *The Collage of Indignation*, a 10-foot-by-120-foot canvas composed of 150 individual panels, protesting the war. Throughout "Angry Arts" week, New York University's Loeb Student Center displayed the *Collage*, which included contributions by such notable artists as Petlin, Richard Serra, Mark di Suvero, and Jim Rosenquist. Though artists worked together on the *Collage*, they did not embrace collective creativity in the same way the Living Theatre, for instance, collaborated to formulate a unified and coherent work. The various panels of the *Collage* comprised the work of many different individual painters and sculptors who shared an opposition to the war. Various artists departed from their usual aesthetics to produce their panels. For instance, Petlin, who possessed strong feelings against the war and participated in protest activities, but whose art didn't necessarily address this opposition or make it clear to an audience, contributed an unflattering image of LBJ suggesting that his exclusive preoccupation with economic concerns led him to trample on the rest of the globe. Petlin signed his painted panel and included an inscription immediately above his signature: "LBJ, infant people burner / Long may you roast in History's Hell!"[11] Petlin's panel exemplifies how the *Collage* allowed artists who usually kept their artwork apart from politics, to break the barriers that separated the two. The painter Leon Golub, who contributed to the *Collage*, wrote, "This is not political art, but rather an expression of popular revulsion. . . . essentially the work is angry—against the war, against the bombing, against President Johnson, etc. The *Collage* is gross, vulgar, clumsy, ugly." Golub argued that the bulk of contemporary art poorly suited antiwar protest because its artists remained "autonomous" and "concerned with perfectibility."[12] The *Collage* sanctioned artists to abandon many of the aesthetic, formal, and technical concerns of their daily work, liberating themselves to produce collectively a bold, indignant political statement.

By 1968 the efforts of groups such as Artists and Writers Protest, the Artists Protest Committee, and collaborators in "Angry Arts" week, combined with the growing unpopularity of the Vietnam War and the radicalization of the student movement, generated increasing momentum for collective political dissent by artists. In the fall of 1968 a group of fourteen minimalist artists, who normally eschewed overt political content, mounted an exhibition at the Paula Cooper Gallery in New York City's emerging SoHo art community as a benefit for the Student Mobilization Against the War. Lippard called it "a striking show of major Minimal art whose content had absolutely nothing to do with the war."[13] Just as the SNCC Freedom Singers served as effective fundraisers in the early sixties, the group of minimalists who contributed to the show at the Cooper Gallery mobilized their art to raise $30,000 for antiwar activists. The exhibit organizers' statement, however, tellingly defended these artists for maintaining a separation between aesthetics and politics in an age increasingly given to direct action and asserted that they showed their commitment against the war "in the strongest manner open to them by contributing major examples of their current work," implying that artists wield their greatest social and political power by donating work for fundraising purposes rather than by politicizing their art. Yet a few months later, circumstances coalesced that spurred artists to engage politics to an extent not witnessed since the thirties. Growing antiwar activism together with the nascent impulse to combat discrimination against women and African Americans in the art world found a "meeting point" in the AWC.[14]

The AWC: From Artistic Freedom to a Broader Agenda

In January 1969 the kinetic sculptor Takis Vassilakis boldly removed his *Tele-sculpture 1960* without permission from the Museum of Modern Art (MoMA) exhibit entitled "The Machine as Seen at the End of the Mechanical Age" because he believed the museum improperly displayed the piece. Takis pursued this course because MoMA ignored his written explanation that the piece was outdated and no longer represented his work. This direct action suggested elements of public performance as the *Village Voice* art critic John Perrault remarked that the removal was "very well rehearsed" and resembled a "movie jewel robbery." If Takis's action represented a kind of guerrilla theater, it is also true that its performative qualities did not end with the mere removal of the sculpture, but rather continued in a way that reflected the protest culture of the age. After liberating the sculpture from its pedestal, Takis and several supporters staged a sit-in in MoMA's outdoor garden until the museum's director, Bates Lowry, conferred with them. The group conceived of themselves as defending artists' freedom to control the exhibition of their work, regardless of whether they had sold the work. This event catalyzed a flurry of meetings and protests as the group adopted the name Art Workers Coalition. "I like the term art-worker," the sculptor Carl Andre remarked, ". . . not because it's any kind of camp Marxism, but it includes everybody who has a contribution to make in the art world." Accordingly, the AWC welcomed not just artists but critics, museum and gallery personnel, and even art audiences.[15] This effort to renounce the implied elitism of an artists-only organization typified New Left–inspired grassroots participation.

That concerns with artistic freedom sparked the AWC's genesis was a logical outcome of the art world's recent history. In the fifties, Cold War politicians invoked abstract expressionist painting as the ultimate freedom, that is, "the freedom to create controversial works of art." Moreover, important abstract expressionist artists themselves, along with influential art critics and museum directors, explicitly linked modern abstract art to freedom and liberation in their writings and discourse. This stance introduced a vocabulary into artists' lives that placed a premium on artistic freedom and even positioned American artists as exemplars of the superiority of the American way of life, as contrasted with Soviet artists who were forced to labor within the confines of Socialist realism.[16] Not surprisingly, then, many artists entered the sixties with a confidence about their inalienable right of free expression (an irony given the use of such artists in the Unites States's anticommunist propaganda campaign).

A notable aspect of the Takis protest is that Lowry not only acceded to the protesters' request for a meeting; he also agreed to remove Takis's sculpture from the show. Lowry gave no explanation for his decision, and he tended to respond to subsequent AWC protests by channeling them away from the public view, so as not to disrupt museum business. In the Takis protest, Lowry asked the protesters, who were seated in a circle around the sculpture in MoMA's outdoor garden, to adjourn to his fifth-floor office, where the parties reached an agreement to place the sculpture in storage.[17] MoMA's compliance reflected a cultural moment where direct action protest in the artistic sphere often yielded tangible results, as it could rely on at least some degree of sympathetic reception from museum staff, with whom artists usually shared a liberal humanist outlook that privileged freedom of expression. Yet the Takis protest also showed the confidence with which artists exercised their right to freedom of expression. It was as though artists such as Takis and his friends who later formed the AWC felt that artistic freedom already had reached the status of birthright, secured and sanctified by a previous generation of American artists.

Emboldened by its initial success at MoMA, the AWC submitted a list of thirteen demands to Lowry, which included the creation of a black and Puerto Rican artists section in the museum, two free evenings a week for working people, and equal gender representation among artists whose works were exhibited and purchased. One demand called for bringing art exhibits to proposed museum branches in poor and minority communities. "All museums should decentralize to the extent that their activities and services enter Black, Puerto Rican and all other communities," the AWC argued. "They should support events with which these communities can identify and that they can control."[18] The language of this demand, especially such terms as "decentralize," "identify," and "control," suggested its origins. The Coalition's concern with bringing the art world into minority communities reflected the entry into art world politics of the New Left goal of decentralization through participatory democracy, and the civil rights movement's agenda of promoting pos-

itive cultural identity, as the AWC sought to make the art world more accessible to a broader racial and economic cross-section of the public and expand
opportunities for minority artists to exhibit their work. The Coalition was
joined in this effort to exert pressure on behalf of artists of color by a separate
but "intertwined" group of black artists that had formed within a week of the
AWC itself, the Black Emergency Cultural Coalition.[19]

The AWC followed up its social and political rhetoric with direct action.
On March 30, 1969, three hundred AWC-organized protesters convened at
MoMA to protest the museum's lack of representation of black artists. (The
New York Times account of this demonstration observed that the protesters
were "overwhelmingly white.") Once again, the AWC prevailed upon Lowry
to accommodate protesters, by letting them past museum guards who tried to
block their entrance and allowing them access to MoMA's outdoor garden to
make speeches.[20] Though Lowry ostensibly sought to prevent protesters from
disturbing the 6,500 paying visitors at MoMA, his commitment to finding a
forum for the AWC on museum grounds emerges as striking in an era when
the mobilization of municipal law enforcement to neutralize demonstrators
had become commonplace. Lowry's acquiescence suggests that visual artists
possessed greater cultural prestige than, for instance, the antiwar protesters at
the 1968 Chicago Democratic Convention, and that direct action protest
among artists constituted a new and surprising development that unnerved
museum officials and caught them off guard.

The AWC's demands that day—better representation of black artists, a
black artists' wing, and decentralized MoMA branches in black and Latino
communities—as well as its criticism of MoMA for admission fees that excluded black and minority communities, reflected the civil rights movement's
shift by the late sixties from integration and voting rights to economic justice
and cultural autonomy. The AWC included a strong black contingency led by
Tom Lloyd, but the fact that the white majority of AWC protesters so actively
agitated for these goals demonstrated both how politicized some artists had
become in a brief period of time and how effectively the civil rights movement
had ingrained its goals in the consciousness of the white Left. Irving Petlin
traced the link between the AWC's use of direct action and the civil rights
movement to events of the early sixties. "Techniques of mechanical reproduc-
tion allowed us to see what happened in Birmingham the next day," Petlin
noted, adding that the protesters' activities inspired sixties artists. "The Civil
Rights Movement, Happenings, Rudy Burckhardt [a Swiss-born, New York
City–based artist, photographer, and filmmaker]," Petlin commented, were
among a number of cultural forces involved in "using the street more directly."

Leon Golub concurred, explaining that though art world developments such as Happenings and Fluxus certainly played a large role in artists' changing relationship to the public space, "we were also influenced by the media and current events." Golub recalled that artists started to ask themselves, "Why are we passive when people who have so much less opportunity and fewer resources are active?," noting the Civil Rights Movement's influence on artists' willingness to engage in direct action protest.[21]

The AWC gained confidence in its use of public spaces in protests, though MoMA did not always accommodate its demands. The AWC's original list included a demand for a public hearing at MoMA regarding "The Museum's Relationship to Artists and Society," yet the Coalition's persistent demonstrations on MoMA's grounds soured the museum's administration on holding the hearing there. As a result, the hearing took place at the School of Visual Arts on April 10. An audience of approximately 250 people heard more than fifty speakers discuss topics such as MoMA's role in the contemporary art world, the representation of black and Puerto Rican artists, museum admission fees that discriminated against the poor, extending museum branches to local communities, and better representation of contemporary artists' work. The hearing lasted for over four hours, exemplifying a phenomenon that typified 1960s oppositional politics, epic meetings in which all present could express their views in a wide-ranging cultural and political discourse.[22] Such meetings pervaded New Left politics, from SDS to Berkeley, but also the artistic sphere. The meeting at the School of Visual Arts resembled the Living Theatre's *Paradise Now*, both in its extended duration and in the breadth of ideas discussed.

Not all who attended the meeting agreed on the agenda outlined in the AWC's original thirteen demands. A film editor named Bill Gordy criticized the idea of establishing a special portion of MoMA dedicated to black and Puerto Rican artists, sarcastically deriding it as a "darkies wing." Gordy's comment testifies to the AWC's reality as a forum for diverse, and sometimes divergent, opinions. The AWC was a coalition, joining sporadically for shared causes on which all individuals did not necessarily agree. Gordy rejected the cultural pluralist demand of a wing dedicated to minority artists' work, suggesting that it encouraged the further marginalization and separation of those artists. Yet within the AWC, Gordy's position was in the minority, since the Coalition consistently advocated mechanisms for greater minority representation and opportunity. He also showed a lack of prescience, given the momentum and legitimacy the women's art movement gathered in the seventies, when he added the ironic query, "How about a wing for women?" Although

Gordy sought to portray the AWC's concern with black artists as absurd, which is evident in his subsequent quips that "WASPs over 30" and "Jewish Heterosexual Magic Realists" might deserve special treatment, in general the AWC's efforts fostered sensitivity about the representation of minority artists. Furthermore, members of the AWC became active in the seventies in the Ad Hoc Women Artists Committee, Women Artists in Revolution, and the Heresies Collective, organizations that promoted the work of women artists and publicized feminist concerns in the art world.[23]

Throughout its existence the AWC pared and fine-tuned the list of thirteen demands, trimming them first to eleven and then in March 1970 to nine. The issue of artists' rights remained strong, epitomizing the pervasive 1960s idea that confronting social and political implications of issues of direct personal importance represented the key to radical liberation.[24] This idea also accounts for the anti-institutional aspect of the AWC's challenges, which targeted MoMA and other prominent New York museums. The Coalition believed it could be most useful in transforming the art world institutions that closely affected the lives of its members, an idea that invokes the New Left's call for shaping institutions to meet human needs.[25] Of the nine demands, five addressed issues of pressing interest to artists: artists' representation on the museum's board of trustees; the creation of an artists' registry at the museum; mobilizing the museum staff to become advocates for artists' welfare and housing; exhibitions for artists not represented by commercial galleries; and artists' control over the exhibition of their work, regardless of whether it has been sold.[26]

The other four demands illustrated the breadth of the AWC's vision in addressing the need for greater museum accessibility for a broader socioeconomic cross section of the public, and for the work of artists it believed were excluded based on race or gender. These demands included free admission to museums; nighttime hours for museums to accommodate working people; museum programs in black and Puerto Rican communities to be controlled by those groups and to promote positive cultural identity; the creation of a museum section dedicated to the work of black and Puerto Rican artists; and equal representation for women artists in exhibitions and in the acquisitions of new artwork.[27] Reaction to the AWC's demands varied, as its program represented a kind of art world litmus test. Several art critics such as the *Village Voice*'s John Perrault sympathized with the AWC's agenda, supported the demands, and were even moved to join the Coalition. Yet establishment critics such as Hilton Kramer of the *New York Times*, though willing to grant that the AWC played a healthy role in generating needed art world debate, viewed such demands as "radical proposals" that were "at a considerable distance from the establishment" and threatened the continued existence of museums as institutions. Grace Glueck, who covered the AWC extensively for the *Times*, took a more centrist position, characterizing the Coalition as a "loosely structured group of dissident artists" representing diverse opinions, which nevertheless shared a "point of unity" in its "Anti-Establishmentarianism." Museum staff similarly split over the AWC's program. For instance, when the AWC initially proposed free admission to MoMA, at the March 1969 protest, Bates Lowry had responded that that request was "absolutely impossible and can't be considered." Yet Lowry's successor as MoMA director, John Hightower, not only sympathized with the eventual settlement of this demand—one free day per week—but ventured so far as to credit the AWC and GAAG for their roles in bringing it about.[28]

The AWC made progress in several areas, achieving "Free Mondays" at MoMA and community programs in black and Puerto Rican neighborhoods, and beginning to pressure museums toward greater representation of women. Even in its partial accommodation of the AWC's demands, the art establishment usually contested and resisted them, imposing a "discretionary" admission fee on visitors to Free Mondays, refusing to create a museum section for minority artists, and failing to implement full gender-based equality in representation. Though it did not achieve all of its demands, the political and social program of the AWC cut a wide swath. The group's willingness to employ direct action reflected the influence of the civil rights movement's struggle over public spaces and institutions, and its formulation of identity politics and the relationship between culture and power owed much to black nationalism's "pursuit of group solidarity" to "restructure America's public and political culture."[29] Although AWC artists remained vigilant about individual artistic rights, they increasingly pursued group solutions to issues that concerned a broad cross section of the art world.

The AWC realized that by focusing the terms of debate and establishing dialogue, it exerted greater influence on institutions within the art world than on external political matters. But beginning in April 1969, spurred by their opposition to the Vietnam War, the AWC and GAAG initiated a series of direct action protests designed to broaden the audience for their ideas beyond traditional museumgoers, a step that served to expand artists' public profile.

Artists in the Streets: The AWC, GAAG, and Guerrilla Theater

The meeting at the School of Visual Arts signified artists' growing need to connect with the public more directly; Lucy Lippard commented on the meeting's uniqueness: "art world complaints are made loudly, but in the relative privacy of studios and bars, rarely in public." Increasingly, artists found public space the best place to engage the public politically. On April 2, 1969, the same "political momentum" that turned a majority of Americans' opinions against the war after the 1968 Tet Offensive propelled the AWC, collaborating with Artists and Writers Protest, into the streets to inaugurate a more visible, symbolic style of protest with an event called the "Mass Antiwar Mail-In."[30] The two groups shared several key members, which reflected the AWC's continuity with its forerunner in providing a forum for artists' political activism. The Mass Antiwar Mail-In featured mailable antiwar artworks addressed to "The Joints Chiefs of War," among them a papier-mâché "bomb" and a disheveled papier-mâché Statue of Liberty, which the two groups paraded to the Canal Street post office and mailed to Washington, D.C. Inspired by his contemporaneous *Napalm* series of paintings, which used red oxide paint to symbolize the deadly incendiary, Leon Golub contributed a napalm toilet seat as part of what the protesters called "Gifts to the Pentagon." "To our absolute amazement, the post office clerks took everything and stamped it," Golub remembered. "What they did with it afterward, I don't know." Golub's remark illustrates the freshness of this approach to protest, in its creation of a symbolic public spectacle, confirmed by the postal employees' reaction of not diverging from the "script," dutifully processing the antiwar artworks, and presumably sending them on their way. In May 1969 the two groups staged a second street action, a march up Sixth Avenue to the Columbus Circle war memorial. Members of the AWC and Artists and Writers Protest carried black body bags identical to those used in Vietnam, inscribed with the totals of American and Vietnamese dead, and white cloth runners stretching over a block in length with the names of the dead. Lippard noted this protest's effect on the audience: "people threw flowers on the bags; even the police . . . were respectful."[31] The sympathetic, or at least neutral, police response Lippard described illustrated a growing shared discontent with the war in the post–Tet Offensive era which made such a public theatrical moment possible.

Heartened by its initial experience with street protest, the AWC continued to stage street actions throughout the remainder of 1969 until 1971, when the group disbanded. These actions incorporated theatrical performance elements, yet they also demonstrated a visual arts sensibility in the papier-mâché bombs, block-long banners, and "big, poster-like paintings." The AWC's more radical cousin, the Guerilla Art Action Group, heightened this connection between art, politics, and performance in its public actions, which began in late 1969.

Jon Hendricks and Jean Toche, both young visual artists affiliated with the AWC, were the two main forces behind GAAG. In the fall of 1969, Hendricks and Toche became angered with the AWC, frustrated that a picket at the Guggenheim Museum collapsed when Coalition members "all went out to lunch." Hendricks, Toche, and Poppy Johnson subsequently created GAAG as "a separate identity from" the AWC, though the three remained members of the Coalition. Although art critics and historians usually discuss the AWC and GAAG together, important discontinuities existed. "We started out of the differences," Hendricks remembered. "The AWC was more concerned about position in the art world, GAAG had nothing we wanted to get into museums," he commented, exposing a key distinction. Though both groups created public spectacles to challenge the art world's modus operandi, the AWC sought to reform existing policies through such efforts as pressuring MoMA to exhibit and acquire more works by contemporary, less well-established artists. Aspirations such as this reflected the AWC's willingness to countenance certain elements of the art world status quo such as its veneration of individual artists. At its core, the AWC wanted to enhance opportunities for contemporary artists and to promote their well-being. The AWC's political statements that reached beyond the art world, most notably the antiwar protests, were constrained by Coalition members' reluctance to jeopardize their primary identities as artists and art workers.

GAAG favored a more radical position. "GAAG felt the AWC's picketing was ineffectual," Hendricks remarked. "GAAG wanted to be able to risk arrest because of our beliefs, the AWC largely wasn't going to risk arrest." This difference dictated the logic of forming a smaller group since, as Hendricks recalled, he and Toche were "a little paranoid" and suspected the New York City police had "spies" within the AWC.[32] Whereas the AWC maintained an inclusive attitude toward new members and was open to all art workers, GAAG was consciously created as a more exclusive group to make politicized art, usually involving public performance, whose members were undaunted by the possibility of being arrested. GAAG's approach recalls the Diggers' injunction to assume freedom rather than demand it; the Living Theatre's conception of *Paradise Now* as commencing the "beautiful nonviolent anarchist revolution"; and civil rights workers' efforts to achieve desegregation by creating situations, such as the lunch counter sit-ins, in which demonstrators acted "as-if" integrated society already existed. That is, GAAG's public performances tended to refrain from making demands in the style of the political Left, in favor of aggressively appropriating public space as a forum for its art and symbolic political commentary.

Whereas the AWC was a "political group" rather than an aesthetic one, GAAG viewed its actions as actual artworks. "We saw what we did as art,"

Hendricks recalled. At a time when performance art struggled for recognition, GAAG's actions addressed the most pressing issues. In a March 1970 statement of purpose, GAAG outlined its intentions: "Our Art Actions are a concept . . . We see ourselves as questioners. Our intention is never to impose our own point of view, but to provoke people into a confrontation with the existing crises. Our methods are only a few of the possible ways to dramatize the problem." Though Hendricks maintained that GAAG's actions were "art not street theater," the group's provocative, confrontational style of dramatizing social and political problems reverberated with that of the Living Theatre and the Diggers. Ideological similarities among these groups surface in GAAG's statement of purpose, including a commitment to nonviolence that echoes the Living Theatre's pacifism. Furthermore, GAAG affirmed that "our concern is with people, not property. . . . We question the order of priorities in this country, the fact that property—how to defend property and how to expand property—always seems to have priority over people and people's needs."[33] GAAG's affirmation of people over property in its public actions, articulated a critique of materialism resonant with The Living Theatre and the Diggers.

Though GAAG eventually conveyed its political ideas through public performance, the group's earliest actions targeted museums and occurred within museum walls. In October 1969, Hendricks and Toche removed Kasamir Malevich's painting *White on White* from a gallery wall at MoMA and posted in its place a list of demands, including one that the museum sell a million dollars' worth of its artworks and redistribute the proceeds to the poor. Whereas the AWC had called for free museum admissions as part of its original list of demands, GAAG's program went further, suggesting actual redistribution of wealth, although GAAG still did not approach the Diggers and the Living Theatre, who advocated the abolition of the money system altogether. GAAG's press release explained that the group chose the Malevich specifically as an example of a piece that had once possessed "revolutionary" meaning but now was exhibited stripped of its political context and reduced to a mere "valuable object." The list of demands also opined: "There is no justification for the enjoyment of art while we are involved in the mass murder of people." This reference to the Vietnam War successfully linked GAAG's critique of the museums to its antiwar position. GAAG elaborated, "Today the museum serves not so much as an enlightening educational experience, as it does a diversion from the realities of war and social crisis." Like the other groups in this study, GAAG believed that art should directly address rather than attempt to transcend social problems, and accordingly it acted proactively to bring moral issues such as involvement in the Vietnam War into the museum to prevent the diversionary function it claimed museums served. GAAG explained that it advocated the end of art's "sanctification," rather than its eradication.[34]

GAAG's ability to synthesize its critique of the contemporary art world and its views on Vietnam hinged on a recognition of how the underwriters of the art world often were enmeshed with the business of making war. For instance, on November 10, 1969, GAAG issued "A Call for the Immediate Resignation of All the Rockefellers from the Board of Trustees of the Museum of Modern Art." Hendricks and Toche signed this letter, as did Poppy Johnson and Silvianna, two women who participated intermittently in GAAG actions. GAAG's letter exposed the Rockefellers' involvement with the "war machine," citing their controlling interest in Standard Oil, which leased facilities for the manufacture of napalm; their partial interest in McDonnell Aircraft Corporation (recently renamed McDonnell Douglas Corporation), which was "deeply involved" in chemical and biological weapons research; and MoMA board chairman David Rockefeller's position as chairman of the board of Chase Manhattan Bank, which participated in the Defense Industry Advisory Council, a liaison between domestic arms manufacturers and the Pentagon.

GAAG's call for the Rockefellers' resignation from the MoMA board illustrated the mechanics of the Left's critique of business during the Vietnam era and extended its insights into the realm of corporate patronage of the arts. On the one hand, the group criticized Rockefeller interests linked if only indirectly, to the war-making apparatus. For instance, Rockefeller-controlled Standard Oil had only leased its plant to another concern, the United Technology Center, and UTC manufactured the napalm. Furthermore, GAAG's letter indicated that this arrangement had occurred three years earlier, in 1966, and did not mention whether Standard Oil's relationship with UTC continued to exist. It is clear, however, that by the time GAAG's letter appeared, UTC had ceased manufacturing napalm.[35] On the other hand, this document demonstrated how by the late sixties, arts groups, the antiwar movement, and the general public increasingly held corporations publicly responsible for their actions, as Students for a Democratic Society had advocated in the 1962 Port Huron Statement.[36] GAAG alleged that the Rockefellers used their art patronage as "a cover for their brutal involvement in all spheres of the war industry," in order to gain "social acceptability."[37] In any other context it would be absurd to suggest that the Rockefellers, one of the nation's most prominent families, needed to do anything extra to court social acceptability, but by late 1969 the Vietnam War's unpopularity made GAAG's interpretation seem plausible. Perhaps even closer to the art world's pulse, GAAG compellingly linked the Rockefellers' private business concerns and ties to the war industry with their public role as patrons of modern art and MoMA board members with the power to make decisions affecting artists' lives and livelihoods. The AWC sculptor Carl Andre explained, "The economic and political interests of artists are very much in contradiction to those of Nelson Rockefeller," who also served on the MoMA board.[38]

Andre was one of the few AWC artists who had read Marx, and the Coalition maintained no formal ideological opposition to capitalism. Rather, AWC artists shared a "general detestation of money's role in the art world." This view stemmed from a tension between the need to raise money to create art, including protest art, and the need to stay separate from the corporate affiliations in which wealthy patrons and major foundations were enmeshed. This dilemma resembles the one that caused the Living Theatre to "exile" itself to Europe in the mid-sixties rather than raise ticket prices and be forced to rely on admissions revenues from upscale theatergoers whose political sensibilities they sought to provoke. The AWC found a unique way to circumvent this dilemma, and one that enacted a redistributive politics within the art world, by raising money from wealthier, established artists to support its activities. For instance, Andre donated to the AWC a $1,000 prize he won for his artwork, for "future expenses."[39]

In its efforts to embody a politics of equality in its daily life and activities, the movement culture of the AWC resembled SNCC's efforts to function as a "leaderless" organization and the Living Theatre's "collective creation." Though SNCC's strategy was designed to maximize the organization's potential for developing grassroots leadership, it also reflected a strong opposition to "any hierarchy of authority such as existed in other civil rights organizations."[40] The AWC similarly resisted hierarchy. Though not venturing as far as the Diggers, who resisted individual leadership responsibilities, remained anonymous, and insisted on authentic personal choice, the AWC sought a nonauthoritarian way of conducting its affairs. One observer of the art world referred to the AWC as "a well established non-institution and non-organization." The AWC held weekly meetings at the cooperatively run Museum for Living Artists, and members passed a hat to collect contributions for special events, posters, flyers, and other supplies. As with SNCC's central figures, Robert Moses, James Forman, John Lewis, and later Stokely Carmichael, "leading personalities" also emerged within the AWC, such as Andre, Lippard, Hans Haacke, Fraser Dougherty, Tom Lloyd, and Alex Gross, as the AWC encompassed a remarkably wide range of perspectives.

Though a Latino contingent within the AWC tended to embrace a Marxist perspective, generally no "downbeat Marxist impulse" prevailed within the group. Significantly, the AWC never favored the eradication of art world institutions as some conservative critics alleged, but rather it sought reform of existing institutions that would better serve artists and a more widely construed public. When the opportunity presented itself, the AWC proved capable of mobilizing established cultural institutions in the art world to its advantage, and most Coalition members never gave up what Petlin termed "wanting to work with the world we had." For instance, the AWC secured $17,000 of financial aid from the Rockefeller Foundation and the New York State Council for the Arts for community cultural centers in eight black and Spanish-speaking sectors of the New York metropolitan area.[41] For all its uneasiness with the relationships between museum and foundation trustees and business concerns that profited from the Vietnam War, the AWC believed artists should be supported financially and that art should be accessible to the public. It considered persuading MoMA to implement a policy of free Mondays as one of its most important achievements.[42]

A week after calling for the Rockefellers' resignation from the MoMA board, GAAG followed up its ideological critique with direct action, or rather, direct action performance art. Hendricks, Toche, Silvianna, and Poppy Johnson entered MoMA and hurled one hundred copies of their November 10 letter to the lobby floor. Next they began to cry "Rape!" and rip off one another's clothes, which had hidden bags containing packs of beef blood, which burst on the floor. Then the artists lowered themselves to the floor and began moaning and writhing in attitudes of what a GAAG "communique" called "individual anguish." Reminiscent of "The Plague" scene in the Living Theatre's *Mysteries and Smaller Pieces*, this scene continued with GAAG members gradually lowering their voices and slowing down their movements to a silent tableau. As the four broke the tableau and rose, the audience applauded "as for a theater piece." The GAAG members then silently put on their street clothes and overcoats and asked the audience to "help us clean up this mess." Because of the strewn leaflets linking the Rockefellers and MoMA to the war, audiences could grasp this request as an allusion to Vietnam. Later that month GAAG repeated this action, which came to be known as the "Blood Bath" demonstration (fig. 5), at the Whitney Museum.

Like the Living Theatre's productions of the *Paradise Now* era, "Blood Bath" broke down the theatrical "fourth wall" to address the audience directly, presenting an Artaudian graphic or "cruel" representation of violence for the purpose of eliminating violence. Echoing the assertion of *Paradise Now* that

FIG. 5. As an antiwar piece, GAAG's "Blood Bath," performed here in the MoMA lobby, resembled "The Plague" scene from the Living Theatre's *Mysteries and Smaller Pieces* and embodied New Left ideology in holding art underwriters accountable for their roles in war profiteering. Photo © Ka Kwong Hui.

"the theatre is in the street," some of GAAG's protests spilled into the streets, such as its May 1970 demonstration in support of Students and Artists United for a Martin Luther King Jr.–Pedro Albizu Canpos Study Center for Black and Puerto Rican Art at the Museum of Modern Art. Hendricks, Toche, and collaborators performed an elaborate representation of the "racist mental attitudes" of MoMA's "controlling forces," which through "myths, fears and their protective fantasies . . . have historically exploited and excluded the art and life-styles of Puerto Rican and Black people." GAAG staged this action, which spoofed MoMA's elitism, in public, directly outside the museum entrance. Hendricks and Toche, dressed in formal wear to represent "The Director" and "The Trustee," "yelled hysterically paranoid harangues" at a group of demonstrators from the Black and Puerto Rican Artists Coalition who were collaborating with GAAG. Hendricks and Toche delivered dialogue drawn from actual comments opposing the study center, such as the remark by Arthur

Drexler, MoMA's Architecture and Design Department Head, that "there is no such thing as Black and Puerto Rican Art." The action also featured a "siege" in which Hendricks and Toche exchanged fire with toy rifles, hurled tomato juice, and set off smoke-bombs.[43] The demonstration epitomized GAAG's synthesis of art and action, uniting public performance with political and cultural protest.

The art historian Alan Moore contends that GAAG's actions derived their potency from bringing sixties artistic movements such as Destruction art, conceptual art, and performance art into public spaces and into "direct confrontational engagement with authorities and institutions."[44] In so doing, GAAG contributed to a growing trend that, by the late sixties, established public performance as the prevailing aesthetic among arts and theatrical groups that viewed their work as a form of political action. In a 1969 article in *Art in America*, the critic Dore Ashton commented: "The pressure of circumstances had much to do with the emergence of spectacle and the importance of theater in the visual arts." Ashton suggested that the war in Vietnam, race relations, and social inequality played instrumental roles in forcing artists to feel so "futile" and "exasperated" that they started to combine guerrilla theater tactics with their artistic expression. Not surprisingly, Ashton explicitly mentioned the Living Theatre as a key influence in this development.[45] The AWC's and GAAG's chosen tactics responded to the upheaval in the late 1960s and further exemplified the theatricalization of protest culture.

The AWC sometimes deployed a macabre sense of humor to dramatize its position. In a January 1971 guerrilla action, the group stormed a trustees' banquet at the Metropolitan Museum of Art and poured a jar of cockroaches on the table. Dinner guests including the Met's director, Thomas Hoving, were reduced to "swatting the cockroaches with their napkins." The AWC rebuked the trustees for showing contempt for the public by closing off the museum's Louis XVI Room to hold a private dinner. The AWC's Ann Arlen remarked: "Our purpose is to point out that there is a very big gap between art and what you people are about." For her, the Met's trustees lived in a world of class privilege, in which lavish banquets abounded and no cockroaches existed. According to Lucy Lippard, one AWC protester explained the protest to the Met's trustees as an attempt "to keep Harlem on your minds," a reference to a controversial 1969 exhibit at the museum. The AWC sought to show Met trustees how "the other half" lived, in this case contemporary New York artists and the urban poor. Other AWC members reinforced this position with the statement that the museum was "preoccupied with acquiring art rather than helping to communicate the spirit that produced it." When the museum secretary Ashton Hawkins met with demonstrators offering meetings and a dialogue, Arlen reaffirmed what the AWC viewed as the value of direct action over talk: "when we sit around and discuss is when we get co-opted because absolutely nothing happens."[46] Arlen's comments highlighted an increasingly common distrust of liberal tactics of mediating dissent that had emerged by the late sixties and early seventies, and more specifically the AWC's frustration with the Met's staid, intransigent way of doing business—especially after the Met refused to participate in a one-day art strike that the AWC and other artists had organized after the United States' invasion of Cambodia and the shootings at Kent State University and Jackson State College in May 1970.

The AWC and the Vietnam War: Bringing the Horror Home to the Streets

At least initially, AWC artists resisted suggestions that the political and social turbulence of the late sixties should be expressed in their individual artistic creations. This reluctance reflected artists' traditional vision of their craft as a bastion of individual freedom and "independence from conventional structures." Lippard clarified the AWC's position on political art: "It has always been a non-aesthetic group involved in ethics rather than aesthetics." From this concern with ethics the AWC formulated an idea of how art could be political without making its subject matter overtly political. "It's how you give and withhold your art that is political," Lippard asserted.[47] Carl Andre, for instance, created his modular minimalist sculptures out of small wire pieces, rusting steel pieces, and nails; recalling Julian Beck's approach to scene design for the Living Theatre, Andre procured many of these materials from the streets or from construction sites, and he described his incorporation of found objects as "trying to make a zero-zero economic vector," which he explained as his ethic to "work as if you were poor." Artists' ability to create, he believed, should not be primarily governed by their access to economic resources. Andre also sold his sculptures for one percent of the buyer's annual income, a strategy designed to make his works more accessible to other artists rather than solely to collectors.[48]

Whereas Andre exemplified Lippard's distinction about giving his art politically, other AWC artists withheld their art in ways that dramatized conditions affecting artists' everyday lives. Indeed, the Takis protest, the event that spurred the formation of the AWC, illustrated this principle. Yet AWC members withheld art politically for causes other than artistic freedom. For instance, in December 1969, Toche withdrew his proposed "Air Pollution Project," a tunnel of air full of noxious gas fumes whose pollution level fluctuated daily according to New York City's actual levels, from the "Software" show at the Jewish Museum. Toche took this action because the show was sponsored by the American Motors Corporation, which he attacked as a "major contributor to air pollution." Toche explained his decision with an archetypal rationale: "Art must not serve the function of bettering the corporate images of those who help to destroy human beings and all forms of life by deliberately manufacturing automobiles which spew off poisonous fumes."[49] Toche echoed the imperative of SDS's "Port Huron Statement" that corporations must be made publicly accountable, an idea that enjoyed cultural currency in actions such as the antiwar protests against the napalm manufacturer Dow Chemical.

AWC artists applied this idea of accountability to the federal government when its members joined twenty-four other artists, including renowned figures such as Robert Morris, Roy Lichtenstein, Robert Rauschenberg, Claes Oldenburg, Robert Motherwell, Frank Stella, and Andy Warhol, in withdrawing from the summer 1970 Venice Biennale because they wanted to dissociate from U.S. government sponsorship. "Our decision to withdraw," remembered Irving Petlin, represented an "effort to make a strong statement that we would not stand for using artists as a cultural fig leaf."[50] The artists sacrificed prestige and pecuniary reward rather than allow their art to "sanctify" a war they deemed morally reprehensible.

Although the AWC politicized the giving and withholding of art rather than its aesthetic qualities, they nonetheless sustained attacks from the critical establishment for politicizing art. Charging that the AWC did not "believe in the principle of museums," the New York Times critic Hilton Kramer criticized the group's suggestion that MoMA disperse its permanent collection so that the museum could feature more work by contemporary artists. Museums, Kramer asserted, should function as repositories for "the finest works of art that the human species has produced." This remark tellingly revealed Kramer's status as an establishment art critic untroubled by the emerging revelations, in movements for black cultural identity and women's liberation, that what constitutes "the finest" art and literature might not be a matter of objective reality but rather one of socially constructed value systems based on the preferences and prejudices of dominant socioeconomic groups. Museums should be free from political pressures, Kramer continued, deriding what he viewed as the AWC's role in politicizing art.[51] Responding on behalf of the AWC, Lippard, Fraser Dougherty, and Hans Haacke repudiated Kramer's portrait of the AWC as "a museum-burning, art-defacing, collection-crushing boogie man." The

AWC's letter of reply answered Kramer's charges of politicizing art by affirming that the form and content of art should be the concern of individual artists. In other words, the AWC explicitly disavowed any unified program geared toward producing "political art." This response underscored the AWC's commitment to individual artists' freedom at the same moment that the Coalition's individual members escalated their political activism. The letter pointed out that as a collection of artists, the AWC had a greater stake in the well-being of museums than anyone. The AWC's suggestion that MoMA present fewer major loan exhibitions in favor of a greater number of smaller showcases for individual contemporary artists sought to make MoMA, an institution devoted to advancing public appreciation of modern art, more responsive to the fundamental needs of modern artists.[52] The AWC's patient, carefully explained proposals for modifying MoMA's policies suggested the Coalition's desire to present itself as a moderate force seeking to reform the museum rather than abolish it. These proposals reflected the interests of modern artists with a stake in MoMA's continuation and improvement, a group that was well represented in the AWC's membership. Yet this moderation applied only to MoMA's acquisition, exhibition, and admissions policies. To the AWC, the museum's relationship to larger political issues represented quite another matter.

The AWC's letter charged that Kramer's indictment of the Coalition for politicizing art ignored the "conservative politicization" of the museum itself. The letter argued that the museum's policy of retaining historical works of art with a guaranteed market value threatened MoMA's modernity, and that the museum depended on funding "from the profits of the Vietnam war, of South African Apartheid, of Latin American colonization."[53] This concluding point stemmed from the AWC's observations about the economic interests of MoMA's trustees, whom Coalition members argued were inextricably linked to the nation's war-making apparatus. Various AWC members had articulated this point of view since the group's inception. At the April 1969 School of Visual Arts hearing, the AWC's Gregory Battcock had charged, "The trustees of the museums direct NBC and CBS, the *New York Times* and the Associated Press . . . AT&T, Ford, General Motors, the great multi-billion dollar foundations, Columbia University, Alcoa . . . besides sitting on the boards of each others' museums. . . . The implications of these facts are enormous," Battcock contended. "Do you realize that it is those art-loving, culturally committed trustees of the Metropolitan and the Modern museums who are waging the war in Vietnam?"[54] In responding to Kramer, the AWC continued this analysis, pointing out what it saw as the fundamental interestedness of MoMA's governing board in the United States' intervention in Vietnam. "If the men now controlling the Museum of Modern Art are not politically involved, who the hell is?" the AWC asked.[55]

Obviously the AWC's perception conflicted with Kramer's. Whereas Kramer viewed museums as essentially neutral and apolitical institutions, the AWC regarded them as enmeshed in politics through numerous and complex relationships of finance, patronage, and governance. Wealthy trustees with vested interests in defense contractors served among the chief funders and policy makers of MoMA, and to the AWC this constituted the "conservative politicization" of the museum. Although Kramer acknowledged that trustees "are likely to be conservative in their social values" and "not always disinterested in their decisions," he concluded that such characteristics did not amount to politicization.[56] This debate typifies the opposing positions on cultural politics during the sixties. Whereas conservative cultural critics such as Kramer adhered to a traditional notion of politics, the AWC—like the New Left and the emerging women's liberation movement—insisted on a broader definition. If MoMA relied on funding that originated from profits from a war that was immoral and unjust, it was implicated in this immorality and injustice.

The AWC's strategy to expose the inherent politicization of museums involved pressuring them to make public statements on political issues. The success of this initiative relied on museum staff, who tended to sympathize with much of the AWC's agenda, as opposed to its trustees, who often were linked to corporate America and government defense contracts. In one action, the AWC attempted to force MoMA to lend its name to a joint condemnation of the 1968 My Lai massacre of hundreds of Vietnamese civilians including women and children, which provoked outrage when it was revealed after an attempted cover-up in the fall of 1969. The AWC's Poster Committee created a poster using *Life* photographer Ronald Haeberle's graphic color photograph of a trench strewn with corpses, with a caption that read, "Q: And Babies? A: And Babies." (These words appeared in the transcript of a Mike Wallace interview with Paul Meadlo, a participant in the massacre.) Three AWC members, including Dougherty, Hendricks, and Petlin collaborated on the offset color lithograph created for the poster.[57]

Significantly, the AWC conceived of the poster as "nonartistic." By this the Coalition meant that no individual artist's name should be connected with the work, and that it should use a documentary photograph rather than an illustration in order to avoid creating a commodifiable art object. This position reflected the AWC's contention that it stood for an *ethics* defined as "philosophizing about artists," as distinct from an *esthetics* or "philosophizing about art."[58] In other words, the AWC believed artists' roles in society were governed by moral and ethical imperatives, such as opposing Vietnam War atrocities. At the same time, however, the AWC sought to maintain freedom for individual artists to pursue their aesthetic lives as they wished. "The Coalition is under no illusion that the poster is art," wrote the AWC. "It is a political poster, a documentary photograph treating an issue that no one, not even the most ivory tower esthetic institution, can ignore."[59] The Coalition's words answered charges that it was politicizing art, while at the same time pressuring art institutions to follow the exemplary statements of its artists against the war. The AWC presented the *Q: And Babies? A: And Babies* poster as a response to the My Lai Massacre by artists who believed the war affected their everyday lives, as opposed to developing a political art against the war which might be subject to the same commodification as other works of art.

The AWC's goal was to get fifty thousand copies of the poster distributed free, and to persuade MoMA to cosponsor the distribution. Encouragingly, MoMA's Executive Staff Committee endorsed this project, for which they received donations of paper from a private businessman and gratis printing from the Amalgamated Lithographers Union. Yet when the staff brought a mock-up of the poster to MoMA board president William S. Paley, who also served as president of the CBS television network, Paley refused to commit the museum to any position not directly related to its mission. So the AWC released the poster without museum sponsorship. "Practically, the outcome is as planned," an AWC press release explained. "An artist-sponsored poster protesting the . . . massacre will receive vast distribution. But the Museum's unprecedented decision to make known, as an institution, its commitment to humanity, has been denied it."[60] Though the AWC did not achieve its goal of securing the museum's joint sponsorship of the poster, and thus its condemnation of American atrocities in Vietnam, the Coalition did expose MoMA's inability to express itself freely on political matters because of the conflict of interest of some of its trustees. Grace Glueck of the *New York Times* argued that this incident illustrated the "considerable distance" between MoMA staff and trustees and suggested that the trustees led "dangerously sheltered lives."[61] The controversy over sponsorship of the *Q: And Babies? A: And Babies* poster demonstrated the AWC's value as a catalyst of discourse concerning social responsibility in the art world, which even hostile critics such as Kramer were forced to admit.

MoMA's lack of support nonwithstanding, fifty thousand copies of the *Q: And Babies? A: And Babies* poster were distributed with the help of sympathetic students and the larger antiwar movement. Since these volunteers passed out copies of the poster free in the streets, it was "visible at street level," accessible to the general public without having to enter a museum or gallery.[62] The poster gained considerable attention, as the AWC further used it as a backdrop for direct action protests in museums. At MoMA, the AWC and GAAG twice protested the museum's lack of sponsorship by staging a "lie-in," and by holding copies of the poster as sandwich boards in front of Pablo Picasso's famous antiwar mural *Guernica*. AWC member Joyce Kozloff and her young son participated in one of these protests, effectively juxtaposed against the color photograph of slaughtered Vietnamese children. The AWC poster derived further publicity through a campaign to get four major New York–based art magazines to use a photo of AWC members holding the poster in front of *Guernica* as a cover for their fall 1970 issues. Ultimately, *Studio International* and *Arts Magazine* used the shot; *ARTnews* and *Art in America* declined.[63] Thus the *Q: And Babies? A: And Babies* poster enhanced the AWC's reputation as a force spurring the art world to acknowledge social and political issues, even as it resisted politicizing the art itself.

The Judson Flag Show and the New York Art Strike

In 1970, however, several artists within the AWC increasingly incorporated explicit political content regarding Black Power, women's liberation, and especially the Vietnam War into their artwork. The conceptual artist and founding AWC member Hans Haacke installed a work entitled *Visitors' Poll* at MoMA's 1970 "Information" show. This piece consisted of a poster board that read, "Would the fact that Governor Rockefeller has not denounced President Nixon's Indochina policy be a reason for you not to vote for him in November?" Museumgoers were instructed to cast "yes" or "no" ballots into one of two clear boxes beneath the poster board, an arrangement which allowed visitors to assess how their sentiments compared to those of other museum patrons. A photograph of *Visitors' Poll* in Lippard's *A Different War* shows the "yes" box approximately seven-eighths full while the "no" box is only about one-third full, signifying the unpopularity of both Rockefeller and the war by 1970, at least among MoMA's audience. In a 1971 show in Milwaukee, one of Haacke's questions was, "Do you think the moral fabric of the U.S. is strengthened or weakened by its involvement in Indochina?" Haacke phrased his questions in an ostensibly neutral way rather than suggest overt condemnation of the war, to avoid preaching to an already converted public since "appeals and condemnations don't make you think."[64] But public opinion had turned decisively against the war, and Haacke's antiwar position was fairly obvious.

In another, more explicit use of art to condemn the war, Hendricks, Toche, and Faith Ringgold helped organize "The People's Flag Show," which opened at Judson Memorial Church on November 9, 1970. A flyer explained that the show intended to "challenge the repressive laws governing so-called flag dese-cration." The show was designed as an "Open Exhibition," and the AWC organizers circulated flyers and posted an announcement in the *New York Times* soliciting works making use of the flag from "concerned artists and citizens." All submissions for the show, over 150 works, were accepted without alteration; one art critic commented that many of the works displayed "genu-ine artistry," thereby also implying the amateurish nature of other entries.[65] By accepting submissions from the general public, however, "The People's Flag Show" organizers democratized this opportunity to exhibit art, privileging antiwar politics above artistic technique and reputation in a manner similar to the Living Theatre's policy of valuing political commitment over formal acting training. The subject of "The People's Flag Show," was "a classic artist's issue," involving both artistic freedom and antiwar imagery. Before the show, artists had already incorporated the flag as "a staple of antiwar posters and art," wrote Lippard, "its stars and stripes reduced to guns, bombs, coffins, skulls, prison bars, and so forth." The issue of artists' appropriations of the flag loomed in the public eye because of a pending U.S. Supreme Court case involving Ste-phen Radich, a New York art dealer who had been convicted in 1967 for exhibiting works by an artist who used various reinterpretations of the flag to criticize U.S. involvement in Vietnam. A poster for "The People's Flag Show" asserted that "a flag that does not belong to the people to do as they see fit should be burned and forgotten," adding that the organizers objected to the flag's use to "sanctify killing." The poster reasoned that if the flag could be used in a pro-Vietnam context, it should also "be available to the people to stop killing."[66] Thus, the flag show's publicity invoked for antiwar forces within the art community, a claim of representing "the people," echoing the militant New Left's attempts to cast itself as "the people" at events such as the demonstrations at the 1968 Chicago Democratic Convention.[67]

"The People's Flag Show" included items such as a baked flag cake, a flag constructed of soft drink cans, and a flag in the shape of a penis. Several notable figures participated in this week-long show. The women's liberationist and writer Kate Millett draped an actual flag over a toilet bowl; the postmod-ern artist and choreographer Yvonne Rainer and the dance troupe Grand Union performed a nude dance with flags; and the Yippie activist Abbie

Hoffman spoke to the audience clad in his flag shirt, which he had been arrested for wearing in 1968, and "on the cuff of which he ostentatiously made a gesture of wiping his nose." On November 13, one day before the show's closing, authorities arrested the "Judson Three"—Hendricks, Toche, and Ringgold—and closed the Judson Memorial Church, though the show ran the next day "in defiance of the D.A.'s orders." A federal court convicted the three of flag desecration, whereupon they appealed and lost, despite legal defense by the American Civil Liberties Union. Like the Living Theatre's Julian Beck and Judith Malina in their 1964 tax trial, the Judson Three mobilized the courtroom as a forum for theatrical condemnations of the hypocrisy of mainstream American institutions. Responding to the charges, the AWC said, "Look what the U.S. Post Office does to our flag every day!" For its part, the court curiously ruled that visual art did not constitute a form of communication, and thus was not protected under the First Amendment.[68]

The crisis of Vietnam increasingly impelled politically inclined artists to confront the war in their work, and "The People's Flag Show" and the case of the Judson Three pushed the envelope. Sometimes this new, more political antiwar art took the form of what one critic called a single "token work," created "perhaps as a kind of exorcism." The sculptor Claes Oldenburg's *Lipstick Ascending on Caterpillar Tracks*, a twenty-four-foot-high red lipstick in a gold container mounted on what resembles the base of a tank, installed at Yale University in the spring of 1969, exemplified this kind of one-time contribution to political art in its juxtaposition of images of a classic consumer product with militarism.[69] The phallus-like structure of *Lipstick* illustrated the observation by the historian Richard Candida Smith that sixties artists and poets attempted to undermine "the forces that coerced identification with the power of the state" by portraying "American military policy as an outgrowth of repressed sexual drives."[70] While some artists addressed the war only in discrete works, AWC-affiliated artists such as Edward Kienholz, Nancy Spero, Leon Golub, and Rudolf Baranik returned to anti-Vietnam themes in their work on repeated occasions. Such artists, compelled by deeply felt opposition to the war, crossed the threshold into explicitly political artwork, illustrating Jon Hendricks's opinion that "if the art wasn't political, then the art would be a lie." [71]

Unsettling developments in the war motivated increasing numbers of artists to become involved with politics. On May 18, 1970, following the invasion of Cambodia that month and the subsequent shootings of student demonstrators at Kent State and Jackson State, approximately fifteen hundred artists met at New York University's Loeb Student Center and formulated the idea of an art strike, which was officially titled "The New York Artists' Strike Against Racism, Sexism, and Repression." Poppy Johnson of the AWC and GAAG made a speech that typified the spirit of this occasion, suggesting that artists should "stop what they were doing and just totally concentrate on doing something else" since "everything was so terrible." Accordingly, the meeting adopted the idea, first proposed by the School of Visual Arts faculty, of a one-day art strike and sent telegrams to the city's museums and galleries asking them to close on May 22. The Whitney Museum, the Jewish Museum, and fifty private galleries closed on the appointed day. MoMA and the Guggen-heim remained open but charged no admissions. The Metropolitan Museum of Art stayed open, and protesters responded by targeting the Met with a major protest on the day of the strike. Over five hundred artists participated, carrying black-and-white signs reading "Art Strike Against Racism, War, and Repression," blocking the museum entrance for twelve hours, and garnering extensive local newspaper and television coverage. Corinne Robbins of *Arts Magazine* termed the Art Strike an "immense success."[72]

The Art Strike demonstrated the ability of politicized artists to make in-roads into the mainstream art world and to wield influence on art institutions. Cindy Nemser of the *Village Voice* depicted the Art Strike's diverse participants at the initial NYU meeting:

> They were all there—bearded, wild-eyed, hollow-cheeked artist revolutionaries; bearded, crafty-eyed, well-fed pseudo artist revolutionaries; smoothly shaven, haggard-eyed, slightly paunchy museum curators; meticulously kempt, sharp-eyed, nattily attired dealers; tangled-haired, glassy-eyed, non-bra-wearing female artists—all the exotic individuals who make up that strange creature designated the New York Art World.

Nemser's account suggested that the expansion of the Vietnam War into Cambodia and the domestic unrest caused by the Kent State and Jackson State incidents compelled many more artists to involve themselves politically. For instance, artists at this meeting chose the established sculptor Robert Morris to serve as chairman (Poppy Johnson was co-chair). Morris had earned a reputation through shows in museums around the country and at New York's prestigious Leo Castelli Gallery, and had most recently terminated a show at the Whitney Museum two weeks before its scheduled closing to protest the events of early May 1970. Though several participating artists were already politically active and even veterans of the AWC, many more made their first foray into political consciousness with the New York Art Strike. The veteran AWC member Alex Gross opined: "The New York Artists Strike is a group of artists that only decided there was some connection between art and politics when they were confronted by . . . corpses." Not surprisingly, the strike articulated an eclectic agenda of demands. Most members agreed with the demand for the strike that took place on May 22, as well as with Morris's idea of a 10-percent tax on the sale of artworks to be earmarked for a fund to promote peace activities, but subgroups within the Art Strike, such as the AWC, Artists and Writers Protest, and Women Artists in Revolution suggested more radical demands, reflecting a broader critique of the art world's modus operandi. The radicals within the Art Strike singled out dealers and curators, arguing that a one-day strike represented insufficient action and that the situation required a longer-term response to the art world's complicity in the war machine. Other radicals proffered the idea that artists should stop making art that "consisted of decadent artifacts which were merely toys for the affluent" and focus instead on creating more political propaganda-style art. Nemser conveyed that this view represented the minority; strike members with a stake in maintaining established art world institutions constituted the majority.[73]

Though the Art Strike registered several successes—drawing public and media attention; closing several museums and galleries on May 22; sponsoring an alternative "liberated" Venice Biennale; influencing the Met and the Jewish Museum to present shows with political themes—its more radical platform never materialized. The Art Strike itself, which emerged as a unique forum for artists to address social and political issues, soon "reduced back to the hard core of the AWC, from whence it had come." At the moment of its greatest potential influence, the artists' movement suffered its greatest internal strife. Though the crises of May 1970, the widening of the Vietnam War through the invasion of Cambodia and the killings of antiwar demonstrators at Kent State and Jackson State, had mobilized scores of previously apolitical artists, many quickly abandoned their newfound activism and were, in Lippard's words, "all too happy to turn their back on it" once the initial shock of the crises abated and political momentum ebbed.[74] At this point, such artists typically realized that their identity as artists with a stake in museums and galleries outweighed their commitment to using their art as a tool of political struggle, which frequently required the sacrifice of personal goals.

A similar dynamic emerged within the AWC itself, pitting members with a stake in the established art world against those who sought fundamental change and "wished to tear it down." One faction of the AWC remained convinced that artists should work to transform the art world so as to secure increased representation for women and artists of color, while others believed that "the important thing was stopping the war." This latter group favored using the established art world to bring about social and political change rather than destroying it, and the group conceded a certain lack of egalitarianism. Irving Petlin remarked, "The art world wouldn't satisfy every artist who wanted a show . . . there was no democracy possible." Instead these artists continued attempts to "reorient" the art world to persuade as much of the American public as possible of the Vietnam War's injustice. GAAG continued to stage its art actions on issues ranging from the war to freedom of expression to minority representation in, and access to, the art world. As the seventies progressed, however, nonperformance forms such as letters, petitions, and posters predominated in the group's work. Internal division typified the larger political Left as well, where radical elements often proved too threatening for the mainstream. In late 1971 the AWC disintegrated, in some respects because of these internal divisions, but also because many AWC activists transferred their energies to the emerging women's art movement. This development, in part, represented women's repudiation of what Lippard called the "male-run process" of the AWC, a reference to the tendency of decision-making power within the AWC and the ability to represent the group publicly, to revert to the more well known male artists. That these AWC men might have achieved such superior reputation because of gender bias in representation in museum shows and galleries was not lost on AWC women, who left the Coalition for the women's art movement in increasing numbers. Far from abandoning earlier concerns about art and politics, such women tended to echo Poppy Johnson's assertion that sexism constituted "the central oppressive force to contend with," and they used this realization to foster an art movement that, if anything, incorporated politics even more overtly than did the AWC.[75]

Beyond the AWC: The Women's Art Movement, Artists Meeting for Cultural Change, and Politicized Performance Art

Women artists and issues of women's liberation had figured centrally in the AWC from the group's outset. The AWC's beginnings paralleled the emergence of the women's liberation movement chronologically, as developments within the Coalition often reflected the dynamics of feminist thinking and politics. For instance, though the AWC's initial list of thirteen demands to MoMA in February 1969 did not feature equal gender representation in exhibitions among the group's most important concerns, by March 1970, when the AWC revised its demands list, the Coalition called for equal representation of female artists in exhibitions, museum purchases, and on selection committees. Leon Golub noted that women in the AWC realized that "the protests men were making weren't necessarily helping women get equal representation in shows." Just as historians of the women's liberation movement have pointed out that women needed to separate from the male-dominated protest movement to address issues that affected their everyday lives, women artists in the AWC increasingly examined their dual reality as artists and women, often participating in consciousness-raising sessions focused on improving their position within the art world.[76]

In the fall of 1970 women in the AWC, the Art Strike, and others formed the Ad Hoc Women Artists Committee. This group founded the Women's Slide Registry and launched a campaign for equal representation of women artists in the Whitney Museum's Annual Exhibition as its most important action. The approximately fifty women who initially composed the group, including notable members of the AWC and GAAG such as Faith Ringgold, Lucy Lippard, and Poppy Johnson, demanded not only that the 1970 Whitney Annual feature 50 percent women artists, but also that half of the women's slots be reserved for black women. The Ad Hoc Women Artists Committee cited "a history of willful negligence" on the Whitney's part, as women's representation in the Annual historically ran between 5 percent and 10 percent, while "53 per cent of the American population is female." They argued that the lack of equal representation denied women artists essential economic rights in their profession.[77]

After receiving no substantive response to these demands, the committee women employed guerrilla tactics to compel the Whitney to alter the demographic makeup of the Annual. They posted notices on the museum's bulletin board criticizing its policies, littered the floors with small pieces of paper that read "50 per cent women in this year's Annual," placed raw eggs and tampons in corners and staircases around the museum, and distributed hard-boiled black-painted eggs to signify the racial stipulation of the 50 percent demand. The women persuaded sympathetic male artists such as Robert Morris, Carl Andre, Jon Hendricks, Jean Toche, and Hans Haacke to send telegrams to the Whitney supporting their demands, and they performed "consciousness-raising" exercises on museum premises and discussed the issue of equal representation with museum visitors. The two-and-a-half-month campaign of public pressure on the Whitney also included weekly Saturday protests involving picketing, singing, whistle-blowing, and even a "snake dance in the lobby." When the show finally opened on December 11, 1970, it featured 20 women of a total of 100 artists, including 2 black women. Though this tally appeared to be only modest progress toward the goal of equal representation for women, the previous Annual had featured the work of only 8 women out of 151 artists (4 percent.)[78] This incremental progress appeared to vindicate Lippard's philosophy that the 50-percent "quota" should function as the central demand because "you have to ask for something definite or you get nothing."[79] The Committee's call for greater representation of women artists reflected the rising tide of women's liberation in the early seventies, and prefigured the theatricalized media savvy pressure politics the Guerrilla Girls, a New York City–based anonymous group of women artists, have employed since the mid-1980s to agitate for more egalitarian representation for women and minority artists, such as public postering campaigns targeting prestigious museums and galleries, which cite specific statistical evidence of underrepresentation.[80] "Eventually the Whitney changed its policies," Golub noted. "The Whitney pretended it wasn't influenced by all this, but obviously it was."[81] At the same time, then, that the antiwar movement's impact was diminishing, the women's art movement was gathering steam.

Within the activist art world, Women Artists in Revolution and the Ad Hoc Women Artists Committee "formed from the ribs of the AWC." Lippard cited the "neglect by the women" as one of the main factors in the demise of the AWC during 1971, along with internal divisions over goals and tactics.[82] Yet, despite the end of the AWC, these women did not abandon politics; instead the women's art movement reformulated its vision of politics to encompass a variety of concerns that directly affected their lives as women and artists. The art historian Irving Sandler has noted that feminism supplanted antiwar protest as "the most powerful polemical and political force in the art world."[83] Performance, with its capacity to engage its audience more immediately than painting or sculpture and often charged with feminist politics implicit or explicit, figured centrally in the women's art movement. Artists such as Faith Wilding, Elenor Antin, Hannah Wilke, and Lynda Benglis used feminism's insight that "the personal is political" to create powerful performance pieces with autobiographical elements, serving, along with Carolee Schneemann, whose Happenings-inspired performances dated back to the mid-sixties, as forerunners for later feminist-influenced artists such as Cindy Sherman and Laurie Anderson.

The women's art movement moved to the forefront of political art, as Lippard commented; outside the feminist movement, art of the seventies was "depressingly apolitical." Though no longer on the cutting edge, from time to time AWC veterans reconvened under other auspices, such as Artists Meeting for Cultural Change (AMCC), which formed in 1975 to revive artists' political activity for societal change and to analyze artists' social roles. AMCC's most notable action was its protest of the Whitney's plan to celebrate the U.S. Bicentennial with an exhibition of the collection of John D. Rockefeller III. The AMCC charged that the Rockefeller collection tended to ignore the art of dissent as well as art by minorities and women that deserved inclusion in a Bicentennial commemoration. AMCC's Hans Haacke explained that the Rockefeller collection represented the "liberal funding of socially innocuous art" which serves to convey the message to the public that "good art is apolitical."[84]

By the mid-seventies the public, performative dimension of artists' concern with social and political issues had receded from the level of visibility it had enjoyed earlier. Golub quipped that "Artists Meeting for Cultural Change was artists *meeting*, rather than doing anything about cultural change."[85] Hendricks and Toche were a notable exception to this trend. The two artists continued to reassemble periodically as GAAG well into the 1980s, reprising the *Q: And Babies? A: And Babies* poster as a satire on President Ronald Reagan's gaffe in 1984, which was inadvertently broadcast on radio, in which he jokingly declared: "My fellow Americans, I am pleased to tell you that I just signed legislation that would outlaw Russia forever. We begin bombing in five minutes."

The emergence of the women's art movement and AMCC in the seventies, the Guerrilla Girls' continuation of the AWC's and GAAG's legacy as agents of conscience within the art world, the rise of movements such as media art and deconstruction art, and art's attempts to confront issues such as AIDS, multiculturalism, and the post–September 11, 2001, War on Terror demonstrate the persistence of artists' commitment to politically oriented material. The wide-ranging subject matter of these movements reflects the expanded definition of politics their sixties predecessors produced. Often these art movements involved performance, an innovation whose roots resided not just in art world developments but in the street theater and protest culture of the sixties. The resonance of public performance within the art world demonstrates that political consciousness among artists did not die with the sixties. Indeed, the story of the AWC after 1971 stands as a microcosm for what many historians have argued became of sixties protest culture after Kent State. With the AWC, as with the New left, protest and political consciousness did not wither away under violent authoritarian backlash, as earlier historians of the era have suggested. Rather, the transition from the AWC to feminist art groups, performance art, deconstructionist art, and other politically oriented art illustrates the process of fragmentation evident in the larger New Left at the end of the sixties. Those who minimize the protest culture's legacy contend that it imploded under the weight of its own rhetoric, but they do so only by ignoring the impact on political awareness by women's liberationists, black activists, and gay rights advocates among others, who continued to struggle for social change in the seventies and beyond.

EPILOGUE

The Continuing Value of Public Performance

The careers of the SNCC Freedom Singers, the Living Theatre, the Diggers, the Art Workers Coalition, and the Guerrilla Art Action Group document the emergence of public, politically oriented performance as an important and influential cultural force during the sixties. During the civil rights era, freedom singing figured prominently in a constellation of social, cultural, and political developments that opened public spaces to various forms of cultural expression that lay dormant amidst the climate of suspicion that surrounded radical political expression after World War II. This transformation paved the way for the Living Theatre's civil disobedience "play-in" of *The Brig*, the revelation of *Paradise Now* that "the theatre is in the street," and the company's street theater in the seventies. The Diggers' parades, Free Food, and free stores similarly embodied this combination of cultural and political expression in public spaces. Likewise, led by Happenings, art world developments in the early sixties gave rise to public performance as a vehicle for visual artists. The AWC and GAAG staged wide-ranging protests and actions using public performance to communicate their goals, demands, and visions in the politically charged atmosphere of the late sixties. By then, as the urgency of the antiwar movement, women's liberationists, and politically oriented artists escalated, public performance was firmly established as a vehicle for oppositional and alternative political statements.

The personal histories of the individuals in these groups contradict the popular notion of sixties activists as "selling out" their idealism after the decade ended. Most of the key figures among these groups retained their commitment to the quest for social transformation, even if they professionalized their activism. Bernice Johnson Reagon of the Freedom Singers became a preeminent scholar of African American studies and is now curator emeritus at the Smithsonian Institute. Reagon's trajectory parallels the transition of the civil rights movement from focusing on integration and assimilation to addressing broader issues of cultural identity. This continued involvement with black culture is apparent in her work with the singing group Sweet Honey in the Rock, whose music embodies a dedication to "preserving and celebrating African-American culture and singing traditions." Cordell Reagon performed as a Freedom Singer until his death in 1996 and remained active in a range of causes—opposing the Vietnam War, supporting nuclear disarmament, and founding the environmental group Urban Habitat.[1] Charles Neblett, the manager and musical director for the current version of the Freedom Singers, still tours and performs a repertoire of freedom songs, interspersing a narrative of the movement and its music. Bernard Lafayette, co-writer of several early freedom songs, now serves as director of the Center for Nonviolence and Peace Studies at the University of Rhode Island and has been known to break into a freedom song or two during the course of an interview. Hollis Watkins periodically tours and sings freedom songs and runs Southern Echo, a Mississippi-based "leadership development, education and training organization." Watkins's work with this group, the latest in a "lifetime of empowerment efforts," represents an organic evolution from his work with SNCC.[2]

The Living Theatre, through its various phases and despite the death of its cofounder Julian Beck, survives as a theatrical collective concerned with politics and social transformation. During the seventies especially, street theater was the most vital part of the company's work. Though the economic necessity of sustaining a dozen to twenty core company members has forced the Living Theatre to return to proscenium theaters, the company still often participates in public performances and workshops, particularly in Europe. In 2003 the company was in residency in Genoa, where it led workshops on the performance techniques and creative processes involved in making political theater. Though the Living Theatre's work has traditionally found greater receptivity and financial support in Europe, reflecting on openness there to a broader spectrum of political discourse and a longer tradition of political art, the company recently announced plans to resume its efforts in the United States by opening a theater in New York City in 2004.

Far from abandoning the counterculture at the end of the sixties, the Diggers were at the forefront of the hippies' movement out of urban enclaves such as Haight-Ashbury and the Lower East Side into rural communes in northern California, New Mexico and Vermont. Though many of these experiments with communal life expired quickly, some persisted into the seventies and beyond and contributed to the counterculture's wide influence on food, health, and spirituality. Peter Coyote's autobiography underscores the thinking that led the Diggers from their Haight-Ashbury role as "social activists of the street" into the vanguard of the rural communard movement.[3] "The practice of doing things 'for free' was fine social theater, useful for highlighting values and relationships to commodities, wealth, and fame," Coyote remarked, ". . . but not a practice that would support what was now a loose confederation of several hundred people."[4] Just as the Living Theatre's 1970s street theater failed to generate the necessary income to support a large collective, the Diggers' impasse with public performance resulted from its inability to provide adequate economic support. Ironically, it was precisely the shortcomings of the money system that the Diggers' street theater (and that of the Living Theatre) struggled to articulate. Such a catch-22 highlights both the limitations and the value of public performance. The groups featured here confronted the contradictions of making creative expressions that opposed mainstream institutions while at the same time attempting to derive sustenance from the mainstream's abundance. This tension marginalized these groups financially, but it did not deter them from continuing to produce art, music, theater, and participatory events that envisioned society's transformation toward greater freedom and equality.

The terminus of the AWC's career coincided with the rise of the women's art movement as two significant groups, Women Artists in Revolution and the Ad Hoc Women Artists Committee, emerged from the AWC.[5] The AWC's demise and the concurrent ascendancy of the women's art collectives recall the historian Doug Rossinow's observation that "it is difficult to see how one can view the post-1968 Left as a complete disaster unless one is unsympathetic or unaware of the women's liberation movement."[6] The radical art critic Lucy Lippard exemplifies this trend of women in the AWC who shifted their energies to applying the insights of women's liberation to art world dynamics. Since the sixties, feminist and politically oriented performance art have figured as vibrant, vital forms. For its part, GAAG continued to perform unannounced public "art actions" in the eighties, even as Jon Hendricks and Jean Toche pursued artistic careers separate from the group.[7]

Not only did the prominent individuals in these groups persist in their commitment to combining artistic and political expression, but the public performance aesthetic they pioneered survives as well. Some observers argue that in the seventies, the outward-looking political and artistic collectives of the sixties turned inward and evolved "into something like therapeutic communities whose collective strength could enable each member to grasp and embrace the depths of his or her individual life."[8] Though seventies performance art often rooted itself in autobiographical narratives and reflected self-absorption, more recent developments reveal a return to addressing the most pressing issues of the day through public performance. In late January 1991, as the United States military intensified its prosecution of the Persian Gulf War, significant domestic protests emerged despite the overwhelmingly pro-war public opinion. The alternative media collective Paper Tiger Television sponsored one of the most striking protests in New York City, "Operation Storm the Media," which criticized media coverage of the war.[9] This demonstration featured protesters dressed as cheerleaders with the letters of the three major television networks (CBS, NBC, ABC) printed on their sweaters. The cheerleaders vividly illustrated the point that in an age when, for instance, General Electric, a leading military contractor, possesses a controlling interest in NBC, journalistic objectivity might be another of the war's casualties. The demonstrators concluded their march at the ABC headquarters where they projected visual images onto the facade of the building, including juxtapositions of President George Bush and Adolf Hitler. "Operation Storm the Media" blurred the lines between art, theater, and political protest to create an innovative statement against media coverage of the war, continuing a trend initiated in the sixties through spectacles such as the 1968 Chicago Democratic Convention demonstrations, where activists transformed politics into a more symbolic, theatrical, media-oriented affair that pitted powerful and impersonal government war makers against "the people" in the streets.[10] The Paper Tiger demonstration exposed television's dominant role in interpreting modern war and questioned whether it is even possible to protest the media monopoly on information effectively when the networks control the images of protest available for public consumption. Indeed, in recent years media coverage has abetted the mainstreaming of sixties-style theater, presenting such spectacles as though audiences are expected to "get" the idea that the fourth wall is a mere convention. The proliferation of reality television such as the *Jerry Springer Show*, *Survivor*, and *The Osbournes* threatens to numb audiences to the transformative potential of sixties-era sensibilities of combining performance and politics, since it mobilizes some of the same techniques—eroding the boundaries between performers and audiences and by using "ordinary people" to democratize performance while leaving power relations essentially unchallenged. The capacious ability of mass media to co-opt and transform oppositional and dissenting forms may pose the largest obstacle to the legacy of sixties-style public performance.

Yet certain characteristics of this form suggest that public performance will endure as part of the usuable past and carry with it the possibility of subversion and dissent.[11] Attempts to use live performance as a catalyst for political change are especially important in the more recent cultural climate, an era when government has sought, as it did in the late forties and the fifties, to exert control over political artists. In 1989 the federal government, expressing the views of the religious Right and congressional conservatives, pressured the National Endowment for the Arts to revoke artists' grants for failing to conform to "general standards of decency." Four of the artists—Karen Finley, Tim Miller, John Fleck, and Holly Hughes—sued, charging that the NEA made its decision on political rather than artistic grounds, as the cases deemed "indecent" all dealt with issues pertinent to the gay community. The NEA controversy suggests how seriously people take the political impact of art; if the political impact of art were negligible, why would it be deemed such a threat?

Moreover, a salient feature of the current cultural moment is the consolidation of information media and resources among a small number of large corporations. Though the Internet represents a degree of hope for the democratization of information, the resources of independent website operators are dwarfed by the power of ever-growing media conglomerates in the contemporary merger prone environment. In such a landscape, public performance emerges as a medium fraught with possibilities for contemporary relevance. This potential is not solely limited to groups on the Left; Operation Rescue, the anti abortion movement, has proven among the most successful organizations at combining street-level politics and dramatic spectacle, underscoring the reality that this approach is available to groups representing divergent, and even competing, political impulses. Public performance maximizes art's potential for social impact since it minimizes mediating factors between performers and audience, such as dependence on granting agencies, high ticket prices, and cultural inhibitions to entering theaters, concert halls, and museums. Furthermore, live street performance resists the common tendency to turn "alternative" forms of artistic expression into just another commercial product of mainstream culture—the way the underground spirit of "grunge" rock or rap music, for example, is vulnerable to co-optation as a fashion statement and as a high-profit media commodity. At its core, performance in the streets joins performers and audience on an immediate level, with minimal governmental, corporate, and electronic filtering, offering communion and transformation as tangible possibilities.

The protests at the 1999 World Trade Organization meeting in Seattle demonstrated the enduring cultural currency of symbolic, theatricalized protest. Two activists rappelled down a five-story banner depicting "two one-way signs going in opposite directions (WTO one way, DEMOCRACY the opposite)." Led by a mock cheerleading squad composed of men and women wearing lipstick and red skirts, protesters held a banner atop an Interstate 5 retaining wall, which read, "Caution: Corporate Rule Ahead. Shut down the WTO." Though some protesters lacked the erudition of sixties New Left critics of corporate America—certain protesters objected to the WTO with comments such as "It's a general question of oppression," and "I don't know what a WTO is . . . but I hate rich people"—the value of these protests and their true theatricality stemmed from the diverse cross section of the world's people represented by the protesters. The *Wall Street Journal* reported that five hundred "nongovernmental organizations" participated in the Seattle protest, including the "Vegan Dykes," the Kuna Youth Movement of Panama, the Fourth World Association of Finland, students, labor union representatives, animal rights activists, communists, and environmental groups ranging from moderate to radical.[12] The sheer diversity on display in the Seattle protests amounted to a public, theatrical spectacle which mobilized the dominant language of symbolic politics, pitting "the people" against the faceless forces of globalization. Though many media accounts of the Seattle protest emphasized the incivility and a vandalism of a minority of protesters, even network television and mainstream newspapers acknowledged that the protesters scored a point in questioning the hegemony of free trade.

In an era characterized by declining voter turnout and by a generation-long series of events—Watergate, the Iran-Contra scandal, the Clinton sex scandal, the controversial events in Florida during the presidential election of 2000— that have caused Americans to question the legitimacy of the political process, the developments in Seattle provide a model for the reanimation of politics by ordinary people. Today's advocates for environmental causes, workers' rights, human rights, and women's issues are frequently compared to sixties activists, but they are not restricted to sixties scripts. Veterans such as GAAG's Jon Hendricks urge contemporary groups to be "wary of using a formula," and contend that with political art "the form each time has to be different."[13] During a symposium entitled "Visions for a Changing Theatre" in New York in 2003, Judith Malina praised what she viewed as the hopeful state of political theater, citing exclusively examples of public performance, including Genoa,

New York City during anti–Iraq War protests, and the WTO protests in Seattle. If her chosen examples signified that the theater, or at least the theater she views as having the greatest impact, is indeed in the streets, she also clarified the role of the artist in shaping such expressions. "Artists have an obligation to bring out the artist in everyone else," she exclaimed, suggesting the value artists have in infusing contemporary oppositional politics with creative sensibilities.[14] If contemporary groups of artists must create their own forms to bring out the artist in others, the public performances of the Freedom Singers, the Living Theatre, the Diggers, the AWC, and GAAG constitute a valuable part of the "usable past," spectacles of participatory democracy which underscore the importance of public space as a forum for free speech and public discourse.

NOTES

Introduction

1. Cited in Marshall Berman, *All That Is Solid Melts into Air: The Experience of Modernity* (New York, 1982), 320.

2. Zellner's remarks introduce the music and words of "We Shall Not Be Moved" in Guy and Candie Carawan and the Student Nonviolent Coordinating Committee's collection *We Shall Overcome!: Songs of the Southern Freedom Movement* (New York, 1963), 21.

3. Marvin Carlson, *Performance: A Critical Introduction* (London, 1996), 4–5.

4. Erving Goffman, *The Presentation of the Self in Everyday Life* (Garden City, N.Y.: Doubleday, 1959), 15–16.

5. Schechner's list appears in Richard Schechner, *Performance Studies: An Introduction* (London, 2002), 25. I am heavily indebted to Schechner's discussion of the problem of defining "performance."

6. Mary Ryan, *Civic Wars: Democracy and Public Life in the American City during the Nineteenth Century* (Berkeley, 1997), 15.

7. "Money Is an Unnecessary Evil," in the Digger Archives, San Francisco Diggers page at <http://www.diggers.org/diggers.htm>.

8. In some cases, government initiatives against socially oriented artistic expression predated the Cold War. As early as 1938, the House Committee on Un-American Activities (whose acronym was later changed to HUAC), chaired by Congressman Martin Dies, instituted investigations that led to the abolition of the Federal Theatre Project and other New Deal arts programs. See Michael Denning, *The Cultural Front: The Laboring of American Culture in the Twentieth Century* (London, 1997), 45, 80.

9. *Signals through the Flames*, directed by Sheldon Rochlin and Maxine Harris, Mystic Fire Video, 1983.

10. Serge Guilbaut, *How New York Stole the Idea of Modern Art: Abstract Expressionism, Freedom, and the Cold War* (Chicago, 1983), 200–201.

11. Adele Heller and Lois Rudnick, eds., *1915, The Cultural Moment: The New Politics, the New Woman, the New Psychology, the New Art, and the New Theatre in America* (New Brunswick, N.J., 1991); see introduction, especially 6–11; also in the same volume see Heller's essay on "The New Theatre," 217–31, which mentions the Living Theatre as one of a number of groups who benefited from the Provincetown Players' legacy, as well as Eugene Leach, "The Radicals of *The Masses*," 33–35, which discusses the Paterson Strike Pageant. The Paterson Strike Pageant is discussed in greater detail in Linda Nochlin, "The Paterson Strike Pageant of 1913," *Art in America* (May/June, 1974), 64–68. Nochlin explicitly notes the pageant's "affinities with some of the larger participatory Happenings of the 1960s."

12. Denning, *Cultural Front*, 365–75. Wendy Smith, *Real Life Drama: The Group Theatre and America, 1931–1940* (New York, 1990), provides a comprehensive chronicle of the Group Theatre's career. Smith's account illustrates that the Group Theatre engaged in self-consciously widening its audience to include a working class previously excluded by Broadway's high ticket prices—a trend toward democratizing culture that figures prominently among the groups featured here, especially the Living Theatre, the Art Workers Coalition, and the Guerrilla Art Action Group.

13. The Popular Front was a broad-based alliance between the Communist Party, organized labor, and sympathetic liberals during the 1930s. For the definitive account of its cultural side, see Denning, *Cultural Front*, xiii–xx, 367–69, 403–22, 490 n. 67; Barbara Melosh, *Engendering Culture: Manhood and Womanhood in New Deal Public Art and Theater* (Washington, D.C., 1991) 1–12, 118–21. Melosh chronicles the ascendancy of social commentary of New Deal art and theater, and contends that the New Deal proved unique among "liberal American reform movements" because it lacked a resurgence of feminism. Melosh points out that portrayals of men and women in thirties art and theater reflected the leftist sympathies of the era yet tended to reinforce traditional gender roles and expectations.

14. The Beats were part of an undercurrent of cultural protest during the fifties that included such popular films as *The Wild One, The Man in the Gray Flannel Suit*, and *Rebel Without a Cause*. Such protest fits the model of apolitical cultural rebellion which the Living Theatre pursued as well. Like the Beats, the Living Theatre limited its rebellion to experiments with artistic form during the fifties. Only with its production of *The Brig* (1963) did the Living Theatre begin to infuse its theatrical offerings with overtly political subject matter.

15. Bradford Martin, "The Living Theatre in America: 1951–1969," senior essay, History Department, Yale University, 1988, 18–24.

16. Lucy R. Lippard, *A Different War: Vietnam in Art* (Seattle, 1990), 20–53.

17. Guy and Candie Carawan, eds., *Freedom Is a Constant Struggle: Songs of the Freedom Movement* (New York, 1968), 177–91; interview with Bernard LaFayette, October 3, 2002.

18. Judith Malina and Julian Beck, *Paradise Now: Collective Creation of The Living Theatre* (New York, 1971), 16–17.

19. Charles Perry, *The Haight-Ashbury: A History* (New York, 1984), 97–99, 108–14.

20. For an excellent discussion of the efforts of the New Left, the counterculture, and the women's liberation movement to redefine legitimate corporate behavior, see Terry H. Anderson, "The New American Revolution: The Movement and Business," in *The Sixties: From Memory to History*, ed. David Farber (Chapel Hill, 1994), 175–201.

21. Jerry Hopkins and Danny Sugerman, *No One Here Gets Out Alive* (New York, 1981).

22. *Signals through the Flames.*

23. David Farber, *The Age of Great Dreams: America in the 1960s* (New York, 1994), 4–5; Kenneth Cmiel, "The Politics of Civility," in Farber, *The Sixties*, 271.

24. Doug Rossinow, *The Politics of Authenticity: Liberalism, Christianity, and the New Left in America* (New York, 1998), 4–5.

25. Julie Stephens links the "re-enchantment" of politics to the counterculture in *Anti-Disciplinary Protest: Sixties Radicalism and Postmodernism* (Cambridge, Eng., 1998), 5. Rossinow links "authenticity" to the New Left. The groups in the present study embody both trends and thus suggest the considerable degree of overlap between the New Left and counterculture, resulting in the kind of theatrical political actions I describe. These expressions bear resemblance to Stephens's concept of "anti-disciplinary protest," which, she argues, refuse "the problematic distinctions which shape the most familiar paradigms of the sixties, most notably the boundary between so-called political radicalism and cultural radicalism, between the activist and hippie."

26. Bernice Johnson Reagon, "Songs of the Civil Rights Movement, 1955–1965: A Study in Culture History," Ph.D. diss., Howard University, 1975, 126–75.

27. Martin, "Living Theatre in America," 35–36.

28. "The Ideology of Failure," *Berkeley Barb*, Nov. 18, 1966, 6; "Let Me Live in a World Pure," in "The Early Digger Papers,"; "A-Political Or, Criminal Or Victim Or Or Or Or Or Or," in "Early Digger Papers."

29. Perry, *Haight-Ashbury*, 242–44. Allen J. Matusow, *The Unraveling of America: A History of Liberalism in the 1960s* (New York, 1984), 302. The Digger phrase "media poisoners" became enshrined in the group's lore largely through Joan Didion's essay "Slouching Towards Bethlehem," which originally appeared in *The Saturday Evening Post* and was reprinted in the collection *Slouching Towards Bethlehem* (New York, 1968.) See pp. 114 and 124 for use of the phrase.

30. Lippard, *A Different War*, 21–28.

31. To its credit, John Tytell's *The Living Theatre: Art, Exile, and Outrage* (New York, 1995), discusses the Living Theatre's post-1970 career in some detail, though its level of scholarly merit is compromised by overemphasis on the details of Julian Beck's and Judith Malina's personal lives.

32. Two notable exceptions are Reagon, *Songs of the Civil Rights Movement*, which is a valuable repository of anecdotes about the singers' use of freedom songs in the civil rights movement, though her main project is placing the songs within a tradition of African American music, and Kerran Sanger, *"When the Spirit Says Sing!": The Role of Freedom Songs in the Civil Rights Movement* (New York, 1995), which analyzes the freedom songs' significance as communications strategy. Clayborne Carson's *In Struggle: SNCC and the Black Awakening of the 1960s*, (Cambridge, Mass., 1981), while an excellent intellectual history of SNCC, is more typical of how historians of the civil rights movement have dealt with singing. *In Struggle* contains one brief discussion of the Albany movement that acknowledges singing's central role in Albany as well as in the movement as a whole. But there is no sustained attention to singing outside of this section. Popular histories of the civil rights movement often underemphasize the role of singing. For instance, Juan Williams's *Eyes on the Prize: America's Civil Rights Years, 1954–1965* (New York, 1987), the companion volume to the PBS documentary series *Eyes on the Prize*, contains a vignette entitled "Freedom Singing: An Interview with Bernice Johnson Reagon" (176–77) that consists primarily of Reagon's personal reflections on singing and the Albany movement, but again there is little comprehensive attention to the overall importance of singing.

33. Though Matusow, *Unraveling of America*, chronicles Digger highlights (300–304), he tends to view their antics as preposterous at best. Farber, *Age of Great Dreams* contains insightful comments about the Diggers (169–72, 186–87), but as a synthesis whose project consists of tracing the main contours of the decade's social, political, and cultural developments, the book does not sustain a detailed analysis of the group's ideological perspectives and street theater actions. Todd Gitlin, *The Sixties: Years of Hope, Days of Rage* (New York,

1987) also offers perceptive commentary on the Diggers (222–41), but he mainly uses the group to illustrate what he views as the Diggers' clearer understanding of the cultural moment than that of the New Left. Stephens, *Anti-Disciplinary Protest*, gives serious attention to the Diggers' ideas and actions (31, 42–46, 79–92, 115–24), but her discussion is enmeshed in an analysis of a wide range of "anti-disciplinary" groups, without allotting the space for protracted commentary on the Diggers themselves. The Diggers receive more nuanced consideration in two recent works: Dominick Cavallo, *A Fiction of the Past: The Sixties in American History* (New York, 1999), 97–144; and Michael William Doyle, "Staging the Revolution: Guerrilla Theater as Countercultural Practice, 1965–68," in *Imagine Nation: The American Counterculture of the 1960s and '70s*, ed. Peter Braunstein and Michael William Doyle (New York, 2002), 78–85.

34. See, for instance, Lippard's *A Different War* and *Get the Message?: A Decade of Art for Social Change* (New York, 1984.) It is also worth mentioning Alan W. Moore's "Collectivities: Protest, Counterculture, and Political Postmodernism in New York City Artists Organizations, 1969–1985," Ph.D. diss. City University of New York, 2000, which positions both the AWC and GAAG in relation to significant contemporary political and aesthetic currents in the art world.

35. Matusow, *Unraveling of America*, with two chapters entitled "Rise and Fall of a Counterculture" and "Rise and Fall of the New Left," epitomizes this approach, and Rick Perlstein's article "Who Owns the Sixties?: The Opening of a Scholarly Generation Gap," *Lingua Franca* 6 (May/June 1996): 32–33, persuasively argues that Matusow "exerted a quiet influence on the writing of movement veterans," citing examples such as Gitlin's *The Sixties*, James Miller's *Democracy Is in the Streets: From Port Huron to the Siege of Chicago* (New York, 1987), and Maurice Isserman's *If I Had a Hammer: The Death of the Old Left and the Birth of the New Left* (New York, 1987). Gitlin stands out as an exception among New Left veterans in his acknowledgment of the Diggers' allure and grasp of the cultural moment, but more typical, for instance, is David Harris's memoir *Dreams Die Hard: Three Men's Journey through the Sixties* (New York, 1982), which voices considerable skepticism about the efficacy of the counterculture's broadly construed notions of politics and yet manages to depict a considerable degree of overlap between countercultural practices and the New Left's movement culture. A variation on the "separate phenomena" interpretation emerges in Timothy Miller, *The Hippies and American Values* (Knoxville, 1991), 10–15. Miller claims that "the hippie counterculture and the New Left pitched their tents in distinct but adjacent campsites," though he concedes that "a substantial minority" of the hippies "saw the two groups as more alike than different, because they were both sworn opponents of the established regime; therefore, they were to be considered as fingers on one hand, distinct but sharing a common role." A new generation of scholarship on the sixties has seen a marked convergence of political and cultural rebellions. Some examples include Farber's *Age of Great Dreams*, Rossinow's *Politics of Authenticity*, Stephens's *Anti-Disciplinary Protest*, Warren Belasco's *Appetite for Change: How the Counterculture Took on the Food Industry*, 2d ed. (Ithaca, N.Y., 1993), and two collections: Barbara Tischler, ed., *Sights on the Sixties* (New Brunswick, N.J., 1992), and Braunstein and Doyle, *Imagine Nation*.

36. The portraits I cite of the New Left and the counterculture as destructive of each other are drawn from Perlstein, "Who Owns the Sixties?," 32–33.

37. Farber, *Age of Great Dreams*, 220–22; Perlstein, "Who Owns the Sixties?," 32–33.

38. Gitlin, *The Sixties*, 208, 287, 307; David Farber, *Chicago '68* (Chicago, 1988), 207. Some of the most nuanced discussions of convergence and conflict between the New Left and the counterculture can be found in the memoirs of participants in these movements. Gitlin's *The Sixties* is the most comprehensive and broadest in scope, but Harris's *Dreams*

Die Hard, Mary King's *Freedom Song: A Personal Story of the 1960s Civil Right Movement* (New York, 1987), and Peter Coyote's *Sleeping Where I Fall* (Washington, D.C., 1998) are memoirs that serve as excellent windows into this issue.

39. Gitlin, *The Sixties,* 202, 209; Jay Stevens, *Storming Heaven: LSD and the American Dream* (New York, 1987), viii–xvi, 308, 329–30; and James Miller, *Democracy Is in the Streets,* 277–78, 307. Gitlin and Stevens suggest that at certain times psychedelic drugs constituted a source of division between activists and hippies, with purist activists charging that drugs represented a self-oriented, hedonistic diversion from the more important collective social and political arenas of struggle. It is reasonable to conclude that the hippie/activist affinity amounted to what Gitlin termed a "fragile paradise" which endured numerous vicissitudes amid the turbulence of the late sixties.

40. Gitlin, *The Sixties,* 353–61.

41. George Lipsitz, "Who'll Stop the Rain?: Youth Culture, Rock 'n' Roll, and Social Crises," in Farber, *The Sixties,* 206–31.

42. Gitlin's *The Sixties* describes this conference in detail (222–32).

43. The introduction to Robin D. G. Kelley's *Race Rebels: Culture, Politics, and the Black Working Class* (New York, 1994), offers a thoughtful and provocative assertion of the need not only to redefine what is political but to question the assumption that only certain movements and modes of resistance are authentic.

44. See George Lipsitz, *Time Passages: Collective Memory and American Popular Culture* (Minneapolis, 1990), 16–17.

45. See Lois Rudnick's definition of "counterculture" in *Utopian Vistas: The Mabel Dodge Luhan House and the American Counterculture* (Albuquerque, 1996), xiii.

Chapter One

1. Bradford Martin, "Politics as Art, Art as Politics: The Freedom Singers, the Living Theatre, and Public Performance," in *Long Time Gone: Sixties America Then and Now,* ed. Alexander Bloom (New York, 2001), 160; Bernice Johnson Reagon, liner notes to *Voices of the Civil Rights Movement: Black American Freedom Songs, 1960–1966,* 2-CD set, Smithsonian Folkways SF40084 1997.

2. On slaves' use of music to "get around and deceive the whites," see Lawrence Levine, *Black Culture and Black Consciousness: Afro-American Folk Thought from Slavery to Freedom* (New York, 1977), 8–19; Eileen Southern, *The Music of Black Americans: A History,* 2d ed., (New York: Norton, 1983), 142–43; and Frederick Douglass, *My Bondage and My Freedom* (New York, 1855), 278–79. Robin D. G. Kelley, " 'We Are Not What We Seem': Rethinking Black Working-class Opposition in the Jim Crow South," *Journal of American History* 80:1 (June 1993): 75–112, includes singing, along with folklore, jokes, and daily conversation, as part of a "hidden transcript" of a "dissident political culture" among working-class African Americans under Jim Crow that often helped them resist to the dominant southern power structure. On the use of "Oh Freedom" in the 1906 Atlanta riots and the Southern Tenant Farmers Union's version of "We Shall Not Be Moved," see Reagon, *Songs of the Civil Rights Movement,* 38–39, 56.

3. Reagon, *Songs of the Civil Rights Movement,* 110–12; also see Southern, *Music of Black Americans,* 284–87.

4. Guy and Candie Carawan and the Student Nonviolent Coordinating Committee, *We Shall Overcome!,* 5–8; Sanger, *"When the Spirit Says Sing!,"* 25–28; Bernice Reagon, "In Our Hands: Thoughts on Black Music," *Sing Out!,* November 1975, 1–2, 5; Levine, *Black Culture and Black Consciousness,* 162–63.

5. One way of gauging music's centrality to the civil rights movement is to consider the

definitive and award-winning documentary *Eyes on the Prize: America's Civil Rights Years*, Blackside, Boston, 1986. Though the film tends to examine key events, figures, and campaigns, and says little about movement culture directly, freedom songs form a veritable soundtrack. In fact, the series takes its title from a freedom song, and several of the individual episodes, such as "Ain't Scared of Your Jails," borrow their titles from the lyrics of freedom songs.

6. On the freedom houses, see Harris, *Dreams Die Hard*, 35, 66–67. The comment about "organizational glue" is from Sam Block, who is quoted in Pete Seeger and Bob Reiser, *Everybody Says Freedom* (New York, 1989), 179.

7. Carson, *In Struggle*, Sanger, *"When the Spirit Says Sing!"*, have both highlighted the movement's decisive role in promoting a positive black identity, an idea that is evident throughout the *Eyes on the Prize* series as well.

8. Lyrics reprinted in Carawan, Carawan, and SNCC, *We Shall Overcome*, 14, and in Seeger and Reiser, *Everybody Says Freedom*, 29.

9. Nash is quoted in Carawan, Carawan, and SNCC, *We Shall Overcome!*, 14. On the rough treatment lunch-counter demonstrators encountered, see Candie Carawan's and Bernard Lafayette's accounts in Seeger and Reiser, *Everybody Says Freedom*, 30–31, as well as Anne Moody's account of the Jackson, Mississippi, sit-ins in *Coming of Age in Mississippi* (New York, 1968), an excerpt of which is reprinted in Alexander Bloom and Wini Breines, eds., *Takin' It to the Streets: A Sixties Reader* (New York, 1995), 19–23. See also Farber, *Age of Great Dreams*, 79.

10. "If You Miss Me at the Back of the Bus" is reprinted in Carawan, Carawan, and SNCC, *We Shall Overcome!*, 50–51; and in Seeger and Reiser, *Everybody Says Freedom*, 72–73.

11. James Bevel, quoted in Carawan, Carawan, and SNCC, *We Shall Overcome!*, 28–32, and in Seeger and Reiser, *Everybody Says Freedom*, 44–51.

12. Reagon, *Songs of the Civil Rights Movement*, 104. The music and lyrics of "You'd Better Leave Segregation Alone" are printed in Carawan, Carawan, and SNCC, *We Shall Overcome!*, 26–27.

13. Quoted in Reagon, *Songs of the Civil Rights Movement*, 102. The cultural currency of this tune received a further boost from the Impressions' 1964 hit single version of "Amen," which rose to number seven on the pop charts. Curtis Mayfield holds the writer's credit for this version.

14. Quoted in Josh Dunson, *Freedom in the Air: Song Movements of the Sixties* (New York, 1965), 35.

15. My interpretation of "This Little Light" draws from Sanger's perceptive observations in *"When the Spirit Says Sing!"*, 77–78.

16. Reagon, "In Our Hands," 1–2.

17. Quoted in Seeger and Reiser, *Everybody Says Freedom*, 85.

18. Quoted in Robert Shelton, "Rights Song Has Own History of Integration," *New York Times*, July 23, 1963, 21, and in Carawan, Carawan, and SNCC, *We Shall Overcome!*, 11.

19. Quoted in Seeger and Reiser, *Everybody Says Freedom*, 8.

20. Carson, *In Struggle*, 63–65.

21. Reagon, "In Our Hands," 1–2.

22. Julius Lester, "Freedom Songs in the South," *Broadside* 39, February 7, 1964, n.p.

23. Interview with Hollis Watkins, March 14, 1998, Cambridge, Massachusetts.

24. "An Oral History with Mr. Hollis Watkins," interviewed by John Rachal, October 23, 1996, University of Southern Mississippi, Oral History Program, 2000.

25. Quoted in Carson, *In Struggle*, 20.

26. Bob Cohen, "Mississippi Caravan of Music," *Broadside* 51, October 1964, n.p. Reagon, *Songs of the Civil Rights Movement*, 152.

27. Harris, *Dreams Die Hard*, 61; Reagon, *Songs of the Civil Rights Movement*, 96–97, 128.

28. Reagon, "In Our Hands," 2.

29. This incident is recounted in both Carawan, Carawan, and SNCC, "*We Shall Overcome!*, 20, and Seeger and Reiser, *Everybody Says Freedom*, 32.

30. Carawan, Carawan, and SNCC, *We Shall Overcome!*, 53.

31. Ibid., 62.

32. "Moment of History," *New Yorker*, March 27, 1965, 37–38; Reagon, *Songs of the Civil Rights Movement*, 64–89.

33. "Moment of History," 37–38; Reagon, *Songs of the Civil Rights Movement*, 64–89. Seeger explains the change from "will" to "shall" in David King Dunaway, *How Can I Keep From Singing: Pete Seeger* (New York, 1981), 222.

34. Reagon, *Songs of the Civil Rights Movement*, 82; Carson, *In Struggle*, 19.

35. Shelton, "Rights Song Has Its Own History of Integration,"; "Battle Hymn of the Integrationists," *U.S. News & World Report*, August 5, 1963, 8.

36. Reagon, *Songs of the Civil Rights Movement*, 131–32.

37. Ibid., 166–67.

38. Kenneth Cmiel, "The Politics of Civility," in Farber, *The Sixties*, 267.

39. Reagon, *Songs of the Civil Rights Movement*, 101.

40. Henry Hampton and Steve Fayer, eds., *Voices of Freedom: An Oral History of the Civil Rights Movement from the 1950s through the 1980s* (New York, 1990), 97–114; Carawan, Carawan, and SNCC, *We Shall Overcome!*, 57–76; Reagon, *Songs of the Civil Rights Movement*, 128–39. The quoted material attributed to Bernice Johnson Reagon is from *Eyes on the Prize*, episode 4: "No Easy Walk (1962–1966)."

41. Hampton and Fayer, *Voices of Freedom* 73–96; Arthur M. Schlesinger, *Robert Kennedy and His Times* (Boston, 1978), 316–23.

42. Anderson, quoted in Carawan, Carawan, and SNCC, *We Shall Overcome!*, p. 16.

43. On SNCC's strategy of refusing bail and Prichett's for responding, see Carson, *In Struggle*, 56–63, and Williams, *Eyes on the Prize*, 163–79.

44. Carawan Carawan, and SNCC, *We Shall Overcome!* 62. Reagon's discussion of the adaptations of "This Little Light of Mine" appears in "Freedom Singing: An Interview with Bernice Johnson Reagon," in Williams, *Eyes on the Prize*, 176–77.

45. Lester, "Freedom Songs in the South," n.p.

46. Quoted in Carawan, Carawan, and SNCC, *We Shall Overcome!*, 21.

47. Interview with Hollis Watkins.

48. On the Fisk Jubilee Singers, see J. B. T. Marsh, *The Story of the Jubilee Singers; With Their Songs* (1881; reprint New York, 1969); Andrew Ward, *Dark Midnight When I Rise: The Story of the Jubilee Singers Who Introduced the World to the Music of Black America* (New York, 2000); and *The American Experience*, "Jubilee Singers: Sacrifice and Glory," PBS, 2000.

49. Shortly after the formation of the SNCC Freedom Singers, Bernice Johnson married Cordell Reagon and became Bernice Reagon, the name by which she is known as a prominent African American scholar and member of the singing group Sweet Honey in the Rock; she kept "Reagon" as her surname after her 1967 divorce from Cordell Reagon.

50. A second group of SNCC Freedom Singers formed in 1964, and, according to Reagon's liner notes for *Voices of the Civil Rights Movement*, 26–27, included Charles Neblett, Cordell Reagon, James Peacock, Matthew Jones, Marshall Jones, and Rafael Bentham, a guitarist (the group supplemented freedom songs with material from the folk

revival and topical song movement). Reagon and Peacock left this group to form the Freedom Voices, and subsequently the SNCC Freedom Singers experienced a number of lineup changes. According to the liner notes, "The three SNCC ensembles developed to the highest degree the use of music to carry the Movement's message to audiences far removed from the struggle. Through nationwide tours, these groups catalyzed support for SNCC Movement activities at a time when public attention was focused primarily on media-recognized leaders and large direct-action events rather than on the more dangerous and lonely grassroots organizing activities."

51. Quoted in Reagon, *Songs of the Civil Rights Movement*, 140.

52. Reagon, "In Our Hands," 2; Reagon, *Songs of the Civil Rights Movement*, 140.

53. Robert Shelton, "Negro Songs Here Aid Rights Drive," *New York Times*, June 22, 1963, 15.

54. Howard Klien, "Bernstein Joins Stern in Concert," *New York Times*, August 31, 1964.

55. On the controversy over Lewis's speech, see Carson, *In Struggle*, 91–95; Hampton and Fayer, *Voices of Freedom*, 164–67; and John Lewis, "Wake Up America," in Bloom and Breines, *Takin' It to the Streets*, 31–34. On the contrasting musical styles represented at the March on Washington, see Reagon, *Songs of the Civil Rights Movement*, 162–66.

56. "Northern Folk Singers Help Out at Negro Festival in Mississippi," *New York Times*, July 7, 1963, 43; " 'Without These Songs . . . ,' " *Newsweek*, August 31, 1964, 74; Bernice Johnson Reagon, "Songs That Moved the Movement," *Civil Rights Quarterly* (summer 1983): 32–33; Reagon, *Songs of the Civil Rights Movement*, 141–46, 162–66. Seeger's recommendation is reprinted in Pete Seeger, *The Incompleat Folksinger* (New York, 1972), 232–33.

57. " 'Without These Songs . . . ,' " 74; Reagon, "Songs That Moved the Movement," 32–33; Reagon, *Songs of the Civil Rights Movement*, 141–46, 162–66. Seeger's observation is from Seeger, *Incompleat Folksinger*, 11. The main element that marked early sixties popular music as frivolous was its lyrical content, which did not yet show evidence of the social transformations or political conflicts of the sixties. In other aspects, however, popular music was beginning to reflect the influence of the civil rights movement, as Reebee Garofalo points out in his nuanced discussion of the "girl groups" and Motown in *Rockin' Out: Popular Music in the U.S.A.*, 2d ed. (Upper Saddle River, N.J., 2002), 152–62. Garofalo contends that "during this period, then, the influence of the Civil Rights movement on rock 'n' roll is not apparent in the content of its lyrics but in the ascendancy of black producers and black-owned record labels and the appearance of black female vocal groups. There can be no question that the growing Civil Rights movement provided a climate that encouraged these developments." Garofalo also argues, provocatively, of the white "Brill Building" songwriters who penned many of the girl groups' hit songs, that "at their best they accomplished culturally what the early Civil Rights movement only dreamed of politically: white songwriters and black vocalists incorporating the excitement and urgency of rhythm and blues into the mainstream tradition of professional pop." The growing "ascendancy" of black people within popular music in the early sixties is undeniable, yet assessing the political and social substance of the music remains problematic. As George Lipsitz points out, "We may remember the sixties as the decade of Janis Joplin and Jimi Hendrix but forget that Elvis Presley, Brenda Lee, and Connie Francis joined the Beatles and Ray Charles as the five best-selling artists of the decade." See Lipsitz, "Who'll Stop the Rain?," in Farber, *The Sixties*, 208–9.

58. Pete Seeger, *We Shall Overcome: Complete Carnegie Hall Concert*, Columbia CL2101/CS8901, 1963.

59. "Northern Folk Singers Help Out . . . ," 43; " 'Without These Songs . . . ,' " 74;

Reagon, "Songs That Moved the Movement," 32–33; Reagon, *Songs of the Civil Rights Movement*, 141–46, 162–66; Seeger, *Incompleat Folksinger*, pp. 232–33.

60. "Northern Folk Singers Help Out . . . ," 43; " 'Without These Songs . . . ,' " 74; Reagon, *Songs of the Civil Rights Movement*, 141–46.

61. "Northern Folk Singers Help Out . . . ," 43.

62. Reagon, *Songs of the Civil Rights Movement*, 170–73. See also Pat Watters and Reese Cleghorn, *Climbing Jacob's Ladder* (New York, 1967), 248–58.

63. Hampton and Fayer, *Voices of Freedom*, 235.

64. Alice Echols, "Nothing Distant about It: Women's Liberation and Sixties Radicalism," in Farber, *The Sixties*, 155, 170 n. 20; Reagon, *Songs of the Civil Rights Movement*, 174–75.

65. Reagon, *Songs of the Civil Rights Movement*, 175.

66. Lester, "Freedom Songs in the South," n.p.; Julius Lester, "The Angry Children of Malcolm X," *Sing Out!*, October–November 1966, 22–25; Seeger, *Incompleat Folksinger*, 104.

67. Southern, *Music of Black Americans*, comments, "As the black masses began to realize that nonviolence was powerless against the entrenched racism in the United States, the singing stopped" (546–47).

68. "Malcolm Favors a Mau Mau in U.S.," *New York Times*, Dec. 21, 1964, 20; Reagon, *Voices of the Civil Rights Movement*, 34; Taylor Branch, *Pillar of Fire: America in the King Years, 1963–65* (New York, 1998), 547–48.

69. Lewis, "Wake Up America," 31–34.

70. On Collier's and Kirkpatrick's songs, see Reagon, "Songs that Moved the Movement," 35, and Carawan and Carawan, *Freedom Is a Constant Struggle*, 9, 184–91. On the more militant tone of black popular music, see Garofalo, *Rockin' Out*, 177–81, and Burt Korall, "The Music of Protest," *Saturday Review*, November 16, 1968, 36–39.

71. In some cases subsequent movements such as the antiwar and women's movements used the same songs. "We Shall Overcome" and "This Little Light of Mine" are two prominent examples.

Chapter Two

1. Malina and Beck, *Paradise Now*, 140.

2. Charles L. Mee Jr., "Epitaph for The Living Theatre," *Tulane Drama Review* 8:3 (spring 1964): 220.

3. For the transcript of "The Significance and Legacy of the Living Theatre" symposium, see Michael Smith, ed., "The Living Theatre at Cooper Union: A Symposium with William Coco, Jack Gelber, Karen Malpede, Richard Schechner, and Michael Smith," *Drama Review* 31:3 (fall 1987): 103–19. Smith's comments appear on pp. 104–6; Coco's on pp. 112–16.

4. See, for instance, Julian Beck, "How to Close a Theatre," *Tulane Drama Review* 8:3 (spring 1964): 181–82.

5. See Pierre Biner, *The Living Theatre* (New York, 1972), 19, and Tytell, *Living Theatre*, 44–46, for accounts of Beck and Malina's courtship, marriage, and early plans for starting a theater.

6. Judith Malina, *The Diaries of Judith Malina, 1947–1957* (New York, 1984), 50.

7. Biner, *Living Theatre*, 24.

8. See Maria Ley Piscator, *The Piscator Experiment* (New York, 1967), 103, and John Willett, *The Theatre of Erwin Piscator* (London, 1978), 167.

9. Malina, *Diaries*, 2.

10. "Theater in the Room" is discussed in Malina, *Diaries*, 169–85, 221; Biner, *Living Theatre*, 25–29; and Tytell, *Living Theatre*, 71–72. The similarities between the Living Theatre and the Provincetown Players are striking. See, for instance, Adele Heller, "The New Theatre," in Heller and Rudnick, *1915, the Cultural Moment*, 217–32. Heller specifically discusses early dramatic evenings in Provincetown with plays staged in Hutchins Hapgood's living room (229).

11. Quoted in Biner, *Living Theatre*, 25.

12. Julian Beck, "Storming the Barricades," in Kenneth Brown, *The Brig* (New York, 1965), 7.

13. See Tytell, *Living Theatre*, 24–27, for a discussion of Julian Beck's relationship with many of the leading figures of Abstract Expressionism. Malina's *Diaries* offer a rich portrait of the intimate social and artistic connections of the New York avant-garde during the late forties and early fifties.

14. Amram quoted in Dan Wakefield's collective biography of literary and intellectual figures, *New York in the Fifties* (Boston, 1992), 7. Max Frankel, a *New York Times* and *Spectator* editor, used the phrase "dogged kind of centrism" to describe this generation's prevailing political views. Wakefield, in a partisan introduction, explicitly and favorably contrasts this engaged, but moderate, politics with what he portrays as the overly emotional, clamorous sixties, which one of his colleagues appraises as simply "one big party time" (7–8).

15. On Day, see Malina, *Diaries*, 368–71, 375–79, 382–84, 389, 411, 425–26, 441–62; Wakefield, *New York in the Fifties*, 7–8, 75–90; and Tytell, *Living Theatre*, 114–15, 133–37. On Day's involvement in twenties New York bohemian life, see Tytell, *Living Theatre*, 114–15, and Heller and Rudnick, *1915, the Cultural Moment*, 5. Malina's poetic homage to Day, "Whose Mercy Endures Forever," appears in Judith Malina, *Poems of a Wandering Jewess* (Paris, 1982), 22–23. On Harrington, see Malina, *Diaries*, 299, 320–21, 370, 378; Wakefield, *New York in the Fifties*, 5, 76–80; and Tytell, *Living Theatre*, 101, 115, 147. On Mills, see Wakefield, *New York in the Fifties*, 5, 32–36, 271–74.

16. Julian Beck interview in *Yale/theatre* 2:1 (spring 1969): 21; see also Wakefield, *New York in the Fifties*, 247–55.

17. Malina, *Poems*, 22–23.

18. See Tytell, *Living Theatre*, 133–37. Also see Julian Beck's letter to Karl Bissinger of January 28, 1965, published as "Thoughts on Theater from Jail," in the *New York Times*, February 21, 1965.

19. Jack Gelber, *The Connection* (New York, 1957); Kenneth Tynan, Preface to Gelber, *The Connection*, 7–11.

20. Biner, *Living Theatre*, 36–37, 44–45, 54; Tytell, *Living Theatre*, 150–51, Beck, "Storming the Barricades," 22–23.

21. See Beck, "Storming the Barricades," 6.

22. Jack Gelber speaks of "illusionist acting techniques" in Smith, "The Living Theatre at Cooper Union," 108; "murmuring together conspiratorially" appears in John Tytell's description of *The Connection* in *Living Theatre*, 155.

23. Beck, "Storming the Barricades," 26.

24. Clurman is cited in Tytell, *Living Theatre*, 157; all other quotations appear in Louis Calta, "*The Connection*: A Play About Junkies," *New York Times*, July 16, 1959, 30.

25. Tynan, Preface to Gelber, *The Connection*, 8.

26. Beck, "Storming the Barricades," 26–27.

27. Malina, *Diaries*, 452–53.

28. Beck, "Thoughts on Theater from Jail."

29. Gelber, *The Connection*; Tynan, Preface to Gelber, *The Connection*, 7–11.

30. I am indebted to Tytell, *Living Theatre*, 157, for this observation.

31. Robert Brustein, "Junkies and Jazz," *New Republic*, September 28, 1959, 29; Jerry Tallmer, "Theatre: *The Connection*," *Village Voice*, July 22, 1959, 90.

32. On the audiences, see Tytell, *Living Theatre*, 160–61, and 379–80 n. 2. Tynan refers to *The Connection* as a "cultural must" and makes the Moscow Art Theatre comparison in his Preface to Gelber, *The Connection*, 7. All other quoted material is from Tytell.

33. Antonin Artaud, *The Theater and Its Double* (New York, 1958), 13.

34. Quoted in Judith Malina, "Directing *The Brig*," in Brown, *The Brig*, 86.

35. Ibid., 98.

36. Ibid.; also see Biner, *Living Theatre*, 69.

37. Gitlin discusses "as-if" in *The Sixties*, 224.

38. Beck, "How to Close a Theatre," 189–90; Elenore Lester, "The Living Theatre Presents: Revolution! Joy! Protest! Shock! Etc.!," *New York Times Magazine*, October 13, 1968, 94. Denning, *Cultural Front*, 285–93, discusses the Federal Theatre's renegade performances of Marc Blitzstein's *The Cradle Will Rock*. The coincidental similarities with *The Brig* episode are nevertheless uncanny, especially the way in which these impromptu performances necessitated physical participation by the audiences.

39. Lester, "Living Theatre Presents," 94.

40. My discussion of the Living Theatre's tax trial draws heavily from two much fuller accounts: Tytell, *Living Theatre*, 191–94, and Biner, *Living Theatre*, 78–83.

41. Caldwell's letter, Blau and Irving's, and seven others from "the vanguard of the resident professional movement" appear in a forum entitled "The Living Theatre and Larger Issues," *Tulane Drama Review* 8:3 (spring 1964): 191–206.

42. Malina and Beck, *Paradise Now*, 15–19.

43. This point draws from both scholarly analysis and my own experience as a Living Theatre performer from 1988 to 1991, as well an an interview with Tom Walker, a long-time company member, August 15, 2002. Walker observed that the company's haphazard approach to compensating performers intermittently continues to raise problems for the current company, remarking that it has "often alienated actors who don't want to take the risk of being dependent on the kindness of the director." Clearly, a sense of Beck and Malina's paternalism, usually benevolent, pervades the history of the company. Walker echoed this attitude, remarking, "It's a family business in spite of all the politics." He also humorously defended the moral and ethical consistency of Beck and Malina's setting priorities as they wished, about the order of meeting expenses including actors' salaries, noting of the company that "it's not Marxist or Socialist, it's anarchist."

44. Lester, "Living Theatre Presents," 88.

45. Beck, "How to Close a Theatre," 183.

46. Julian Beck, #2 (untitled poem), in *semi-permeable membranes: twenty songs of the revolution* (n.p., 1984), 1.

47. Blau and Irving, letter in "Living Theatre and Larger Issues," 197.

48. Julian Beck, *The Life of the Theatre* (New York, 1972), 84–85.

49. See Adele Heller, "The New Theatre," in Heller and Rudnick, *1915, The Cultural Moment*, 217–31. Heller explicitly and correctly identifies the Provincetown Players as precedents for the Living Theatre (as well as the San Francisco Mime Troupe) although Malina's and Beck's writings indicate that Piscator, Artaud, and the Russian constructivist director Vsevolod Meyerhold were more conscious theatrical influences. Also see, Robert K. Sarlos, "Jig Cook and Susan Glaspell: Rule Makers and Rule Breakers," in Heller and Rudnick, *1915, The Cultural Moment*, 250–58. Sarlos's article includes an excellent discussion of the Provincetown Players' creative process.

50. Beck, *Life of the Theatre*, 85.
51. Ibid., 5.
52. Peter Hartman, quoted in Tytell, *Living Theatre,* 209–10.
53. Beck, *Life of the Theatre*, 84.
54. Jackie Goldberg, for one, uses the phrase "democracy is an endless meeting," commenting on the Berkeley free speech movement in the documentary film *Berkeley in the Sixties,* New York, First Run Features, 1990.
55. Beck, *Life of the Theatre*, 84–85.
56. Laurence Veysey, *The Communal Experience: Anarchist and Mystical Counter-Cultures in America* (New York, 1973), 56–60. Veysey identifies nine "areas of intellectual and emotional engagement" in the tradition of American cultural radicalism: "God (universal coherence), authority, violence (sanctity of life), the individual and the community (intensification and loss of self), sex, maximization of consciousness (clarity/ecstasy), possessions and fixity of abode, bodily and intellectual intake of substances and ideas, optimism/desperation." Veysey's list mirrors the Living Theater's most salient personal and theatrical concerns, and collective creation was a conscious attempt to address many of these ideas. Veysey's list applies with equal appropriateness to the ideas and actions of the Diggers.
57. Aldo Rostagno, *We, The Living Theatre* (New York, 1970), 78–109; Biner, *Living Theatre*, 145; Tytell, *Living Theatre,* 199–201.
58. Julian Beck, "Theatre and Revolution," unpublished essay, 1967, Living Theatre Archives, University of California at Davis, 6.
59. Quoted in Tytell, *Living Theatre,* 269–70.
60. Biner, *Living Theatre*, 160.
61. Quotes are from the "Preparation" section of Malina and Beck, *Paradise Now,* 5–13. See also Beck interview in *Yale/theatre,* 16.
62. Tytell, *Living Theatre,* 235–37; Charles Marowitz, "You Can Go Home Again?," *New York Times,* September 8, 1968, sec.2, 1–5.
63. Quotes are from the "Preparation" section of Malina and Beck, *Paradise Now,* 5.
64. Ibid., 23–25.
65. On the diverse audience reactions to *Paradise Now,* see Judith Malina, *The Enormous Despair* (New York, 1972), 41–228; Malina and Beck, *Paradise Now,* 72–75; Tytell, *Living Theatre,* 236–60; Clive Barnes, "Stage: Living Theatre's 'Paradise Now,' a Collective Creation," *New York Times,* October 15, 1968. 39; Marowitz, "You Can Go Home Again?," sec.2, 1–5; Lester, "Living Theatre Presents," 94; and "Sex as a Spectator Sport," *Time,* July 11, 1969, 61–62.
66. Malina and Beck, *Paradise Now,* 6.
67. On the length of performances, see, for instance, Barnes, "Stage: Living Theatre's 'Paradise Now,'" 39. The quote is from Malina and Beck, *Paradise Now,* 140.
68. Malina, *Enormous Despair,* 42; Malina and Beck, *Paradise Now,* 15–17; William Borders, "Indecent Exposure Charged to Becks," *New York Times,* September 28, 1968, 27.
69. Renfreu Neff, *The Living Theatre, U.S.A.* (New York, 1970), 117; Malina, *Enormous Despair,* 117.
70. Quoted in Neff, *Living Theatre, U.S.A.,* 44.
71. Malina, *Enormous Despair,* 50–51.
72. John Rockwell in *Oakland Tribune,* February 22, 1969, quoted in Rostagno, *We, The Living Theatre,* 170.
73. Malina, *Enormous Despair,* 183.
74. Beck's comments appear in Rostagno, *We, The Living Theatre,* 30. For the Living

Theatre's participation in the events in Paris in May 1968, including the liberation of the Odeon, see Rostagno, *We, The Living Theatre*, 29–36, and Beck, *Life of the Theatre*, 173–75. Tytell, *Living Theatre*, 229–36.

75. Malina, *Enormous Despair*, 180–81.

76. Malina, *Enormous Despair*, 169–70.

77. "Shock Troops of the Avant-Garde," *Time*, September 27, 1968, 66.

78. Beck, *Life of the Theatre*, 221.

79. The other three cells were to be "environmental," "cultural," and "spiritual." While the cells did manage to continue some activities—the cultural cell mounted performances of *Paradise Now* in London that integrated rock music, and the spiritual cell visited India before returning to London and performing under a different name—they were all fairly short-lived.

80. "Living Theatre Action Declaration," reprinted in Biner, *Living Theatre*, 225–27.

81. On the San Francisco Mime Troupe, see R. G. Davis, *San Francisco Mime Troupe: The First Ten Years* (Palo Alto, Calif., 1975), and Michael William Doyle's excellent essay "Staging the Revolution: Guerrila Revolution as Countercultural Practice, 1965–68," in Braunstein and Doyle, *Imagine Nation*, 71–91, which also chronicles the Diggers' emergence from the SFMT and their subsequent career in guerrilla theater. Doyle examines the Yippies in this essay as well.

82. Beck, *Life of the Theatre*, 38–41; Tytell, *Living Theatre*, 275; interview with Tom Walker, August 24, 1998.

83. Tytell, *Living Theatre*, 275–82; interview with Tom Walker, August 24, 1998.

84. Judith Malina, letter to Carl Einhorn, March 28, 1970, reprinted in Beck, *Life of The Theatre*, 75–77.

85. Tytell, *Living Theatre*, 283–84.

86. Ibid., 289–304; interview with Tom Walker, August 24, 1998.

87. Quoted material is from an interview with Tom Walker, August 15, 2002.

88. Tytell, *Living Theatre*, 309, 315, 319, 334. Interview with Tom Walker, August 15, 2002. The Living Theatre was not always able to perform its street theater unmolested, however. Walker recalled a spring 1974 incident in Brooklyn where the company performed the *Strike Support Oratorium* in cooperation with the United Farm Workers, which was interrupted by the police, and another performance of the same piece in New Haven whose audience included some "egg-throwers."

89. Interview with Tom Walker, August 24, 1998; Tytell, *Living Theatre*, 322.

90. Interview with Tom Walker, August 24, 1998; Beck quoted in Tytell, *Living Theatre*, 317.

91. Interviews with Tom Walker, August 24, 1998 and August 15, 2002; Tytell, *Living Theatre*, 321–22.

92. Paul Ryder Ryan, "The Living Theatre's 'Money Tower,'" *Drama Review* 18:2 (June 1974): 9–19; Living Theatre Collective, "'Money Tower' Scenario," *Drama Review* 18:2 (June 1974): 20–25; interview with Tom Walker, August 24, 1998; Tytell, *Living Theatre*, 317–27.

93. Claudio Vicentini, "The Living Theatre's 'Six Public Acts'," *Drama Review* 19:3 (September 1975): 80–93; interview with Tom Walker, August 24, 1998; Tytell, *Living Theatre*, 321–27.

94. This text is reprinted in Vicentini, "Living Theatre's 'Six Public Acts'," 92.

95. Ibid., 80–93; interview with Tom Walker, August 24, 1998; Tytell, *Living Theatre*, 321–27.

96. Beck, *Life of the Theatre*, 221.

97. The quote is from an interview with Tom Walker, August 24, 1998. Walker pro-

vided key information about the Living Theatre's experiences in Europe during 1975–76; this period is also discussed in Tytell, *Living Theatre*, 323–28.

98. Tytell, *Living Theatre*, 345.

99. The Carnegie-Mellon student is mentioned in Malina, *Enormous Despair*, 122. Tytell, *Living Theatre*, 278–304, discusses the Living Theatre's experiences in Brazil. Beck's comment about the company's naiveté is from "Thoughts on Theater from Jail."

100. Interview with Tom Walker, August 24, 1998.

101. Gitlin uses this phrase to describe the Diggers in *The Sixties*, 223.

Chapter Three

1. See George Metevsky, "Delving the Diggers," *Berkeley Barb*, Oct. 21, 1966, 3; Perry, *Haight-Ashbury*, 108; and Farber, *Age of Great Dreams*, 169.

2. Alex Forman, "San Francisco Style: The Diggers and the Love Revolution," *Anarchy* 7:7 (July 1967) (accessible in the Digger Archives, <www.diggers.org>); also see Todd Gitlin, *The Sixties*, 224.

3. "Hippies: Death on a Sunny Afternoon," *Rolling Stone*, November 9, 1967, 11; Perry, *Haight-Ashbury*, 242–44; Matusow, *Unraveling of America*, 302; Miller, *Hippies and American Values*, 106.

4. See, for instance, the title article in Didion, *Slouching Towards Bethlehem*, 84–128. Also see Farber, *Age of Great Dreams*, 186–87.

5. Peter Coyote, *Sleeping Where I Fall* (Washington, D.C.: 1998), xiii.

6. Ibid., 130.

7. R. G. Davis, *The San Francisco Mime Troupe: The First Ten Years* (Palo Alto, Calif., 1975), 70–76, 81, 87, 100, 117. The Peter Coyote quote is from a January 12, 1989, interview with Etan Ben-Ami, which is transcribed in its entirety in the Digger Archives.

8. Davis, *San Francisco Mime Troupe*, 9, 70.

9. "The Early Digger Papers: San Francisco, Fall, 1966 to Spring, 1967," Digger Archives; Davis, *San Francisco Mime Troupe*, 80.

10. "Early Digger Papers"; George Metevsky (a favorite Digger pseudonym), "The Ideology of Failure," *Berkeley Barb*, November 18, 1966, 6; Emmett Grogan, *Ringolevio: A Life Played for Keeps* (Boston, 1972), 236–37.

11. "Burocops Proboscis Probes Digger Bag," *Berkeley Barb*, October 21, 1966, 3; "The San Francisco Riot," *Newsweek*, October 10, 1966, 28–29; Perry, *Haight-Ashbury*, 93–94.

12. See Doyle, "Staging the Revolution," 85–86. Todd Gitlin also took up the Digger/ Yippie comparison in *The Sixties*, 234–37.

13. "Burocops Proboscis Probes Digger Bag," 3.

14. "Time to Forget," Haight Street Diggers Records, MS 3159, box 1, folder 1, California Historical Society, North Baker Research Library; also reprinted in "Early Digger Papers."

15. "Time to Forget," uses the phrase "marketers of expanded consciousness." The other quoted material is from Metevsky, "Ideology of Failure," 6.

16. Perry, *Haight-Ashbury*, 90–91; "Money Is an Unnecessary Evil," in "Early Digger Papers."

17. "A-Political Or, Criminal Or Victim Or Or Or Or Or Or," in "Early Digger Papers."

18. "In Search of a Frame," *Berkeley Barb*, November 25, 1966, 6; Perry, *Haight-Ashbury*, 105.

19. All quoted material is from "In Search of a Frame," 6.

20. Perry, *Haight-Ashbury*, 108.

21. "In Search of a Frame," 6; Perry, *Haight-Ashbury*, 99–100.

22. On the English Diggers' influence, see Grogan, *Ringolevio*, 237–38, and "English Diggers," Digger Archives.

23. Perry, *Haight-Ashbury*, 89–93; Grogan, *Ringolevio*, 238–41.

24. Metevsky, "Ideology of Failure," 6; Perlstein, "Who Owns the Sixties?," 37. Perlstein attributes the argument that "the Sixties' rebel mystique was better suited to retailing than revolution" to Tom Frank, among others. The characterization of baby boomers as "dynamic consumers" was lifted from Frank's then-forthcoming book on sixties advertising, *The Conquest of Cool: Business Culture, Counterculture, and the Rise of Hip Consumerism* (Chicago, 1997).

25. The quoted material is from "In Search of a Frame," 6. In addition to the Diggers, other groups or movements that attempted to galvanize the counterculture as a serious political, social, or spiritual force included the Yippies, John Sinclair's White Panthers, and the rural communards.

26. Metevsky, "Ideology of Failure," 6; see also Perry, *Haight-Ashbury*, 91.

27. Grogan, *Ringolevio*, 245–50; Perry, *Haight-Ashbury*, 99.

28. Grogan, *Ringolevio*, 245–48; Perry, *Haight-Ashbury*, 97–99; Metevsky, "Delving the Diggers," 3; "Burocops Proboscis Probes Digger Bag," 3.

29. Hunter S. Thompson, "The 'Hashbury' Is the Capital of the Hippies," *New York Times Magazine*, May 14, 1967, 121; Grogan, *Ringolevio*, 245.

30. "In Search of a Frame," 6; "Diggers New Game: The Frame," *Berkeley Barb*, November 4, 1966, 1; Grogan, *Ringolevio*, 249–50; Farber, *Age of Great Dreams*, 169–70.

31. Grogan, *Ringolevio*, 246–48, 261–62; Perry, *Haight-Ashbury*, 98.

32. "Free Bread," reprinted under heading "Digger Bread (made with love)," Digger Archives; Stephen M. Pittell, "The Current Status of the Haight-Ashbury Hippie Community (Excerpt)," September 1968, Digger Archives; Warren Belasco, *Appetite for Change: How the Counterculture Took on the Food Industry*, 2d ed. (Ithaca, N.Y., 1993), 17–20, 87.

33. Perry, *Haight-Ashbury*, 136, 167, 212, 226, 271, 284.

34. Grogan, *Ringolevio*, 462–66.

35. Coyote interview with Etan Ben-Ami.

36. Coyote interview with Etan Ben-Ami; Perry, *Haight-Ashbury*, 210, 212, 284; Pittell, "Current Status of the Haight-Ashbury Hippie Community"; "Free Bread"; "Free Food in the Panhandle, 1983," Digger Archives; Arthur Lisch, correspondence with the author, August 4, 1999; "What Is Food Not Bombs?," <www.foodnotbombs.net>; "San Francisco Food Not Bombs," <www.sffoodnotbomb.org>.

37. Gitlin, *The Sixties*, 224.

38. "San Francisco Diggers (1966–68)," "Create the Condition You Describe," Digger Archives.

39. Perry, *Haight-Ashbury*, 108–9; Grogan, *Ringolevio*, 248–49, 472; "The Digger Papers," in Bloom and Breines, *Takin' It to the Streets*, 319; Farber, *Age of Great Dreams*, 169; Gitlin, *The Sixties*, 228.

40. Grogan, *Ringolevio*, 248–49, 472; "Digger Papers," 319.

41. Coyote, *Sleeping Where I Fall*, 89–93; Grogan, *Ringolevio*, 297–303.

42. Coyote interview with Etan Ben-Ami; see also Gitlin, *The Sixties*, 223.

43. For the Diggers' influence on the Yippies, see Gitlin, *The Sixties*, 230–37. For the Krassner incident, see Perry, *Haight-Ashbury*, 109.

44. Forman, "San Francisco Style," n.p.

45. See Gitlin, *The Sixties*, 233, and Grogan, *Ringolevio*, 319–21.

46. "The Splendid Desire for Nothing," *America*, May 20, 1967, 746–47; Harvey Cox, "An Open Letter to Allen Ginsberg," *Commonweal*, April 21, 1967, 147–49.

47. Didion, *Slouching Towards Bethlehem*, 114. Didion recounts that Chester Anderson, the leading force behind the Communications Company, the Diggers' publicity apparatus, showed her a flier announcing this series.

48. Perry, *Haight-Ashbury*, 108–109, 116–18, 136, 200–201.

49. Perry, *Haight-Ashbury*, 108–109, 116–18, 136.

50. Loudon Wainwright, "The Strange New Love Land of the Hippies," *Life*, March 31, 1967, 15–16.

51. The quote and the estimate are from Thompson, "The 'Hashbury'," 122.

52. Grogan, *Ringolevio*, 248–49, 472; "Digger Papers," 319.

53. Grogan, *Ringolevio*, 445–46.

54. Grogan, *Ringolevio*, 248, 264; Didion, *Slouching Towards Bethlehem*, 99.

55. Coyote interview with Etan Ben-Ami.

56. Nicole Wills, correspondence with the author, June 28, 2001.

57. All quoted material is from Coyote interview with Etan Ben-Ami.

58. Nicole Wills, correspondence with the author, July 2, 2001.

59. Coyote interview with Etan Ben-Ami.

60. Ibid.

61. Sam, originally Eileen Ewing, made these comments in a discussion group on the Digger website, <www.diggers.org>, February 25, 2002.

62. Wills correspondence, June 28, 2001.

63. Lynnie's remarks appeared in a discussion group on the Digger website, <www .diggers.org>, March 29, 2002.

64. Coyote, *Sleeping Where I Fall*, 11–12.

65. Grogan, *Ringolevio*, 303.

66. Although some scholars, painting the counterculture as "resolutely nonpolitical," reject the idea that the counterculture and New Left converged as the sixties wore on (see Matusow, *Unraveling of America*, 275–307, for example), such an interpretation relies on too narrow a definition of "politics" and ignores the melding of personal and political concerns that defined these two groups. More convincing are David Farber's account of the infusion of countercultural sensibilities into the antiwar movement in *Age of Great Dreams*, 220–21; Todd Gitlin's analysis of former civil rights workers' participation in the counterculture in *The Sixties*, 168–69; and Hunter S. Thompson's contemporary reporting on how Haight-Ashbury usurped Berkeley's claim as the cutting edge of radicalism while incorporating some of its elements, in "The 'Hashbury'" 29, 120–24.

67. "Public Nonsense Nuisance Public Essence Newsense Public News," in "Early Digger Papers."

68. "Diggers New Game: The Frame," *Berkeley Barb*, November 4, 1966, 1; Perry, *Haight-Ashbury*, 103–5; Grogan, *Ringolevio*, 250–51.

69. "Diggers New Game.

70. Kenneth Cmiel, "The Politics of Civility," in Farber, *The Sixties*, 267–69.

71. The Diggers, "where is PUBLIC at?," in "Early Digger Papers."

72. "Diggers New Game"; Perry, *Haight-Ashbury*, 103–5; Grogan, *Ringolevio*, 250–51.

73. Todd Gitlin advanced this interpretation of the Diggers' "new sense" in *The Sixties*, 222. A glance at the following accounts supports this reading: "Diggers New Game"; Perry, *Haight-Ashbury*, 103–5; Grogan, *Ringolevio*, 250–51; "Public Nonsense," in "Early Digger Papers."

74. "In the Clear," *San Francisco Chronicle*, November 30, 1966, 1; see also Grogan, *Ringolevio*, 253–55.

75. "Diggers New Game"; Perry, *Haight-Ashbury*, 105.

76. Perry, *Haight-Ashbury*, 114–15; see also Grogan, *Ringolevio*, 259–61, and Coyote, *Sleeping Where I Fall*, 96–97.

77. Perry, *Haight-Ashbury*, 114–16; Grogan, *Ringolevio*, 259–63; Coyote, *Sleeping Where I Fall*, 96–97.

78. Perry, *Haight-Ashbury*, 115–16; Grogan, *Ringolevio*, 263; Coyote, *Sleeping Where I Fall*, 96–97 (see photo of Snyder, McClure, Ginsberg, and Kandel onstage at the Human Be-In following p. 178).

79. On Kandel and Fritsch (who was also known as "Sweet William Tumbleweed"), see Coyote, *Sleeping Where I Fall*, 113–29. The Digger "benefit" is described in Grogan, *Ringolevio*, 277–79. On Corso, Welch, and Snyder, see Coyote, *Sleeping Where I Fall*, 126, 205–6, 281–82.

80. Gitlin, *The Sixties*, 225–30; Grogan, *Ringolevio*, 385.

81. Gitlin, *The Sixties*, 225–30; Nicholas von Hoffman, "Hippiedom Meets the New Left," *Washington Post*, June 19, 1967, A3; Grogan, *Ringolevio*, 385–403.

82. Grogan, *Ringolevio*, 274.

83. Ibid., 280–86; "The Invisible Circus," Digger Archives; Perry, *Haight-Ashbury*, 145–47; Coyote, *Sleeping Where I Fall*, 77–79.

84. For the influence of Happenings and Fluxus on groups such as the AWC and GAAG, see Irving Sandler, *Art of the Post-Modern Era: From the Late 1960s to the Early 1990s* (Boulder, Colo., 1998), 35, 50–51. For this point, I also drew from my interviews with Irving Petlin, November 30, 1998; Leon Golub, December 9, 1998; and Jon Hendricks, February 12, 1999.

85. Quoted material is from "Invisible Circus"; also see Grogan, *Ringolevio*, 283–84.

86. Grogan, *Ringolevio*, 280–86; "Invisible Circus"; Perry, *Haight-Ashbury*, 145–47; Coyote, *Sleeping Where I Fall*, 77–79, 86.

87. Grogan, *Ringolevio*, 284–85.

88. Coyote, *Sleeping Where I Fall*, 350.

89. Perry, *Haight-Ashbury*, 145–47; Grogan, *Ringolevio*, 280–86; Coyote, *Sleeping Where I Fall*, 77–79. The quote is from "Invisible Circus."

90. Didion, *Slouching Towards Bethlehem*, 124. Mainstream press accounts heralding the hippie phenomenon and the Summer of Love include Wainwright, "Strange New Love Land," 15–16; "Love on Haight," *Time*, March 17, 1967, 27; and Thompson, "The 'Hashbury'." See also Martin Arnold, "Organized Hippies Emerge on Coast," *New York Times*, May 5, 1967, 41–42. The popularity of "San Francisco (Be Sure to Wear Flowers in Your Hair)" is chronicled in Perry, *Haight-Ashbury*, 201, 212.

91. Perry, *Haight-Ashbury*, 204, 211–12, 216; Grogan, *Ringolevio*, 412–16; Earl Shorris, "Love Is Dead," *New York Times Magazine*, October 29, 1967, 27, 113–16; Coyote interview with Etan Ben-Ami.

92. Miller, *The Hippies and American Values*, 106. Didion provides acidic and somewhat defensive comments on the Diggers' views of "media poisoners" in *Slouching Towards Bethlehem*, 114, 124. The anecdote about the reporters is from Gitlin, *The Sixties*, 223.

93. This event is discussed in both Grogan, *Ringolevio*, 354–55, and Gitlin, *The Sixties*, 231–32.

94. Gitlin, *The Sixties*, 225.

95. Perry, *Haight-Ashbury*, 243; "Hippies: Death on a Sunny Afternoon," 11; Grogan, *Ringolevio*, 445–46; Abe Peck, *Uncovering the Sixties: The Life and Times of the Underground Press* (New York, 1985) 52–53.

96. "Hippies: Death on a Sunny Afternoon," 11; Shorris, "Love Is Dead," 27, 113–16; Shelley Muzzy, correspondence with author, April 23, 1999; Perry, *Haight-Ashbury*, 242–44; Grogan, *Ringolevio*, 445–46; Peck, *Uncovering the Sixties*, 52–53; Coyote, *Sleeping Where I Fall*, 135.

97. Shorris, "Love Is Dead," 27, 113–16.

98. Russell Baker, "Observer: The Latest Crisis in Hashbury," *New York Times*, Novem-

ber 9, 1967, 46; also see "Parade in Haight-Ashbury Marks 'Death of Hippie,'" *New York Times*, October 7, 1967, 26.

99. Perry, *Haight-Ashbury*, 272, 292–94; Coyote, *Sleeping Where I Fall*, 167–215, 347–51.

100. Coyote, *Sleeping Where I Fall*, 179–80

101. Davis, *San Francisco Mime Troupe*, 163. The Matusow chapter is in *Unraveling of America*, 275–307. Farber generously assesses the fate and legacy of the counterculture in *Age of Great Dreams*, 187–89, and I am indebted to several of his insights. Coyote's comments on the counterculture's accomplishments appear in the Afterword to *Sleeping Where I Fall*, 347–51. The quote appears on p. 349.

102. Coyote, *Sleeping Where I Fall*, 350.

Chapter Four

1. Lippard, *A Different War*, 20–53; interview with Irving Petlin, November 30, 1998.

2. Lucy Lippard, "The Art Workers' Coalition: Not a History," *Studio International*, November 1970, 171–74.

3. On the abstract expressionists' sponsorship of *Dissent*, see David Craven, *Abstract Expressionism as Cultural Critique: Dissent during the McCarthy Period* (New York, 1999), esp. 4–6.

4. Robert Motherwell's essay "The Modern Painter's World," *DYN* 1:6 (November 1944):9–14, is a particularly strong expression of the rationale for the movement away from politics and toward aesthetics. This essay is reprinted in Patricia Hills, *Modern Art in the USA: Issues and Controversies of the 20th Century* (Upper Saddle River, N.J., 2001), 164–68. The Hills quote is from her introduction to this essay (165).

5. Guilbaut, *How New York Stole the Idea*, 200–201.

6. Craven, *Abstract Expressionism* 31.

7. Artists and Writers Protest, Open Letter, *New York Times*, June 26, 1962, 12.

8. Artists and Writers Protest, "End Your Silence," *New York Times*, April 18 and June 2, 1965; Lippard, *Different War*, 12.

9. Lippard, *Different War*, 12–13; interviews with Petlin, November 30, 1998, and September 10, 1999. The *New York Times* advertisement appeared on February 26, 1966.

10. Craven's *Abstract Expressionism* analyzes the political sensibilities of the Abstract Expressionists at great length, relying on, among other sources, FBI files on such prominent artists as Robert Motherwell, Ad Reinhardt, and Mark Rothko. Craven also discusses the "lifelong leftism" of Jackson Pollock, the preeminent abstract expressionist, citing Robert Motherwell's comment that "Pollock in fact had very leftist views that seemingly had little to do with his art." See Craven, *Abstract Expressionism*, esp. 46–48. Interview with Petlin, November 30, 1998.

11. Interview with Lucy Lippard, September 30, 1999. Petlin produced this panel with Roberto Matta, though the two divided the panel into two unequal parts, with Petlin's image on the left and Matta's on the right. Petlin's panel is pictured in Lippard, *Different War*, 15.

12. Leon Golub, "The Artist as Angry Artist," *Arts Magazine*, April 1967, 48.

13. Lippard, *Different War*, 18.

14. Interview with Petlin, November 30, 1998.

15. See John Perrault, "Whose Art?," *Village Voice*, January 9, 1969, 16–17; "Sculptor Takes Work Out of Museum Show," *New York Times*, January 4, 1969, 24; Grace Glueck, "Artists Threaten Sit-in at the Modern," *New York Times*, March 7, 1969, 26; Grace Glueck, "J'accuse, Baby! She Cried," *New York Times*, April 20, 1969, sec. 2, 28; Lippard,

Different War, 20; Lucy R. Lippard, *Get the Message?: A Decade of Art for Social Change* (New York, 1984), 11. See also Alan W. Moore, "Collectivities: Protest, Counter-Culture, and Political Postmodernism in New York City Artists Organizations 1969–1985," Ph.D. diss., City University of New York, 2000, 5–6. The quote is from Carl Andre, "Carl Andre: Artworker," interview by Jeanne Siegel, *Studio International*, November 1970, 175–79.

16. On politicians' positioning of the abstract expressionists as exemplars of the American way, see Guilbaut, *How New York Stole the Idea*, esp. 201. For an excellent sampling of the discourse of abstract expressionist artists, along with that of important critics such as Meyer Schapiro and the Museum of Modern Art's first director, Alfred Barr, see chap. 4 in Hills, *Modern Art in the USA*. It is worth noting that not all cold war politicians saw freedom when they looked at abstract expressionism. For instance, Hills's collection contains the text of a 1949 speech by the Michigan congressman George Dondero, who saw modern art, with abstract expressionism at the forefront, as "shackled" to Communism, since, as Hills paraphrases his argument, "all the 'isms' are Communist inspired, and, therefore, deny men their freedom" (190–92).

17. "Sculptor Takes Work Out," 24. Lowry's pattern of deflecting protest away from public forums was also evident in his handling of a March 30, 1969, protest when he "especially" created a white-ribboned corridor for protesters so as not to disturb paying visitors. This incident is described in Robert Windeler, "Modern Museum Protest Target," *New York Times*, March 31, 1969, 33. Lowry also rejected the AWC's call for a large open hearing to publicize the needs and opinions of artists, advocating instead an ongoing committee which would have met privately; see Glueck, "Artists Threaten Sit-in," 26. A hearing was ultimately held at the School of Visual Arts on April 10, 1969, and is discussed later in this chapter.

18. Glueck, "Artists Threaten Sit-in," 26; Windeler, "Modern Museum Protest Target," 33. The AWC's list of demands is reprinted in Lippard, "Art Workers' Coalition," 171–74, and Lippard, *Get the Message?*, 12–13.

19. See Moore, "Collectivities," 7 n. 16.

20. Windeler, "Modern Museum Protest Target," 33.

21. Interview with Petlin, November 30, 1998; interview with Leon Golub, December 9, 1998.

22. Grace Glueck, "Dissidents Stir Art World," *New York Times*, April 12, 1969, 41; Glueck, "J'accuse, Baby!" Lippard, *Different War*, 22; Lippard, *Get the Message?*, 10–15; Art Workers Coalition, *Open Hearing* (New York, 1969).

23. Glueck, "Dissidents Stir Art World," 41; Grace Glueck, correspondence with author, August 4, 2001; Lippard, *Different War*, 42; Lippard, *Get the Message?*, 24–25.

24. For versions of this idea, see the SDS Port Huron Statement and Casey Hayden and Mary King, "Sex and Caste: A Kind of Memo," in Bloom and Breines, *Takin' It to the Streets*, 61–74 and 47–51, respectively, and Alice Echols, "Nothing Distant about It: Women's Liberation and Sixties Radicalism," in Farber, *The Sixties* 149–74. See also Sara Evans, *Personal Politics: The Roots of Women's Liberation in the Civil Rights Movement and the New Left* (New York, 1979), and Robin Morgan, ed., *Sisterhood Is Powerful: An Anthology of Writings from the Women's Liberation Movement* (New York, 1970).

25. SDS, Port Huron Statement, and Hayden and King, "Sex and Caste," are excellent examples of this New Left initiative.

26. Lippard, "Art Workers' Coalition," 171–74.

27. Lippard, *Get the Message?*, 12.

28. Hilton Kramer, "Artists and the Problem of 'Relevance,'" *New York Times*, May 4, 1969, sec. 2, 23; Glueck, "J'accuse, Baby!" Glueck, "Dissidents Stir Art World," 41; Windeler, "Modern Museum Protest Target," 33; Grace Glueck, "Hightower Meets Museum's

Critics, *New York Times*, March 4, 1970, 38; Lil Picard, "Interview with John Hightower," *Arts Magazine*, May 1970, 20–24.

29. The phrases cited appear in David R. Colburn and George E. Pozzetta's article about the rise of identity politics, "Race, Ethnicity, and the Evolution of Political Legitimacy," in Farber, *The Sixties*, 121.

30. Lippard, *Different War*, 24; Lippard, *Get the Message?*, 11. In an interview on September 30, 1999, Lippard used the phrase "political momentum" to describe what propelled the AWC. For a discussion of the Tet Offensive as the turning point in American public opinion against the Vietnam War, see Chester J. Pach Jr., "And That's the Way It Was: The Vietnam War, on the Nightly Network News," in Farber, *The Sixties*, 90–112.

31. Interview with Golub, December 9, 1998; interview with Petlin, November 30, 1998; Lippard, *Different War*, 24; Lippard, *Get the Message?*, 16.

32. "Some of the Events That Led to GAAG's Creation," in *GAAG: The Guerrilla Art Action Group, 1969–1976* (New York, 1978), n.p. Interview with Jon Hendricks, February 12, 1999.

33. The original statement was notarized on March 4, 1970, and the addendum about prioritizing people over property on March 18, 1970. Both are reprinted in *GAAG*; all other quoted material is from the interview with Hendricks, February 12, 1999.

34. Interview with Hendricks, February 12, 1999; *GAAG*, Action Number 2, n.p. contains both the press release and the list of demands; Grace Glueck, "Yanking the Rug from Under," *New York Times*, January 25, 1970, sec. 2, 25; Lippard, *Different War*, 25–26.

35. According to Anderson, "New American Revolution," 180–81, by 1967 Dow Chemical was the only company producing napalm. The GAAG letter cites Seymour Hersh, *Chemical and Biological Warfare: America's Hidden Arsenal* (Indianapolis, 1968), among other sources in its indictment of the Rockefellers. Hersh's book contains a discussion of the roles of Standard Oil, UTC, and Dow in napalm production (258–62).

36. Anderson, "New American Revolution," 175–205, provides an excellent overview of this trend.

37. "A Call for the Immediate Resignation of All the Rockefellers from the Board of Trustees of The Museum of Modern Art," *GAAG*, Action Number 3, n.p.; also reprinted in Lippard, *Different War*, 123. By the late sixties, Nelson Rockefeller's record of antagonism toward political artists reached back over three decades. In 1933, as director of the New York Museum of Modern Art, he donated space in Rockefeller Center for the Mexican painter Diego Rivera to create a mural, but the commission was revoked and the painting destroyed because Rockefeller opposed the mural's positive depiction of Lenin. See Denning, *Cultural Front*, xvi, 490 n. 67, and Laurance P. Hurlburt, *The Mexican Muralists in the United States* (Albuquerque, 1989), 159–74.

38. Andre, "Carl Andre: Artworker," 175.

39. Lil Picard, "Protest and Rebellion: The Function of the Art Workers Coalition," *Arts Magazine*, May 1970, 18–20; interview with Petlin, November 30, 1998.

40. Carson, *In Struggle*, 30.

41. Picard, "Protest and Rebellion," 18–20; interview with Petlin, Nov. 30, 1998. Jon Hendricks pointed out that neither the AWC nor GAAG secured any grant for its own activities; rather, money was raised by passing the hat at meetings. "If you had $5 to put in, fine, if you didn't, fine," Hendricks explained during an Aug. 12, 1999 interview.

42. Later MoMA started to renege on free Mondays, instituting a "discretionary admission charge" that Lippard characterized as "pay what you wish, but pay." MoMA suggested a payment of one dollar or more, but the AWC argued that this unfairly stigmatized poor people and pressured them into making contributions they could not afford or refraining

from entering the museum altogether. "The poorer you are, the less you're likely to cry poor," Lippard explained. In response, the AWC staged an action distributing pennies to people in line for admission to MoMA, and it tried to persuade potential museumgoers to give only a penny to combat this discriminatory "compulsory contributions" policy. See Lippard, *Get the Message?*, 20–21.

43. The "Communique" is printed in *GAAG*, Action Number 3, n.p.; *GAAG*, Action Number 10, n.p.; interview with Hendricks, February 12, 1999.

44. See Moore, *Collectivities*, esp. 20–21.

45. Dore Ashton, "Response to Crisis in American Art," *Art in America*, January / February 1969, 24–35.

46. Timothy Ferris, "A Creepy Protest at Museum," *New York Post*, January 13, 1971 (reprinted in *Artforum*, February 1971, 31); Lucy Lippard, "Charitable Visits by the AWC to MoMA and Met," *The Element*, January 1971 (reprinted in *Get the Message?*, 21). The 1969 "Harlem on My Mind" exhibit at the Met provoked controversy because of an essay in the exhibit's catalog that contained sentiments many construed as dangerously anti-Semitic. The catalog drew the wrath of the New York Jewish community, Mayor John Lindsay, and ultimately the Met's trustees themselves, who feared a possible decline in the museum's financial support stemming from the controversy. See Thomas Hoving, *Making the Mummies Dance: Inside the Metropolitan Museum of Art* (New York, 1993), 164–80.

47. Lippard, "Art Workers' Coalition," 171–74.

48. Andre, "Carl Andre: 'Artworker,'" 175–79; Lippard, *Different War*, 22.

49. Grace Glueck, "The Cast Is a Flock of Hat Blocks," *New York Times*, December 21, 1969, sec. 2, 35.

50. Paul Hoffman, "35th Art Biennale Beset by Problems at Venice Opening," *New York Times*, June 24, 1970, 38; Lippard, *Different War*, 33; interview with Petlin, November 30, 1998.

51. Hilton Kramer, "Do You Believe in the Principle of Museums?," *New York Times*, January 18, 1970, sec. 2, 25.

52. Frazer Dougherty, Hans Haacke, Lucy Lippard, Art Workers Coalition, Letter to the Editor, in "Art Mailbag: Why MoMA Is Their Target," *New York Times*, February 8, 1970, sec. 2, 23–24; interview with Petlin, November 30, 1998.

53. Dougherty et al., Letter, 23–24.

54. Quoted in Lippard, "Art Workers' Coalition," 173.

55. Dougherty et al., Letter, 23–24.

56. Hilton Kramer, "About MoMA, the AWC, and Political Causes," *New York Times*, February 8, 1970, sec. 2, 23.

57. Lucy Lippard, "The Dilemma," *Arts Magazine*, 1970, 27–29; Lippard, *Different War*, 33; interview with Petlin, November 30, 1998; interview with Hendricks, February 12, 1999.

58. Lippard, "Dilemma," 27–29.

59. Dougherty et al., Letter, 23–24.

60. Excerpts from this press release are reprinted in Lippard, "Art Workers' Coalition, 171–74, and in Lippard, *Get the Message?*, 15. Events surrounding the distribution of the poster are also discussed in Glueck, "Yanking the Rug from Under," 25, and Lippard, *Different War*, 27–28.

61. Glueck, "Yanking the Rug," 25.

62. Lippard, "Dilemma," 27–29.

63. Lippard, *Different War*, 28; Glueck, "Yanking the Rug," 25; *GAAG*, Action Number 6, n.p.; See covers of *Studio International*, November 1970, and *Arts Magazine*, November 1970.

64. Haacke is quoted and his *Visitors Poll* is pictured and discussed in Lippard, *A Different War*, 31.

65. Grace Glueck, "A Strange Assortment of Flags Is Displayed at 'People's Show,'" *New York Times*, November 10, 1970, 53; Clark Whelton, "The Flag as Art: Bars and Stripes Forever," *Village Voice*, November 19, 1970, 1, 20; Lippard, *Different War*, 26–27; Grace Glueck, "Art Notes," *New York Times*, November 1, 1970, sec. 2, 22.

66. Quotes are from Lippard, *Different War*, 26–27; see also Glueck, "Strange Assortment of Flags," 53.

67. See, for instance, Farber, *Chicago '68*, 226–35.

68. Judson 3 Defense Committee, "Historical Background of the People's Flag Show," 1–6, reprinted in *GAAG*, Action Number 12, n.p.; Lippard, *Different War*, 26–27, 34–62, 119 n.

69. Lippard, *Different War*, 34–35; Grace Glueck, "Soft Sculpture or Hard—They're Oldenburgers," *New York Times Magazine*, September 21, 1969, 21, 100–115.

70. Richard Candida Smith, *Utopia and Dissent: Art, Poetry, and Politics in California* (Berkeley, Calif., 1995) 357–60.

71. Interview with Hendricks, February 12, 1999.

72. Corinne Robbins, "The N.Y. Art Strike," *Arts Magazine*, September/October 1970, 27; John Perrault, "On Strike," *Village Voice*, May 28, 1970, 17; Cindy Nemser, "Artists and the System: Far from Cambodia," *Village Voice*, May 28, 1970, 20–21. Poppy Johnson is quoted in Lippard, *Different War*, which discusses the Art Strike on pp. 32–33.

73. Nemser, "Artists and the System," 20–21; Alex Gross, "Do Artists Want Change?," *Arts Magazine*, September / October 1970, 28.

74. Robbins, "N.Y. Art Strike," 27; Lippard, *Different War*, 30–34; interview with Lippard, September 30, 1999.

75. Interview with Petlin, November 30, 1998; interview with Golub, December 9, 1998; interview with Lippard, September 30, 1999; *GAAG*, "Statement of Poppy Johnson. June 16, 1976," n.p.

76. Golub made his comments in an interview on Dec. 9, 1998. For an excellent overview of women's need to separate from the larger, male-dominated protest movement, see Echols, "Nothing Distant About It," 149–74. On the rising tide of feminism within the art world, see Sandler, *Art of the Postmodern Era*, 114–18, and Lippard, *Different War*, 30, 42.

77. Grace Glueck, "At the Whitney, It's Guerrilla Warfare," *New York Times*, November 1, 1970, sec. 2, 22; Lippard, *Get the Message?*, 24; Therese Schwartz, "The Political Scene," *Arts Magazine*, December 1970 / January 1971, 16; Andrew Ross, *Real Love: In Pursuit of Cultural Justice* (New York, 1998), 118–19.

78. Schwartz, "The Political Scene," 16; Glueck, "At the Whitney"; Therese Schwartz, "The Political Scene," *Arts Magazine*, February 1971, 17; Therese Schwartz "The Political Scene," *Arts Magazine*, March 1971, 16; Sandler, *Art of the Postmodern Era*, 117–18.

79. Quoted in Glueck, "At the Whitney," 22.

80. Ross's *Real Love*, 117–48, links the Guerrilla Girls to the legacy of the Art Workers Coalition, GAAG, and the Ad Hoc Women Artists Committee. Though the Guerrilla Girls' identities are anonymous, the continuity between their concerns, tactics, and language and that of these three earlier groups suggests a strong possibility of overlapping personnel, or, at the very least, a clear chain of influence.

81. Interview with Golub, December 9, 1998.

82. Lippard, *Different War*, 42; Lippard, *Get the Message?*, 24.

83. Sandler, *Art of the Postmodern Era*, 114.

84. Hans Haacke, interview by Margaret Sheffield, *Studio International*, March / April 1976, 117–23. See also Moore, "Collectivities," 37–45.

85. Lippard, *Get the Message?*, 24; interview with Golub, December 9, 1998.

Epilogue

1. The quote on Sweet Honey in the Rock is from the group's official website, <www .sweethoney.com>. The material on Cordell Reagon is from Lawrence Van Gelder, "Cordell Hull Reagon, Civil Rights Singer, Dies at 53," *New York Times*, November 19, 1996, sec. D, 25, and "In Memoriam: Cordell Hull Reagon, 1943–1996," *Black Scholar* (spring 1997): 3. See also Seeger and Reiser, *Everybody Says Freedom*, 85.

2. Information on Neblett and Watkins is drawn from "The Music of the Civil Rights Movement," program notes for a March 15, 1998, Freedom Singers concert, Kennedy Library Civil Rights History Project at the Kennedy Library, Boston; and from "Teacher Forum to Feature Movement Veteran," *Bill of Rights Network* 10, newsletter of the Bill of Rights Education Project, Boston (winter 1998): 1, 7.

3. R. G. Davis uses this phrase in *San Francisco Mime Troupe*, 70.

4. Coyote, *Sleeping Where I Fall*, 130.

5. Lippard, *Different War*, 42.

6. Doug Rossinow, " 'The Break-through to New Life': Christianity and the Emergence of the New Left in Austin, Texas, 1956–1964," *American Quarterly* 46:3 (September 1994): 332–33, n. 3.

7. Because of their similar name, the Guerrilla Girls are often confused with GAAG. An anonymous, feminist-oriented artists' collective founded in 1985 as the self-proclaimed "conscience of the art world," the Guerrilla Girls may possess no formal link to GAAG, though their anonymity makes it problematic to assert this definitively. When I asked Jon Hendricks, in the February 12, 1999, interview, if a relationship existed between the groups, he was flattered and clearly honored to be compared with the Guerrilla Girls. The comparison is not so far-fetched. Indeed, AWC and the Guerrilla Girls share tactics and ideologies, from a conscious determination to challenge the art world status quo to using postering and theatrical elements such as costuming to convey their messages.
The Guerrilla Girls maintain a website, <www.guerrillagirls.com> which is an excellent starting place to learn more about the group. When I visited this website, I began an e-mail correspondence with a woman who identified herself as one of the Guerrilla Girls' founders, who wrote: "There may have been an early member who was part of the Women's Artist Committee, but we were a different generation. As for influences, we were inspired by activist groups that came before us, including those you name [AWC and GAAG], but not just art world activists. . . . We were also inspired by the Yippies, the Berkeley People's Park demonstrations, and other wild and crazy street activists, as well as by cultural icons like Mad Magazine and Saturday Night Live. We came together with the idea of doing posters employing contemporary advertising techniques, that turned issues around and presented them differently, breaking down viewers' preconceived notions with facts, graphics and humor. In the 1980's, when we began our activities, a backlash was eroding the gains of the 60's and 70's. Artists were afraid to speak up. Women were disavowing feminism. We wanted to make feminism and activism fashionable again."

8. Marshall Berman makes this observation in *All That Is Solid Melts into Air: The Experience of Modernity* (New York, 1982), 335–37. His main piece of evidence consists of his interpretation of the Performance Group's 1977 production of Spalding Gray's *Rumstick Road*, but his argument here reflects a familiar narrative, grafted onto the realm of

performance, of the sixties sensibilities of social activism and beloved community in decline, eclipsed by the ascendant "Me Generation" mentality of the seventies.

9. My account of the Paper Tiger protest is drawn both from personal memory and from Paper Tiger's video of the event, *Operation Storm the Media*, Paper Tiger Television, New York, 1991.

10. Farber, *Chicago '68*, xv–xvi.

11. The Paper Tiger Manifesto, the collective's mission statement, asserts, "The power of mass culture rests on the trust of the public. This legitimacy is a paper tiger. Investigation into the corporate structures of the media and critical analysis of their content is one way to demystify the information industry. Developing a critical consciousness about the communications industry is a necessary first step towards democratic control of information resources." This call for scrutiny of corporate media clearly owes a debt to the New Left's attempts to hold business publicly accountable and to redefine what constitutes legitimate corporate behavior.

12. "Protesters Arrested After Hanging Banner from I-5," *Seattle Post-Intelligencer*, November 27, 1999, accessed at <http://seattlepi.nwsource.com/>; Helene Cooper, "Some Hazy, Some Erudite and All Angry, WTO Protesters Are Hard to Dismiss," *Wall Street Journal*, November 30, 1999, A2; Kim Murphy, "In the Streets of Seattle, Echoes of Turbulent '60s," *Los Angeles Times*, December 1, 1999, A1; Timothy Egan, "Free Speech vs. Free Trade," *New York Times*, December 5, 1999, sec. 4, 1; Geov Parrish, "The Day the WTO Stood Still," *Seattle Weekly*, December 2–8, 1999, 1, 22.

13. Interview with Hendricks, February 12, 1999.

14. Judith Malina, remarks as presenter on panel "Decoding Utopia," at "Visions for a Changing Theatre" symposium, October 9, 2003, Fales Library, New York University, New York.

BIBLIOGRAPHY

Interviews

Leon Golub, December 9, 1998, telephone interview
Jon Hendricks, February 12, 1999, New York; and August 12, 1999, telephone interview
Bernard LaFayette, October 3, 2002, South Kingstown, R.I.
Lucy Lippard, September 30, 1999, telephone interview
Judith Malina, April 13, 1988, New Haven, Conn.
Charles Neblett, March 15, 1998, Boston
Irving Petlin, November 30, 1998, and September 10, 1999, telephone interviews
Hanon Reznikov, April 13, 1988, New Haven, Conn.
Tom Walker, August 24, 1998, and August 15, 2002, Cornwall, Conn.
Hollis Watkins, March 14, 1998, Cambridge, Mass.

Archival Collections

Mark Amitin Papers, Special Collections, Bobst Library, New York University, New York
Chester Anderson Papers, Bancroft Library, University of California at Berkeley
Civil Rights in Mississippi Digital Archive, McCain Library and Archives, University of Southern Mississippi, Hattiesburg, <http://www.lib.usm.edu/spcol/crda/index.html>
The Digger Archives: "San Francisco Diggers (1966–68 . . . and beyond)," <http://www.diggers.org>
Haight Street Diggers Records, North Baker Research Library, California Historical Society, San Francisco
Living Theatre Archives, Performing Arts Collection, Special Collections, University of California at Davis
Living Theatre Records, 1945–1991, Billy Rose Theater Collection, New York Public Library for the Performing Arts, New York

191

Books, Articles, and Other Source Materials

Anderson, Terry. "The New American Revolution: The Movement and Business." In Farber, *The Sixties*, 175–205.

Andre, Carl. "Carl Andre: Artworker." Interview by Jeanne Siegel. *Studio International*, November 1970, 175–79.

"A-Political Or, Criminal Or Victim Or Or Or Or Or Or Or." In "The Early Digger Papers." <http://www.diggers.org/digger_sheets.htm>.

Arnold, Martin. "Organized Hippies Emerge on Coast." *New York Times*, May 5, 1967, 41–42.

Artaud, Antonin. *The Theater and Its Double*. New York: Grove Press, 1958.

Art Workers Coalition. *Open Hearing*. New York: Art Workers Coalition, 1969.

Artists and Writers Protest. "End Your Silence." *New York Times*, April 18, 1965, and June 2, 1965.

———. *Open Letter*. *New York Times*, June 26, 1962.

Ashton, Dore. "Response to Crisis in American Art." *Art in America*, January/February 1969, 24–35.

Baker, Russell. "Observer: The Latest Crisis in Hashbury." *New York Times*, November 9, 1967.

Barnes, Clive. "Stage: Living Theatre's '*Paradise Now*,' a Collective Creation." *New York Times*, October 15, 1968.

"Battle Hymn of the Integrationists." *U.S. News & World Report*, August 5, 1963, 8.

Beck, Julian. "How to Close a Theatre." *Tulane Drama Review* 8:3 (spring 1964): 180–90.

———. Interview in *Yale/theatre* 2:1 (spring 1969): 16–21.

———. Letter to Karl Bissinger. January 28, 1965. Printed as "Thoughts on Theater from Jail." *New York Times*, February 21, 1965.

———. *The Life of The Theatre*. New York: Proscenium, 1972.

———. *semi-permeable membranes: twenty songs of the revolution*. Nashville, Tenn.: Bliss Press, 1984.

———. "Storming the Barricades." In Brown, *The Brig*, 1–35.

———. "Theatre and Revolution." Unpublished essay, 1967. Living Theatre Archives.

Belasco, Warren. *Appetite for Change: How the Counterculture Took on the Food Industry*. 2d edition. Ithaca, N.Y.: Cornell University Press, 1993.

Bentley, Eric. "I Reject The Living Theatre." *New York Times*, October 20, 1968, 35.

Berman, Marshall. *All That Is Solid Melts into Air: The Experience of Modernity*. New York: Simon and Schuster, 1982.

Biner, Pierre. *The Living Theatre*. New York: Horizon Press, 1972.

Bloom, Alexander. *Long Time Gone: Sixties America Then and Now*. New York: Oxford University Press, 2001.

Bloom, Alexander, and Wini Breines, eds. *Takin' It to the Streets: A Sixties Reader*. New York: Oxford University Press, 1995.

Borders, William. "Indecent Exposure Charged to Becks." *New York Times*, September 28, 1968, 27.

Branch, Taylor. *Pillar of Fire: America in the King Years, 1963–65*. New York: Simon and Schuster, 1998.

Braunstein, Peter, and Michael William Doyle, eds. *Imagine Nation: The American Counterculture of the 1960s and '70s*. New York: Routledge, 2002.

Brown, Kenneth. *The Brig*. New York: Hill and Wang, 1965.

Brustein, Robert. "Junkies and Jazz." *New Republic*, September 28, 1959, 29.

"Burocops Proboscis Probes Digger Bag." *Berkeley Barb*, October 21, 1966.

"A Call for the Immediate Resignation of All the Rockefellers from the Board of Trustees of The Museum of Modern Art." In *GAAG: The Guerrilla Art Action Group, 1969–1976*. Action Number 3. New York: Printed Matter, 1978.

Calta, Louis. "*The Connection*: A Play About Junkies." *New York Times*, July 16, 1959, 30.

Carawan, Guy, and Candie Carawan, eds. *Freedom Is a Constant Struggle: Songs of the Freedom Movement*. New York: Oak Publications, 1968.

Carawan, Guy, Candie Carawan, and the Student Nonviolent Coordinating Committee. *We Shall Overcome!: Songs of the Southern Freedom Movement*. New York: Oak Publications, 1963.

Carlson, Marvin. *Performance: A Critical Introduction*. London: Routledge, 1996.

Carson, Clayborne. *In Struggle: SNCC and the Black Awakening of the 1960s*. Cambridge: Harvard University Press, 1981.

Cavallo, Dominick. *A Fiction of the Past: The Sixties in American History*. New York: St. Martin's, 1999.

Cmiel, Kenneth. "The Politics of Civility." In Farber, *The Sixties*, 263–90.

Cohen, Bob. "Mississippi Caravan of Music." *Broadside* 51, October 1964, n.p.

Colburn, David R., and George E. Pozzetta. "Race, Ethnicity, and the Evolution of Political Legitimacy." In Farber, *The Sixties*, 119–48.

Cooper, Helene. "Some Hazy, Some Erudite, and All Angry, WTO Protesters Are Hard to Dismiss." *Wall Street Journal*, November 30, 1999.

Cox, Harvey. "An Open Letter to Allen Ginsberg." *Commonweal*, April 21, 1967, 147–149.

Coyote, Peter. Interview by Etan Ben-Ami, January 12, 1989. Digger Archives.

———. *Sleeping Where I Fall*. Washington, D.C.: Counterpoint, 1998.

Craven, David. *Abstract Expressionism as Cultural Critique: Dissent during the McCarthy Period*. New York: Cambridge University Press, 1999.

Davis, R. G. *The San Francisco Mime Troupe: The First Ten Years*. Palo Alto, Calif.: Ramparts Press, 1975.

Denning, Michael. *The Cultural Front: The Laboring of American Culture in the Twentieth Century*. London: Verso, 1997.

Didion, Joan. *Slouching Towards Bethlehem*. New York: Farrar, Straus and Giroux, 1968.

"Diggers New Game: The Frame." *Berkeley Barb*, November 4, 1966.

"The Digger Papers." In Bloom and Breines, *Takin' It to the Streets*, 316–322.

Dougherty, Frazer, Hans Haacke, Lucy Lippard, and Art Workers Coalition. Letter to the Editor. In "Art Mailbag: Why MoMA Is Their Target." *New York Times*, February 8, 1970.

Douglass, Frederick. *My Bondage and My Freedom*. New York, 1855.

Doyle, Michael William. "Staging the Revolution: Guerrila Theater as Countercultural Practice, 1965–68." In Braunstein and Doyle, *Imagine Nation*, 71–97.

Dunaway, David King. *How Can I Keep from Singing: Pete Seeger*. New York: McGraw-Hill, 1981.

Dunson, Josh. *Freedom in the Air: Song Movements of the Sixties*. New York: International Publishers, 1965.

"The Early Digger Papers: San Francisco Fall, 1996 to Spring, 1967." *Digger Archives*,

Echols, Alice. "Nothing Distant about It: Women's Liberation and Sixties Radicalism." In Farber, *The Sixties*, 149–74.

Egan, Timothy. "Free Speech vs. Free Trade." *New York Times*, December 5, 1999.

Evans, Sara. *Personal Politics: The Roots of Women's Liberation in the Civil Rights Movement and the New Left*. New York: Knopf, 1979.

Farber, David. *The Age of Great Dreams: America in the 1960s*. New York: Hill and Wang, 1994.

———. *Chicago '68*. Chicago: University of Chicago Press, 1988.

————, ed. *The Sixties: From Memory to History*. Chapel Hill: University of North Caro-
lina Press, 1994.
Ferris, Timothy. "A Creepy Protest at Museum." *New York Post*, January 13, 1971.
Forman, Alex. "San Francisco Style: The Diggers and the Love Revolution." *Anarchy* 7:7
(July 1967).
Frank, Thomas. *The Conquest of Cool: Business Culture, Counterculture, and the Rise of Hip
Consumerism*. Chicago: University of Chicago Press, 1997.
"Free Bread." Reprinted as "Digger Bread (made with love)." Digger Archives.
"Free Food in the Panhandle, 1983." Digger Archives.
GAAG: The Guerrilla Art Action Group, 1969–1976. New York: Printed Matter, 1978.
Garofalo, Reebee. *Rockin' Out: Popular Music in the U.S.A.* 2d edition. Upper Saddle River,
N.J.: Prentice-Hall, 2002.
Gelber, Jack. *The Connection*. New York: Grove Press, 1957.
Gitlin, Todd. *The Sixties: Years of Hope, Days of Rage*. New York: Bantam, 1987.
Glueck, Grace. "Artists Threaten Sit-in at the Modern." *New York Times*, March 7, 1969.
————. "At the Whitney, It's Guerrilla Warfare." *New York Times*, November 1, 1970.
————. "The Cast Is a Flock of Hat Blocks." *New York Times*, December 21, 1969.
————. "Dissidents Stir Art World." *New York Times*, April 12, 1969.
————. "Hightower Meets Museum's Critics." *New York Times*, March 4, 1970.
————. "J'accuse, Baby! She Cried." *New York Times*, April 20, 1969.
————. Letter to author. August 4, 2001.
————. "Soft Sculpture or Hard—They're Oldenburgers." *New York Times Magazine*,
September 21, 1969.
————. "A Strange Assortment of Flags Is Displayed at 'People's Show.'" *New York Times*,
November 10, 1970.
————. "Yanking the Rug from Under." *New York Times*, January 25, 1970.
Goffman, Erving. *The Presentation of the Self in Everyday Life*. Garden City, N.Y.: Double-
day, 1959.
Golub, Leon. "The Artist as Angry Artist." *Arts Magazine*, April 1967, 48.
Grogan, Emmett. *Ringolevio: A Life Played for Keeps*. Boston: Little, Brown, 1972.
Gross, Alex. "Do Artists Want Change?" *Arts Magazine*, September/October 1970, 28.
Guilbaut, Serge. *How New York Stole the Idea of Modern Art: Abstract Expressionism, Free-
dom, and the Cold War*. Chicago: University of Chicago Press, 1983.
Haacke, Hans. Interview by Margaret Sheffield. *Studio International*, March/April 1976,
117–23.
Hampton, Henry, and Steve Fayer. *Voices of Freedom: An Oral History of the Civil Rights
Movement from the 1950s through the 1980s*. New York: Bantam Books, 1990.
Harris, David. *Dreams Die Hard: Three Men's Journey through the Sixties*. New York: St.
Martin's, 1982.
Heller, Adele. "The New Theatre." In Heller and Rudnick, *1915*, 217–32.
Heller, Adele, and Lois Rudnick, eds. *1915, The Cultural Moment: The New Politics, the
New Woman, the New Psychology, the New Art, and the New Theatre in America*.
New Brunswick, N.J.: Rutgers University Press, 1991.
Hersh, Seymour. *Chemical and Biological Warfare: America's Hidden Arsenal*. Indianapolis:
Bobbs-Merrill, 1968.
Hills, Patricia. *Modern Art in the USA: Issues and Controversies of the 20th Century*. Upper
Saddle River, N.J.: Prentice-Hall, 2001.
"Hippies: Death on a Sunny Afternoon." *Rolling Stone*, November 9, 1967, 11.
Hoffman, Paul. "35th Art Biennale Beset by Problems at Venice Opening." *New York
Times*, June 24, 1970.

Hopkins, Jerry, and Danny Sugerman. *No One Here Gets Out Alive*. New York: Warner, 1981.

Hoving, Thomas. *Making the Mummies Dance: Inside the Metropolitan Museum of Art*. New York: Simon and Schuster, 1993.

Hurlburt, Laurance P. *The Mexican Muralists in the United States*. Albuquerque: University of New Mexico Press, 1989.

"In Memoriam: Cordell Hull Reagon, 1943–1996." *Black Scholar* 27:1 (spring 1997): 3.

"In Search of a Frame." *Berkeley Barb*, November 25, 1966.

"In the Clear." *San Francisco Chronicle*, November 30, 1966.

Isserman, Maurice. *If I Had a Hammer: The Death of the Old Left and the Birth of the New Left*. New York: Basic Books, 1987.

Kelley, Robin D. G. *Race Rebels: Culture, Politics, and the Black Working Class*. New York: Free Press, 1994.

———. " 'We Are Not What We Seem': Rethinking Black Working-class Opposition in the Jim Crow South." *Journal of American History* 80:1 (June 1993): 75–112.

King, Mary. *Freedom Song: A Personal Story of the 1960s Civil Rights Movement*. New York: Morrow, 1987.

Klein, Howard. "Bernstein Joins Stern in Concert." *New York Times*, August 31, 1964.

Korall, Burt. "The Music of Protest." *Saturday Review*, November 16, 1968, 36–39.

Kramer, Hilton. "About MoMA, the AWC, and Political Causes." *New York Times*, February 8, 1970.

———. "Artists and the Problem of 'Relevance.' " *New York Times*, May 4, 1969.

———. "Do You Believe in the Principle of Museums?" *New York Times*, January 18, 1970.

Leach, Eugene. "The Radicals of *The Masses*." In Heller and Rudnick, *1915*, 33–35.

Lester, Elenore. "The Living Theatre Presents: Revolution! Joy! Protest! Shock! Etc.!" *New York Times Magazine*, October 13, 1968, 52–53, 87–96, 100–107, 110.

Lester, Julius. "Freedom Songs in the South." *Broadside* 39, February 7, 1964, n.p.

Levine, Lawrence. *Black Culture and Black Consciousness: Afro-American Folk Thought from Slavery to Freedom*. New York: Oxford University Press, 1977.

Lewis, John. "Wake Up America." In Bloom and Breines, *Takin' It to the Streets*, 31–34.

Lippard, Lucy. "The Art Workers' Coalition: Not a History." *Studio International*, November 1970, 171–74.

———. "Charitable Visits by the AWC to MoMA and Met." *The Element* January 1971, 10–11.

———. *A Different War: Vietnam in Art*. Seattle: Whatcom Museum of History and Art and Real Comet Press, 1990.

———. "The Dilemma." *Arts Magazine*, November 1970, 27–29.

———. *Get the Message?: A Decade of Art for Social Change*. New York: Dutton, 1984.

Lipsitz, George. *Time Passages: Collective Memory and American Popular Culture*. Minneapolis: University of Minnesota Press, 1990.

———. "Who'll Stop the Rain?: Youth Culture, Rock 'n' Roll, and Social Crises." In Farber, *The Sixties*, 206–34.

"Living Theatre Action Declaration." January 1970. Reprinted in Biner, *Living Theatre*, 225–27.

"The Living Theatre and Larger Issues." *Tulane Drama Review* 8:3 (spring 1964): 191–206.

The Living Theatre Collective. " 'Money Tower' Scenario." *Drama Review* 18:2 (June 1974): 20–25.

"Love on Haight." *Time*, March 17, 1967, 27.

"Malcolm Favors a Mau Mau in U.S." *New York Times,* December 21, 1964.
Malina, Judith. *The Diaries of Judith Malina, 1947–1957.* New York: Grove Press, 1984.
———. "Directing *The Brig.*" In Brown, *The Brig.*
———. *The Enormous Despair.* New York: Random House, 1972.
———. Letter to Carl Einhorn. March 28, 1970. Reprinted in Beck, *Life of the Theatre,* 75–77.
———. *Poems of a Wandering Jewess.* Paris: Handshake Press, 1982.
Malina, Judith, and Julian Beck. *Paradise Now: Collective Creation of The Living Theatre.* New York: Random House, 1971.
Marowitz, Charles. "You Can Go Home Again?" *New York Times,* September 8, 1968.
Marsh, J. B. T. *The Story of the Jubilee Singers; With Their Songs.* 1881. Reprint, New York: Negro Universities Press, 1969.
Martin, Bradford. "The Living Theatre in America: 1951–1969." Senior essay, History Department, Yale University, 1988.
———. "Politics as Art, Art as Politics: The Freedom Singers, The Living Theatre, and Public Performance." In Bloom, *Long Time Gone,* 159–87.
Matusow, Allen J. *The Unraveling of America: A History of Liberalism in the 1960s.* New York: Harper and Row, 1984.
Mee, Charles L. Jr. "Epitaph for The Living Theatre." *Tulane Drama Review* 8:3 (spring 1964): 220–21.
Melosh, Barbara. *Engendering Culture: Manhood and Womanhood in New Deal Public Art and Theater.* Washington, D.C.: Smithsonian Institution Press, 1991.
Metevsky, George. "Delving the Diggers." *Berkeley Barb,* October 21, 1966.
———. "The Ideology of Failure." *Berkeley Barb,* November 18, 1966.
Miller, James. *Democracy Is in the Streets: From Port Huron to the Siege of Chicago.* New York: Simon and Schuster, 1987.
Miller, Timothy. *The Hippies and American Values.* Knoxville: University of Tennessee Press, 1991.
"Moment of History." *New Yorker,* March 27, 1965, 37–38.
"Money Is an Unnecessary Evil." In "The Early Digger Papers." <http://www.diggers .org/digger_sheets.htm>.
Moody, Anne. *Coming of Age in Mississippi.* New York: Doubleday, 1968.
Moore, Alan W. "Collectivities: Protest, Counter-Culture, and Political Postmodernism in New York City Artists Organizations, 1969–1985." Ph.D. diss., City University of New York, 2000.
Morgan, Robin, ed. *Sisterhood Is Powerful: An Anthology of Writings From the Women's Liberation Movement.* New York: Vintage, 1970.
Motherwell, Robert. "The Modern Painter's World." *DYN* 1:6 (November 1944): 9–14.
Murphy, Kim. "In the Streets of Seattle, Echoes of Turbulent '60s." *Los Angeles Times,* December 1, 1999.
"The Music of the Civil Rights Movement." Program notes for Freedom Singers concert, March 15, 1998, Kennedy Library Civil Rights History Project at the Kennedy Library, Boston.
Neff, Renfreu. *The Living Theatre, U.S.A.* New York: Bobbs-Merrill, 1970.
Nemser, Cindy. "Artists and the System: Far from Cambodia." *Village Voice,* May 28, 1970.
Nochlin, Linda. "The Paterson Strike Pageant of 1913." *Art in America,* May/June 1974, 64–68.
"Northern Folk Singers Help Out at Negro Festival in Mississippi." *New York Times,* July 7, 1963.
"An Oral History with Mr. Hollis Watkins." University of Southern Mississippi, Oral History Program, 2000. Civil Rights in Mississippi Digital Archive.

Pach, Chester J. Jr. "And That's the Way It Was: The Vietnam War on the Nightly Network News." In Farber, *The Sixties*, 90–112.

"Parade in Haight-Ashbury Marks 'Death of Hippie.'" *New York Times*, October 7, 1967.

Parrish, Geov. "The Day the WTO Stood Still." *Seattle Weekly*, December 2–8, 1999.

Peck, Abe. *Uncovering the Sixties: The Life and Times of the Underground Press*. New York: Pantheon, 1985.

Perlstein, Rick. "Who Owns the Sixties?: The Opening of a Scholarly Generation Gap." *Lingua Franca* 6:4 (May/June 1996): 30–37.

Perrault, John. "On Strike." *Village Voice*, May 28, 1970.

———. "Whose Art?" *Village Voice*, January 9, 1969.

Perry, Charles. *The Haight-Ashbury: A History*. New York: Random House/Rolling Stone Press, 1984.

Picard, Lil. "Interview with John Hightower." *Arts Magazine*, May 1970, 20–24.

———. "Protest and Rebellion: The Function of the Art Workers Coalition." *Arts Magazine*, May 1970, 18–20.

Piscator, Maria Ley. *The Piscator Experiment*. New York: J. H. Heineman, 1967.

Pittell, Stephen M. "The Current Status of the Haight-Ashbury Hippie Community (Excerpt)." September 1968. Digger Archives.

"Protesters Arrested after Hanging Banner from I–5." *Seattle Post-Intelligencer*, November 27, 1999. Accessed at <http://seattlepi.nwsource.com/>.

"Public Nonsense Nuisance Public Essence Newsense Public News." In "The Early Digger Papers." <http://www.diggers.org/digger_sheets.htm>.

Reagon, Bernice. "In Our Hands: Thoughts on Black Music." *Sing Out!*, November 1975, 1–5.

Reagon, Bernice Johnson. "Songs of the Civil Rights Movement, 1955–1965: A Study in Culture History." Ph.D. diss., Howard University, 1975.

———. "Songs That Moved the Movement." *Civil Rights Quarterly* (summer 1983): 26–35.

Robbins, Corinne. "The N.Y. Art Strike." *Arts Magazine*, September/October 1970, 27.

Ross, Andrew. *Real Love: In Pursuit of Cultural Justice*, New York: New York University Press, 1998.

Rossinow, Doug. " 'The Break-through to New Life': Christianity and the Emergence of the New Left in Austin, Texas, 1956–1964." *American Quarterly* 46:3 (September 1994): 309–40.

———. *The Politics of Authenticity: Liberalism, Christianity, and the New Left in America*. New York: Columbia University Press, 1998.

Rostagno, Aldo. *We, The Living Theatre*. New York: Ballantine, 1970.

Rudnick, Lois. *Utopian Vistas: The Mabel Dodge Luhan House and the American Counterculture*. Albuquerque: University of New Mexico Press, 1996.

Ryan, Mary. *Civic Wars: Democracy and Public Life in the American City during the Nineteenth Century*. Berkeley: University of California Press, 1997.

Ryan, Paul Ryder. "The Living Theatre's 'Money Tower.'" *Drama Review* 18:2 (June 1974): 9–19.

"San Francisco Food Not Bombs." <www.sffoodnotbombs.org>.

"The San Francisco Riot." *Newsweek*, October 10, 1966, 28–29.

Sandler, Irving. *Art of the Post-Modern Era: From the Late 1960s to the Early 1990s*. Boulder, Colo.: Westview Press, 1998.

Sanger, Kerran L. *"When the Spirit Says Sing!": The Role of Freedom Songs in the Civil Rights Movement*. New York: Garland, 1995.

Sarlos, Robert K. "Jig Cook and Susan Glaspell: Rule Makers and Rule Breakers." In Heller and Rudnick, *1915*, 250–58.

198   *Bibliography*

Schechner, Richard. *Performance Studies: An Introduction*. New York: Routledge, 2002.
Schlesinger, Arthur M. *Robert Kennedy and His Times*. Boston: Houghton Mifflin, 1978.
Schwartz, Therese. "The Political Scene." *Arts Magazine*, December 1970/January 1971, 16.
———. "The Political Scene." *Arts Magazine*, February 1971, 17.
———. "The Political Scene." *Arts Magazine*, March 1971, 15–16.
"Sculptor Takes Work Out of Museum Show." *New York Times*, January 4, 1969.
Seeger, Pete. *The Incompleat Folksinger*. New York: Simon and Schuster, 1972.
Seeger, Pete, and Bob Reiser. *Everybody Says Freedom*. New York: Norton, 1989.
"Sex as a Spectator Sport." *Time*, July 11, 1969, 61–62.
Shelton, Robert. "Negro Songs Here Aid Rights Drive." *New York Times*, June 22, 1963.
———. "Rights Song Has Own History of Integration." *New York Times*, July 23, 1963.
"Shock Troops of the Avant-Garde." *Time*, September 27, 1968, 66.
Shorris, Earl. "Love Is Dead." *New York Times Magazine*, October 29, 1967, 27, 113–16.
Smith, Michael, ed. "The Living Theatre at Cooper Union: A Symposium with William Coco, Jack Gelber, Karen Malpede, Richard Schechner, and Michael Smith." *Drama Review* 31:3 (fall 1987): 103–19.
Smith, Richard Candida. *Utopia and Dissent: Art, Poetry, and Politics in California*. Berkeley: University of California Press, 1995.
Smith, Wendy. *Real Life Drama: The Group Theatre and America, 1931–1940*. New York: Knopf, 1990.
"Some of the Events That Led to GAAG's Creation." In *GAAG*, n.p.
Southern, Eileen. *The Music of Black Americans: A History*, 2d edition. New York: Norton, 1983.
"The Splendid Desire for Nothing." *America*, May 20, 1967, 746–47.
Stephens, Julie. *Anti-Disciplinary Protest: Sixties Radicalism and Postmodernism*. Cambridge: Cambridge University Press, 1998.
Stevens, Jay. *Storming Heaven: LSD and the American Dream*. New York: Atlantic Monthly Press, 1987.
Tallmer, Jerry. "Theatre: *The Connection*." *Village Voice*, July 22, 1959.
"Teacher Forum to Feature Movement Veteran." *Bill of Rights Network* (newsletter of the Bill of Rights Education Project, Boston) 10 (Winter 1998): 1, 7.
Thompson, Hunter S. "The 'Hashbury' Is the Capital of the Hippies." *New York Times Magazine*, May 14, 1967, 28–29, 120–24.
"Time to Forget." Haight Street Diggers Archive, MS 3159, box 1, folder 1, California Historical Society, North Baker Research Library, San Francisco.
Tischler, Barbara. ed. *Sights on the Sixties*. New Brunswick, N.J.: Rutgers University Press, 1992.
Tynan, Kenneth. Preface to *The Connection*, by Jack Gelber. New York: Grove Press, 1957.
Tytell, John. *The Living Theatre: Art, Exile, and Outrage*. New York: Grove Press, 1995.
Van Gelder, Lawrence. "Cordell Hull Reagon, Civil Rights Singer, Dies at 53." *New York Times*, November 19, 1996.
Veysey, Laurence. *The Communal Experience: Anarchist and Mystical Counter-Cultures in America*. New York: Harper and Row, 1973.
Vicentini, Claudio. "The Living Theatre's 'Six Public Acts.'" *Drama Review* 19:3 (September 1975): 80–93.
von Hoffman, Nicholas. "Hippiedom Meets the New Left." *Washington Post*, June 19, 1967.
Wainwright, Loudon. "The Strange New Love Land of the Hippies." *Life*, March 31, 1967, 15–16.

Wakefield, Dan. *New York in the Fifties*. Boston: Houghton Mifflin, 1992.
Ward, Andrew. *Dark Midnight When I Rise: The Story of the Jubilee Singers Who Introduced the World to the Music of Black America*. New York: Farrar, Straus and Giroux, 2000.
Watters, Pat, and Reese Cleghorn. *Climbing Jacob's Ladder*. New York: Harbinger, 1967.
"What Is Food Not Bombs?" <www.foodnotbombs.net>.
Whelton, Clark. "The Flag as Art: Bars and Stripes Forever." *Village Voice*, November 19, 1970.
"where is PUBLIC at?" In "The Early Digger Papers." <http://www.diggers.org/digger _sheets.htm>.
Willett, John. *The Theatre of Erwin Piscator*. London: Eyre-Methuen, 1978.
Williams, Juan. *Eyes on the Prize: America's Civil Rights Years, 1954–1965*. New York: Viking, 1987.
Windeler, Robert. "Modern Museum Protest Target." *New York Times*, March 31, 1969.
" 'Without These Songs. . . . ' " *Newsweek*, August 31, 1964, 74.

SOUND RECORDINGS
The Newport Folk Festival—1963. The Evening Concerts: Vol. 1. Vanguard 77002–2, 1964.
Seeger, Pete. *We Shall Overcome: Complete Carnegie Hall Concert*. Columbia CL2101/ CS8901, 1963.
Sing for Freedom: The Story of the Civil Rights Movement Through Its Songs. Smithsonian Folkways, SF40032, 1990.
Voices of the Civil Rights Movement: Black American Freedom Songs, 1960–1966. 2-CD set. Smithsonian Folkways, SF40084, 1997.

VIDEOS
The American Experience. "Jubilee Singers: Sacrifice and Glory." PBS, WGBH, Boston, 2000.
Berkeley in the Sixties. Directed by Mark Kitchell. First Run Features, New York, 1990.
Signals through the Flames. Directed by Sheldon Rochlin and Maxine Harris. Mystic Fire Video, New York, 1983.
Operation Storm the Media. Paper Tiger Television, New York, 1991.
Eyes on the Prize: America's Civil Rights Years. Blackside, Boston, 1986.

WEBSITES
The Digger Archives <www.diggers.org>
The Guerrilla Girls <www.guerrillagirls.com>
The Living Theatre <www.livingtheatre.org>

INDEX

Page numbers of illustrations are given in italics.

BRADFORD D. MARTIN was born and raised in Connecticut. He has a B.A. in history with theater studies from Yale University, an M.A. in American Studies from the University of Massachusetts Boston, and a Ph.D. from Boston University's American and New England Studies Program. Prior to his career in academic life, he performed with various theater groups including the Living Theatre, Theater for the New City, and Bread and Puppet Theater. He has taught at University of Massachusetts Boston and Boston University, and is currently assistant professor of history at Bryant College in Rhode Island. He was a recipient of the Clarimond Mansfield Award of the Boston University Humanities Foundation. *The Theater Is in the Street* is his first book. Brad Martin lives in Providence, Rhode Island, with his wife, Heather, and three children, Jackson, Hazel, and Harry.